FICHTE'S SOCIAL AND POLITICAL PHILOSOPHY

In this study of Fichte's social and political philosophy, David James offers an interpretation of Fichte's most famous writings in this area, including his *Foundations of Natural Right* and *Addresses to the German Nation*, centred on two main themes: property and virtue. These themes provide the basis for a discussion of such issues as what it means to guarantee the freedom of all the citizens of a state, the problem of unequal relations of economic dependence between states, and the differences and connections between the legal and political sphere of right and that of morality. James also relates Fichte's central social and political ideas to those of other important figures in the history of philosophy, including Locke, Kant and Hegel, as well as to the radical phase of the French Revolution. His account will be of importance to all who are interested in Fichte's philosophy and its intellectual and political context.

DAVID JAMES is Senior Lecturer in Philosophy at the University of the Witwatersrand, South Africa.

T0371052

MODERN EUROPEAN PHILOSOPHY

General Editor

ROBERT B. PIPPIN, *University of Chicago*

Advisory Board

GARY GUTTING, *University of Notre Dame*
ROLF-PETER HORSTMANN, *Humboldt University, Berlin*

Some recent titles

FICHTE'S SOCIAL AND POLITICAL PHILOSOPHY: PROPERTY AND VIRTUE

DAVID JAMES
University of the Witwatersrand

CAMBRIDGE
UNIVERSITY PRESS

CAMBRIDGE UNIVERSITY PRESS
Cambridge, New York, Melbourne, Madrid, Cape Town,
Singapore, São Paulo, Delhi, Mexico City

Cambridge University Press
The Edinburgh Building, Cambridge CB2 8RU, UK

Published in the United States of America by Cambridge University Press, New York

www.cambridge.org
Information on this title: www.cambridge.org/9781107684447

© David James 2011

First published 2011
First paperback edition 2013

A catalogue record for this publication is available from the British Library

ISBN 978-1-107-68444-7 Paperback

For my son, Benjamin

CONTENTS

ix

ACKNOWLEDGEMENTS

The research for this book was to a large extent made possible by funding from the South African National Research Foundation. I would like to thank Lawrence Hamilton for his comments on material that later came to form part of the book, and Daniel Breazeale and Frederick Neuhouser for their helpful suggestions as to how I might improve the book itself.

The book includes some revised material that has previously appeared elsewhere as 'The Relation of Right to Morality in Fichte's Jena Theory of the State and Society', *History of European Ideas* 35(3) (2009), 'Applying the Concept of Right: Fichte and Babeuf', *History of Political Thought* 30(4) (2009), 'Fichte's Reappraisal of Kant's Theory of Cosmopolitan Right', *History of European Ideas* 36(1) (2010), 'Fichte's Theory of Property', *European Journal of Political Theory* 9(2) (2010) and 'Fichte on the Vocation of the Scholar and the (Mis)use of History', *Review of Metaphysics* 63(3) (2010).

ABBREVIATIONS OF FICHTE'S WORKS

AGN   *Addresses to the German Nation*, trans. Gregory Moore (Cambridge University Press, 2008)

CPR   'The Characteristics of the Present Age', in *The Popular Works of Johann Gottlieb Fichte*, trans. William Smith, 2 vols. (London: Trübner & Co., 1889), vol. II

EPW   *Fichte: Early Philosophical Writings*, trans. Daniel Breazeale (Ithaca: Cornell University Press, 1988)

FNR   *Foundations of Natural Right*, ed. Frederick Neuhouser, trans. Michael Baur (Cambridge University Press, 2000)

GA   *J. G. Fichte – Gesamtausgabe der Bayerischen Akademie der Wissenschaften*, ed. Reinhard Lauth, Erich Fuchs and Hans Gliwitzky (Stuttgart and Bad Canstatt: Frommann-Holzboog, 1964–)

RPP   'J. G. Fichte, Review of Immanuel Kant, *Perpetual Peace: A Philosophical Sketch* (Königsberg: Nicolovius, 1795)', trans. Daniel Breazeale, *Philosophical Forum* 32 (4) (2001), 311–21

SE   *The System of Ethics*, ed. and trans. Daniel Breazeale and Günter Zöller (Cambridge University Press, 2005)

INTRODUCTION

J. G. Fichte played an essential role in the development of the philosophical movement known as German idealism, appropriating the critical philosophy of Kant in a way that came to influence later thinkers such as Schelling and Hegel. Although there has been a renewed interest in Fichte's philosophy in the English-speaking world,[1] the last book in English by a single author on Fichte's political thought dates back to the 1930s.[2] While I hope to remedy this situation, my discussion of Fichte's social and political philosophy will be limited in two important respects. First of all, this book deals mainly with Fichte's writings in this area belonging to the period from his professorship at the University of Jena to the time of the publication of the *Addresses to the German Nation* (*Reden an die deutsche Nation*), a period that extends roughly from 1794 to 1808. Secondly, I limit myself to dealing with two particular themes which I consider to be so integral to Fichte's social and political philosophy that they provide the key to understanding its most basic aims and character. These are the themes of property and virtue, which themselves relate to another concept that is central to Fichte's social and political philosophy and, indeed, to his philosophy as a whole, namely, freedom.[3]

---

1 Two significant examples of this renewed interest are Neuhouser, *Fichte's Theory of Subjectivity* and Zöller, *Fichte's Transcendental Philosophy.*
2 The book in question is Engelbrecht, *Johann Gottlieb Fichte.*
3 The importance of the concept of property and, moreover, its relation to the concept of freedom has been noted before. Cf. Braun, *Freiheit, Gleichheit, Eigentum*, 5 and 16ff. I offer, however, a more detailed and, I hope, more nuanced account of Fichte's theory of property. For example, Braun maintains that Fichte conceives of property as being identical with rightfully constituted freedom, by which he means the legitimate distribution of freedom of action in the external world. Property in this sense would appear to be something very different from property in things. Although, as we shall see, Fichte certainly does conceive of property in terms of an activity in the external world that can

1

To begin to explain why I have chosen to focus on these themes, it will help if I first say something about another theme that has recently provoked interest in Fichte's philosophy, namely, the concept of recognition, though this interest has generally been accompanied by the claim that it is Hegel, rather than Fichte himself, who develops the concept of recognition as a central category in social and political philosophy.[4] Fichte himself introduces the notion of recognition in his attempt to deduce the concept of right (*Recht*) as a condition of self-consciousness, so as to establish this concept's status as a purely rational concept, that is to say, one that is contained within the essence of reason as such, and is not, therefore, present 'through experience, instruction, arbitrary human conventions, etc., but rather in consequence of the being's rational nature'.[5] Rather than concentrating on Fichte's project of offering a transcendental deduction of the concept of right, I intend to show that Fichte develops a number of ideas that are interesting from a political perspective, and which lend themselves to being explained and valued in relative independence of the ambitious project of deducing the concept of right as a condition of self-consciousness. This approach will allow me also to meet some criticisms that have been made of Fichte's political philosophy. These criticisms can be explained with reference to his account of recognition.

Fichte's deduction of the concept of right as a condition of self-consciousness is found in the first main division of what is arguably his most famous and highly regarded work on political philosophy, his 1796/97 *Foundations of Natural Right* (*Grundlage des Naturrechts nach Principien der Wissenschaftslehre*), which has formed the main focus of attention when it comes to recent discussions of his political philosophy in the English-speaking world.[6] Fichte here attempts to show that the concept of right must be presupposed in order to explain how a

---

rightfully be regarded as one's own, and that he even treats this form of property as primary, he also thinks that this form of property to some extent entails and allows for property in things. My account of Fichte's theory of property aims both to show why he treats property in the sense of an activity in the external world that can rightfully be regarded as one's own as primary and how this understanding of the concept of property relates to property in things.

4 For a classic example of this approach, see Siep, *Anerkennung als Prinzip der praktischen Philosophie.*

5 GA I / 3: 358; FNR: 49.

6 See, for example, the collection of articles in Breazeale and Rockmore (eds.), *Rights, Bodies and Recognition.*

finite rational being can become conscious of itself as free, so that in trying to think such a being, we are also forced to think the concept of right. In § 2 of the *Foundations of Natural Right*, Fichte begins by seeking to explain the possibility of self-consciousness in terms of a finite rational being's relation to the material world, especially with regard to such a being's attempts to change this world in accordance with the ends it has formed. Fichte believes, however, that he is able to show that it is possible for a finite rational being to comprehend itself as free only if its object is another finite rational being with the capacity to be self-determining. This brings me to Fichte's theory of a summons (*Aufforderung*) as presented in § 3 of the *Foundations of Natural Right.*

Fichte identifies this summons with an act of self-limitation on the part of one human being in relation to another human being, whereby the human being to whom the summons is addressed is left free to act in the sphere that is made available to him by the other human being's act of limiting his own activity. This act of self-limitation presupposes the rationality and freedom of both parties. On the one hand, the summons presupposes that the human being to whom the summons is addressed is capable of comprehending the intention behind it and of acting freely, or of choosing not to act, as the case may be. On the other hand, the idea of acting in accordance with ends that one has oneself freely adopted is itself already contained in the concept of a summons, in the shape of the end to limit one's activity in favour of the freedom of another human being, an end that the human being who summons another human being must be thought to adopt.

This raises the problem, however, as to how the human being who summons another human being came to comprehend himself as a free and rational being, capable of forming its own ends and acting in accordance with them. In short, the question arises as to how this human being first became conscious of himself as free. Fichte's answer to this question is to introduce the notion of mutual recognition, whereby each human being limits his activity in relation to other human beings whom he recognizes as free and rational. Fichte accordingly describes the relation of free beings to one another as 'a relation of reciprocal inter-action through intelligence and freedom', in which one 'cannot recog-nize the other if both do not mutually recognize each other; and one cannot treat the other as a free being, if both do not mutually treat each other as free'.[7] He terms this relation between free beings 'the relation of

---

7 GA I / 3: 351; FNR: 42.

right' (*das Rechtsverhältniß*), while he calls the formula that describes this relation 'the principle of right' (*der Rechtssaz*).[8] Fichte holds the relation of right also to be a condition of individuality, in the sense that it allows human beings to determine themselves as individuals distinguishable from other individuals in virtue of the different choices that they freely make, as opposed to the differences between one human being and another human being simply resting on their having certain different physical features or psychological characteristics, which are given by nature. Fichte uses the term 'person' to designate the human being who 'exclusively' ascribes to himself a sphere for his freedom, and who 'exclusively' makes choices within this sphere.[9]

Fichte's attempt to show that an individual's relation to others is a constitutive element of this same individual's own understanding of himself as free and rational is richly suggestive, though it is Hegel who is often credited with having developed the fuller implications of this position. Yet Fichte's project of demonstrating the necessity of the concept of right as a condition of self-consciousness, along with the existence of rights, laws and the state as further conditions of this concept, can be viewed in a more negative light. For example, there is the claim that Fichte 'deduces and postulates *a priori* state and legal systems out of his own head as "absolute Ego"', together with the unfavourable comparison that this approach is said to invite between him and Hegel, who is credited with confronting empirical reality in the form of modern civil society, whose emergence is historically linked to the French Revolution.[10]

In what follows, I argue against this characterization of Fichte's political philosophy, by focusing in the first instance on Fichte's theory of property. This theory shows a clear awareness on Fichte's part of the possibility that human beings may fail to recognize the freedom of others. It also involves the construction of a normative account of property which identifies the conditions that need to be met if finite rational beings are to live in harmony with each other, that is to say, in accordance with the idea of a relation of right, whereby human beings limit their own activity in relation to each other. Fichte's acknowledgement of the possibility of conflict between human beings, together with his consideration of how a relation of right can be guaranteed, lead him away from

8 GA I / 3: 358; FNR: 49.
9 GA I / 3: 361; FNR: 53.
10 Ritter, *Hegel and the French Revolution*, 72.

the realm of pure reason towards that of experience; so that, far from simply deducing and postulating *a priori* both the state and laws out of his own head, Fichte can be seen to take into account the empirical relations existing between human beings, which contain the potential for conflict. This in turn prompts him to show how such relations can be rightfully constituted both at the *a priori* normative and at a more empirical level.

This brings me to Fichte's claim that the concept of right, although it is a concept of pure reason, needs to be applied to the conditions of the sensible world, that is to say, to the relations that obtain between finite rational beings existing in certain spatial and temporal relations to each other and to material objects in the world. In the Introduction to the *Foundations of Natural Right*, Fichte refers to the doctrine of natural right as 'a real philosophical science' (*eine reelle philosophische Wissenschaft*).[11] He opposes such a science to '*an empty, formulaic philosophy* [*eine leere Formular-Philosophie*] that believes it has done enough if it has proved that one can think of something at all, without being concerned about the object (about the conditions of the necessity of this thinking)'; whereas a 'real' philosophy 'presents concepts and the object at the same time, and never treats one without the other'.[12] Fichte's reflections on the method of his foundational science, the *Wissenschaftslehre*, provide the background to these claims. This foundational science is 'real' in the sense that it has a 'real' object in the form of the necessary acts through which the mind 'constitutes' or 'constructs' itself and its world as observed by the philosopher, who reflects on these acts. Yet this notion of a 'real philosophical science' introduces a 'serious ambiguity' in the case of the *Foundations of Natural Right*, because in the later parts of this work Fichte appears to justify the claim that it represents a 'real' science in terms of the very different idea that the doctrine of right can be applied to the conditions of the sensible world.[13]

---

11 GA I / 3: 319; FNR: 8.
12 GA I / 3: 317; FNR: 7.
13 Daniel Breazeale, 'The "Mixed Method" of Fichte's *Grundlage des Naturrechts* and the Limits of Transcendental *Reellephilosophie*', in Breazeale and Rockmore (eds.), *Rights, Bodies and Recognition*. As Breazeale points out, one serious problem with Fichte's view of the possibility of applying the principles of right to the empirical world as corroboratory evidence for his claim that his theory of right constitutes a 'real philosophical science', is that this raises questions concerning the claims to necessity made in the *Foundations of Natural Right*. This in turn relates to the problem of the relation of the transcendental, *a priori* aspects of this work to the empirical claims that are also made in it. It is not my intention to argue that Fichte presents us with a consistent account of how these transcendental and empirical elements relate to each other. Rather, I show that notwithstanding such internal problems, Fichte's social and political philosophy is of

Rather than trying to explain away such an ambiguity in Fichte's notion of a 'real philosophical science', so as to make Fichte's theory of right appear more consistent, either internally or in its relation to his *Wissenschaftslehre*, I intend to show that the idea of an application of the concept of right in the second sense, that is, in the sense of showing how this concept can be applied to the conditions of the sensible world, should be welcomed. This is because it amounts to an attempt on Fichte's part to explain the possibility of bridging the gap between the normative, purely theoretical level and the empirical level. Fichte's theory of property will be shown to provide the clearest example of how he attempts to bridge this gap, so as not himself to fall foul of the criticism that 'most theorists of right are content to philosophize formally about the concept of right [*Rechtsbegriff*], and – as long as their concept is merely thinkable – care very little about how the concept can be applied'.[14] Moreover, the idea that the principles of right need to be applied suggests that, if we are fully to understand a political concept such as that of property, which, after all, concerns human beings as they interact with each other in the empirical world, we must have some conception of how it can be applied, given the fact that relations of mutual recognition may fail to obtain between human beings. Fichte's engagement with such issues enables him to develop an original and highly interesting theory of property, which has some important implications when it comes to assessing the viability of a recent tendency in the interpretation of his political philosophy. This is the tendency to interpret the latter in terms of some of the central tenets of modern day liberalism.

An example of this tendency to stress the liberal character of Fichte's political philosophy is provided by Frederick Neuhouser's claim that Fichte views the political realm as having its own distinctive end in the fostering of each citizen's individuality, and that 'it is not difficult to see how a liberal political order – one committed to safeguarding a private sphere demarcated by a set of individual rights – might be understood as fostering the value of individuality'.[15] This interpretation appears to be based on solid grounds insofar as Fichte holds right to be a

interest precisely because it attempts to overcome a purely formalistic standpoint by 'applying' the concept of right to the conditions of the sensible world, and, in so doing, gives rise to a distinctive theory of property, whose implications are rigorously pursued by Fichte himself.
14 GA I / 3: 395; FNR: 92.
15 Neuhouser, 'Fichte and the Relationship between Right and Morality', 163.

condition of individuality, in the sense that it both consists in and guarantees a type of relation in which each person limits his own activity and thereby leaves open to other persons a sphere in which they may come to determine themselves as individuals by exercising their capacity for free choice. Having made this link between Fichte's theory of right and the idea of a liberal political order, Neuhouser goes on to claim that for Fichte 'the rational basis of the liberal political order would reside, most fundamentally, in its ability to form the self-conceptions of its members as free individuals'.[16] According to Neuhouser's careful analysis of Fichte's position, this means that a liberal political order must foster in its members a conception of themselves as having the capacity to engage in conscious, goal-directed activity, and make them conscious of themselves as such and as free, which itself requires being capable of translating one's intended purposes into real actions in the external world, so as to become conscious of oneself as an agent.[17] A liberal political order is thus held to perform a positive as well as a negative function. The latter is that of protecting the rights of its members, while the former is that of helping to form and reinforce their conceptions of themselves as free and rational beings.

It is not my intention to question Neuhouser's account of Fichte's views on what is required of a political order that accords with the demands of right, since I think it is essentially correct and that it throws considerable light on the basic intentions of Fichte's theory of right. I do, however, intend to question the idea that Fichte can be regarded as providing support for the view that a liberal political order is the one best equipped to perform both the negative and positive functions mentioned above. In fact, if we trace the course of Fichte's arguments in sufficient detail, which demands taking seriously the idea that the concept of right needs to be applied, it becomes evident that the kind of political order he thinks is necessary to develop the self-conscious, rational and free agency described by Neuhouser is very different in kind to a liberal one in any meaningful sense of the term. The attempt to situate Fichte's political philosophy firmly in the liberal tradition, and to view him, moreover, as developing a justification of a liberal political order, therefore appears misguided. By a liberal political order I have in mind one that guarantees the right to property, understood as the right to exclude others from the

16 Neuhouser, 'Fichte and the Relationship between Right and Morality', 168f.
17 Neuhouser, 'Fichte and the Relationship between Right and Morality', 163ff.

use or benefit of something, and to dispose of it as one pleases; that regards restrictions on human freedom as something that should be kept to an absolute minimum, which requires establishing firm and effective guarantees against any attempt on the part of the state to inter- fere unduly in the lives of individuals; and that does not rest on any particular conception of the good life, but instead aims to make it possible for individuals to pursue their own personal conceptions of the good life, as long as they do not thereby prevent others from doing the same.

With respect to the concept of property, it is significant that Neuhouser claims that by the time Fichte wrote the *Foundations of Natural Right* he 'had come to view individually owned property as essential to the realization of human subjectivity and as a central concern of a theory of right'.[18] In the absence of any indications to the contrary, I think we can safely assume that the term 'property' is here being understood in its modern sense of something from whose use or benefit one has the right to exclude others, and which one may dispose of as one pleases. We shall see that Fichte does not himself use the term 'property' exclusively in the modern sense of the term. Moreover, although he thinks that a political order in which the right to property is realized must perform the negative function of guaran- teeing this right, so as to perform the more positive function of helping form and reinforce individual human beings' conceptions of them- selves as free and rational, the concept of property that Fichte employs requires a set of institutional arrangements and redistributive meas- ures that liberals would surely find unacceptable. In fact, by suggesting that only a different kind of political order to a liberal one can adequately perform both the negative function of guaranteeing the right to property and the more positive one of enabling human beings to develop a conception of themselves as free and rational, Fichte succeeds in casting doubt on the ability of liberalism to realize some of its own essential aspirations.

This is a point I develop in Chapter 1, in which I look at Fichte's theory of property and its implications, and in which I begin to show that Fichte's further determination of the sphere of activity that is to be guaranteed in accordance with the normative idea of a relation of right undermines the kind of liberal interpretation of his theory of right offered by Neuhouser. Such an interpretation neglects the way in which the need to apply the concept of right leads to a fuller understanding of what the

18 Neuhouser, 'Fichte and the Relationship between Right and Morality', 173.

actualization of this concept really requires. The liberal reading of Fichte's theory of right offered by Neuhouser will be shown, in fact, to depend on taking the first part of the *Foundations of Natural Right* in abstraction from its application to the conditions of the sensible world. This type of reading thus distorts Fichte's position, by ignoring the way in which the application of the concept of right can lead us to modify our understanding of such a central political concept as that of the right to property. Fichte also ultimately appears to advocate a certain conception of the good life based on a view of society that, especially when it is viewed from an historical perspective, sits uncomfortably with the idea of a liberal political order. I show, in short, that it makes little sense to identify Fichte's social and political philosophy with a liberal social and political order, either in conceptual or in historical terms.

In Chapter 2, this rejection of a liberal interpretation of Fichte's political philosophy will be buttressed by an account of the compatibility of his theory of property with the radical phase of the French Revolution, and, in particular, with some of the main doctrines associated with the revolutionary figure of Gracchus Babeuf, who attempted unsuccessfully to initiate a second radical phase of the Revolution at roughly the same time as the first part of Fichte's *Foundations of Natural Right* was published. Consequently, although Fichte's relation to the French Revolution may not, like Hegel's, focus on the idea of civil society, he will be shown to develop a theory of right that in a number of significant respects finds its corresponding expression in some of the main ideas associated with this historical event, especially its most radical phase. In this respect, far from being an abstraction from the historical process that during his own lifetime was helping to determine the shape of the modern world, Fichte's theory of right can be seen to reflect certain ideas that people living in revolutionary France had attempted, or were attempting, to put into practice. Hopefully, this should go some way towards counteracting the image of Fichte as an entirely abstract thinker, whose thought bore little, if any, relation to historical reality, suggested by the claim that he simply deduced and postulated his theory of right *a priori* out of his own head.

Since I pay close attention in Chapters 1 and 2 to Fichte's attempt to 'apply' the concept of right to the conditions of the sensible world, I am led to discuss in some detail a text which represents the final application of this concept, insofar as its application still occurs at the level of theory and has yet to enter the world of actual politics. The text in question is *The Closed Commercial State* (*Der geschloßne Handelsstaat*), which was published in 1800, not long after Fichte's dismissal from the University of Jena in the wake of accusations of atheism that had been levelled against him there.[19] This work has been described, not without good reason, as representing 'perhaps the most extreme utopia of a closed state and society for the task of realizing state-directed socialism and of securing work for every citizen'.[20]

Although such a description by itself suggests that this work must constitute an embarrassment to anyone wishing to offer an interpretation of Fichte's social and political philosophy that caters to an age and society in which liberalism has become the dominant political and economic ideology, I show that it forms an integral part of Fichte's theory of right, and that it must, therefore, be taken into account when considering the compatibility of his theory of right with the central tenets of liberalism. Indeed, some of the main proposals found in *The Closed Commercial State* are already outlined in the second part of the *Foundations of Natural Right*. To ignore this text altogether thus threatens to result in a highly truncated account of Fichte's theory of right, which fails to go beyond a merely formal theory of right; whereas Fichte's own claim that the concept of right needs to be applied clearly signals that he himself wishes to avoid such formalism. For this reason alone, I would dispute the claim that Fichte himself stressed that the transcendental foundations of the concepts of right and the state that he developed in the *Foundations of Natural Right* were to be strictly distinguished from the 'fictional empirical' model of the state found in *The Closed Commercial State*. This claim is not surprisingly made in connection with an attempt to interpret Fichte's theory of right in liberal terms, by arguing that in this theory Fichte develops the most nuanced and interesting concept of the welfare state of his own time on the basis of the liberal tradition.[21]

We may, of course, question whether Fichte's concept of property as developed in the *Foundations of Natural Right* actually requires the specific measures that he outlines in the second part of this work and in *The Closed Commercial State*. Yet, as against the claim that the transcendental ground of the concepts of right and the state can be regarded in complete abstraction from the question of their

19 For a brief account of the so-called Atheism Controversy (*Atheismusstreit*), see Breazeale, 'Editor's Introduction: Fichte in Jena', 40ff.
20 Kohn, 'The Paradox of Fichte's Nationalism', 331.
21 Frischmann, 'Die Herausbildung des Sozialstaatsdenkens im neuzeitlichen Kontraktualismus von Hobbes bis Fichte', 58of.

application to experience, Fichte can be credited with having attempted to develop the full implications of his theory of property, by
developing an empirical model that seeks to realize this theory in
relation to the conditions of the sensible world, in which individuals
confront each other with potentially conflicting claims concerning
their rights to parts of the world and the objects within it. I would
suggest that this places the onus on anyone who wishes to offer a
liberal reading of Fichte's theory of right to show, at the very least, that
his theory of property can be reconciled with the way in which liberal
states actually function. Moreover, as I show in Chapter 3 in relation
to Fichte's views on the theory of cosmopolitan right developed by
Kant, Fichte is able to identify in *The Closed Commercial State* an important issue that is still relevant today concerning the relation of individual states to other states. This issue is the problem of one-sided
forms of economic dependence. I argue that Fichte's identification of
this problem, as compared to Kant's neglect or, as I suggest, simple
acceptance of it, is by itself enough to show that the work in question
does not deserve to be treated as an entirely expendable part of
Fichte's theory of right.

Including as it does an account of the full and systematic application
of the concept of property, Fichte's theory of property represents an
attempt to deal with the problems raised by some of the realistic
assumptions he makes concerning the possible failure and absence of
relations of mutual recognition between human beings, leading him to
argue for the necessity of a state authority that is in the position to
enforce property rights, as he understands them. In line with this
acknowledgement of the essentially contingent nature of mutual recognition at the empirical, if not at the transcendental, level, Fichte
stresses the merely hypothetical nature of the relation of right in the
following passage:

> It is not possible to point to an absolute reason why someone should
> make the formula of right – limit your freedom so that the other
> alongside you can also be free – into a law of his own will and actions.
> This much is clear: a community [*Gemeinschaft*] of free beings as such
> cannot exist if each is not subject to this law; and therefore, whoever
> wills such a community must also necessarily will the law; and thus the
> law has hypothetical validity. *If* a community of free beings as such
> is to be possible, then the law of right must hold.[22]

22 GA I / 3: 387; FNR: 82.

This passage shows that for Fichte the relation of right is contingent on certain human beings actually willing the end of living in community with others. The condition of mutual recognition that Fichte thinks he is able to deduce as a condition of self-consciousness in the first part of the *Foundations of Natural Right* thus turns out to be something merely possible that needs to be actualized by means of human will and action, and he accordingly describes the concept of right as a 'merely technical-practical' one.[23] Since, however, Fichte's theory of mutual recognition implies that human beings must be part of a community of free beings in order to become conscious of themselves as free, there appears to be some inconsistency involved in maintaining that the existence of such a community depends on an act of freedom, in the shape of an individual's decision to limit his freedom in relation to other human beings with the intention of establishing a condition of right. This is a point to which I shall shortly return. First, however, I shall relate the idea that the concept of right is something merely possible to the problem of its merely formal character and Fichte's distinctive claim that the concept of right must be applied to the conditions of the sensible world.

Fichte points to the merely formal nature of the law 'limit your freedom through the freedom of all others', when he claims that, as it stands, this law cannot be applied, because it does not, by itself, provide an answer to the question as to 'just how far should the sphere of each individual extend within which no one may disturb him and beyond which he, for his part, may not go without being regarded as someone who disturbs the freedom of others?'[24] The question of the extent to which each person's freedom extends or may extend is one that needs to be answered, even though the answer given to it presupposes the possibility of the existence of relations of mutual recognition between human beings. After all, even if we accept Fichte's claim that relations of mutual recognition can be discovered *a priori* in human reason as conditions of self-consciousness, this does not rule out the potential for conflict at a more empirical level. This is especially the case when relations between human beings are mediated by external objects and parts of the sensible world, as indeed they must be in the case of finite rational beings. To this extent, relations of mutual recognition

---

23 GA I / 3: 320; FNR: 10.
24 GA I / 3: 326f.; FNR: 15.

between human beings need to be produced and constituted in such a way as to avoid or mitigate potential conflicts over such objects and parts of the world; and this implies that these relations will need to be determined by means of human thought and action.

In the *Foundations of Natural Right*, Fichte adopts what is arguably the most radical expression of the idea that juridical and political relations must be constructed by human beings with the aim of preventing conflict between them, namely, the theory that the state is based on a contract into which each of its members has freely entered. Such an approach may appear to be at odds with Fichte's claim that the concept of right is a concept of pure reason that does not depend on arbitrary human conventions. However, as we shall see in due course, the contract that Fichte has in mind is not an entirely arbitrary one, since it is subject to the normative constraints that stem from his theory of property, which itself represents an attempt to determine further the relation of right that he deduces as a condition of self-consciousness in the first part of the *Foundations of Natural Right*.

The way in which Fichte further specifies and seeks to realize the concept of right in the course of the *Foundations of Natural Right* has led to the accusation that he fails to develop the implications of his theory of mutual recognition as a transcendental condition of right, because he comes instead to develop a theory of the state based on egoism and in which coercion, as opposed to recognition, plays a major role in establishing and maintaining the relation of right.[25] This criticism involves understanding the relation of right, as Fichte presents it in his deduction of the concept of right, as an essentially moral relation based on acts of mutual recognition, which does not, therefore, need to be maintained by means of coercion. See, for example, the following description of the concept of right as expressing a relation that is

> a morally necessary one, i.e., the idea of a rational-moral community, not unlike Kant's kingdom of ends. In his concept of community (*Gemeinschaft*), Fichte reflects the concept of a universal law made by freedom that places restrictions upon the freedom of all, a freely imposed self-restraint.[26]

25 Cf. Williams, 'The Displacement of Recognition by Coercion in Fichte's Grundlage des Naturrechts'.
26 Williams, *Recognition*, 54f.

If, as is done here, one conceives of the relation of right in essentially moral terms, there would indeed appear to be a contradiction between this relation and the amoral conception of the state that Fichte goes on to develop in the later parts of the *Foundations of Natural Right*. It is far from obvious, however, that Fichte himself thought of the relation of right as an essentially moral one at any stage in this work, including his deduction of the concept of right. After all, he stresses that the concept of right is not to be confused with the moral one of duty, which is in fact 'directly opposed to the concept of right in most of its characteristics'.[27] For example, even when a person has the right to something, the moral law or law of ethics (*das Sittengesez*) may forbid this person from exercising the very same right.[28] It is on grounds such as this one that Fichte holds the science of right to be entirely separate from the science of morality, leading him to claim categorically that, 'Both sciences are already – originally and without any help from us – separated by reason itself, and they are completely opposed to one another'.[29]

Admittedly, the problem here arises that Fichte's theory of mutual recognition implies that a human being must be part of a community of free beings if he is to become conscious of himself as free, whereas his contract theory of the state, which rests on the idea that individuals consent to enter into community with others, appears to presuppose that individuals are free even before they enter into community with others. Conceiving the relation of right in moral terms provides one means of solving this problem, insofar as it points to the idea of a form of community that is prior to, and the condition of, any other form of community, including the legal and political one based on consent that we encounter in the *Foundations of Natural Right*. This moral community would, in short, have to be thought of as primary in the sense that it is the condition of a human being's first becoming conscious of himself as free, which is itself a condition of his being in the position to consent to something.

This understanding of the issue raises its own problems, however, including the one that, as we shall see in Chapter 4, Fichte makes the existence of a condition of right into a presupposition of a moral form of community, at least insofar as the possibility of establishing such a community in the sensible world is concerned. This shows not only

27 GA I / 3: 359; FNR: 50.
28 GA I / 3: 359; FNR: 50.
29 GA I / 3: 360; FNR: 51.

that there is an important sense in which Fichte thinks of a legal and political community as being prior in both conceptual and temporal terms to a moral one, but also that he makes an important distinction between the idea of a moral community as an ideal form of community and the idea of such a community insofar as it can be actualized in the sensible world. Thus, although Fichte assumes that mutual recognition between human beings must be possible, he clearly does not view such recognition as something merely given which does not itself need to be produced in the case of finite rational beings, even by means of coercion, if this should prove necessary. Moreover, Fichte conceives of a moral community itself, insofar as its existence in space and time is concerned, as something that must be produced through a process of education, as the following passage makes clear:

> For a species of perfected moral beings, there is no law of right. It is already clear that humankind cannot be such a species, from the fact that the human being must *be educated* and must *educate himself* [*sich selbst erziehen*] to the status of morality; for he is not moral [*moralisch*] by nature, but must make himself so through his own labour.[30]

In any case, even if Fichte does assert the primacy of a moral form of community based on relations of mutual recognition, the question nevertheless arises as to how this community, once its individual members have come to think of themselves as free, can be sustained over time. For, given the existence of human freedom, which entails having the capacity to will or not to will actions that accord with the demands of the moral law, it is conceivable that a state equipped with the authority and power to coerce individuals into recognizing the rights of others might still turn out to be necessary in relation to the end of maintaining the existence of a condition of mutual recognition. Thus, even if, for the sake of argument, we grant that Fichte's transcendental deduction of right as a condition of self-consciousness points to the existence of a moral form of community, this by no means invalidates the theory of the state that he develops on the basis of the concept of right, however difficult it may appear to be to reconcile the self-interest and use of coercion found in Fichte's amoral conception of the state with the uncoerced relations of mutual recognition that characterize a purely moral form of community.

30 GA I / 3: 432; FNR: 132.

It would seem, then, that, rather than accusing Fichte of inconsistency, we need to make sense of his separation of right from morality, if we are to offer an adequate interpretation of his social and political philosophy. What is more, we need to make sense of this separation of right from morality in a way that does justice to the most radical terms in which Fichte expresses it, which are to be found in the following statement:

> In the domain of natural right, the good will has no role to play. Right must be enforceable, even if there is not a single human being with a good will; the very aim of the science of right is to sketch out just such an order of things. In this domain, physical force – and it alone – gives right its sanction.[31]

In Chapter 4, I accordingly discuss Fichte's separation of right from morality in more detail. I shall argue that eliding the differences between right and morality that Fichte identifies, by reducing the relation of right to a moral relation, amounts to neglecting one of his major insights, which is to have identified and expressed in distinct terms the various types of disposition that individuals may have towards each other and the state. I also show how some remarks that Fichte makes in his deduction of the concept of right that might be thought to suggest that he conceives of the relation of right in moral terms are actually compatible with the amoral conception of the state he develops in the *Foundations of Natural Right*.

Although in the first part of the *Foundations of Natural Right* Fichte speaks of human beings as mutually recognizing each other by means of the act of limiting their activity in relation to each other, he does not specify what motivates them to act in this way. Whereas, when we look more closely at the ways in which Fichte goes on to specify the grounds on which individuals may act in the case of right, on the one hand, and in the case of morality, on the other, it becomes possible to appreciate more fully the insights contained in his separation of right from morality, and to show that it is a mistake to conceive of the relation of right in moral terms. Moreover, the kind of disposition that Fichte thinks is characteristic of the realm of right allows his amoral conception of the state to be related to the newly emerging form of society that he, unlike Hegel, is said to have failed to confront, namely, modern civil society. This is not to say that Fichte consciously engaged with this new form of

31 GA I / 3: 359; FNR: 50.

society. As we shall see, he in fact operates with a more traditional conception of society. Yet this does not prevent Fichte from identifying the kind of disposition characteristic of this new form of society, even though the step of linking the disposition in question to the idea of a civil society that is independent of the political state was taken by Hegel.

Notwithstanding this attempt to defend Fichte's separation of right from morality, I go on to question the assumption that the distinction between right and morality found in Fichte's Jena theory of the state and society is in fact an absolute one, by indicating some important ways in which right and morality can be thought to stand in an essential relation to each other. This will be done by relating the *Foundations of Natural Right* to the theory of ethical duties that Fichte sets out in another main work from his Jena period, his 1798 *The System of Ethics* (*Das System der Sittenlehre nach den Principien der Wissenschaftslehre*). It is here that I introduce the concept of virtue. Although this concept does not appear to play an especially prominent role in Fichte's ethical writings, while it is almost completely absent from his Jena theory of right, I show that a social or political form of virtue is in fact something that this theory in a number of respects presupposes. The way in which the essentially ethical concept of virtue is shown to be highly relevant to Fichte's social and political philosophy will allow me once again to relate the latter to certain ideas connected with the radical phase of the French Revolution. The concept of virtue will, moreover, be shown to be central to a fuller understanding of another of Fichte's most famous political texts, his *Addresses to the German Nation*.

The concept of virtue features in these addresses in two main ways. First of all, with respect to Fichte's conception of the scholar's, and thus his own, moral vocation, and, secondly, with respect to the question as to how the kind of virtuous citizen required by Fichte's vision of the moral regeneration of the German nation can be produced. In the *Addresses to the German Nation*, Fichte explains how such citizens can be produced in terms of a German national education. Although this system of education provides one possible answer to the question as to how a truly ethical community might be created, I argue that the particular explanation that Fichte offers shows, in fact, that the idea of such a community, insofar as its actuality in the shape of a particular, historically situated community is concerned, is not necessarily something to be welcomed, whereas the criticism that Fichte's deduction of the concept of right, given the roles played by intersubjectivity and mutual recognition within it, points to the existence of a fully ethical community and is therefore incompatible with the introduction of the concept of coercion into his theory of right, appears to assume the desirability of this type of community. The problems I identify with Fichte's attempt to explain how a genuinely ethical community can be produced suggest, moreover, that the separation of right from morality found in the social and political philosophy of his Jena period should be seen as preferable to his later attempt to moralize the realm of right.

In considering the *Addresses to the German Nation*, this book extends beyond Fichte's Jena period. It does not, however, include extensive discussions of Fichte's other writings on political subjects, such as his early *Contribution towards Correcting the Public's Judgement of the French Revolution* (*Beitrag zur Berichtigung der Urtheile des Publikums über die französische Revolution*) from 1793 and his *Rechtslehre* from 1812. Although the latter represents what is arguably Fichte's most important later work in the area of political philosophy, this fragmentary lecture manuscript constitutes only a new presentation, rather than an entirely original version, of the theory of right that Fichte developed in the *Foundations of Natural Right*. My neglect of such texts, though some mention will be made of them, is motivated by the wish to provide a systematic account of Fichte's social and political philosophy that best brings out the ways in which Fichte can be seen as responding to problems that should still be taken seriously today; and this is something that can be done, I believe, by making the concepts of property and virtue into the main organizing themes of my interpretation of Fichte's social and political philosophy. Although a systematic reading of Fichte's theory of right that aims at bringing out what is of philosophical interest in it today might also be achieved by concentrating on the writings of his Jena period,[32] there are, in my view, at least two solid reasons for extending the discussion of

32 This approach is exemplified by Alain Renaut's interpretation of Fichte's theory of right in his *Le système du droit*. Renaut stresses the systematicity of the theory of right that Fichte developed in the *Foundations of Natural Right* in various ways. To begin with, Renaut argues that right, while itself forming a system of which it constitutes the object of reflection, performs a unifying function in the philosophical system that Fichte sought to develop during his Jena period. This is the function of mediating nature and freedom, so as to effect the transition from theoretical to practical reason. Fichte's theory of right is thus placed at the very centre of his philosophical system. Although the issue of the relation of Fichte's theory of right to the other parts of his philosophical system is not one with which I deal in this book, with the notable exception of its relation to his ethical theory, there is another aspect of this systematic reading of Fichte's theory of right with which I can be seen to engage indirectly. This concerns the idea that,

Fichte's social and political philosophy to include an account of the *Addresses to the German Nation.*

The first reason is that this text is clearly relevant to the problem of the moralization of politics and the consequences it may have in relation to the possibility of human freedom. Secondly, and in connection with the first reason, it has been said that a 'deep rupture' separates the *Foundations of Natural Right* and the *Addresses to the German Nation.* This rupture is explained in terms of a shift in Fichte's views on the relation of right to morality, and, more precisely, in terms of the idea that the later work dispenses with the project of conceiving of the political realization of right in a way that makes no appeal to the morality of the citizens of the state.[33] By showing how the *Addresses to the German Nation* centres on the concept of virtue, which I argue also has an important social and political role, albeit a largely

in order to mediate nature and freedom, the possibility of realizing the concept of right in the sensible world must be demonstrated. This leads Renaut to stress the importance of Fichte's application of the concept of right. Renaut argues, however, that something he calls the antimony of political right arises from Fichte's account of the relation of freedom to constraint in his theory of right. For, on the one hand, the individual is understood as free in relation to the state, insofar as he does not transgress the rights of others; while, on the other hand, the individual is seemingly not free in relation to the state, because he must alienate unreservedly his right to make judgements concerning his rights within the legal and political community of which he is a member. Renaut associates the thesis of this antinomy with liberalism and the antithesis with authoritarianism, and he seeks to show how Fichte resolves the antimony by synthesizing the thesis and antithesis by means of the idea that the all-powerful sovereign is law, which is itself the expression of the sovereignty of the general will, in which there exists a perfect union of all individual wills.

Although Renaut is certainly correct to stress the importance of the applicability of the concept of right, my account of Fichte's theory of property suggests that his characterization of the thesis of the antimony that he identifies is wrong. Renaut identifies Fichte's theory of property primarily with this thesis, which he takes to represent the liberal element in Fichte's theory of right, describing it explicitly as a theory of private property based on the Lockean principle that the incorporation of one's labour into a material object grounds a property right to the same object (302). Although this is true of the early *Contribution towards Correcting the Public's Judgement of the French Revolution*, we shall see that it is certainly not true of the later *Foundations of Natural Right*, which contains a theory of property that appears to have very little in common with a liberal conception of property rights. Moreover, Fichte's theory of property shows that the idea of the application of the concept of right extends to *The Closed Commercial State*, whereas Renaut does not pursue it this far. In this respect, Renaut's defence of the systematicity of Fichte's theory of right, on the grounds that it represents a successful synthesis of liberalism and absolutism – or of liberalism and socialism as he otherwise characterizes it – appears premature.

33 Renaut, 'Fichte: Le droit sans la morale?', 235ff.

concealed one, to play in the writings of Fichte's Jena period, I am able to suggest that it is an exaggeration to speak of a deep rupture here, and that Fichte's social and political thought therefore exhibits a greater degree of continuity than has previously been acknowledged. The *Addresses to the German Nation* is viewed, in fact, as providing a prime example of a later text which tackles issues that already feature in the writings of Fichte's Jena period. An examination of such issues as the relation of right to morality, which is undertaken in Chapter 4, in this respect opens the way for a fuller understanding of the *Addresses to the German Nation* that goes beyond the question of the role played by these addresses in the development of German nationalism and the question of the type of nationalism they contain, which have typically formed the main focus in discussions of this text.

FICHTE'S THEORY OF PROPERTY

The theory of the state that Fichte sets out in his 1796/97 *Foundations of Natural Right* has much in common with earlier theories of the state belonging to the modern natural law tradition, such as the one developed by John Locke, insofar as the state's function is held to be the protection of property. As we shall see, Fichte, like Locke, operates with what, in the light of current linguistic usage, must be regarded as an extended meaning of the term 'property', so that there also appears to be some common ground concerning the precise nature of that which the state protects. I show, however, that such similarities should not be allowed to conceal the originality of Fichte's theory of property, in which a broad conception of property goes together with recognition of the fact that property rights may restrict human freedom, as well as being a means of realizing the latter, leading Fichte to place definite limitations on the ownership of property.

This brings me to a particular reason for regarding Fichte's theory of property as being highly significant, not only with respect to the history of political thought but also with respect to some present day concerns. The reason in question is that Fichte's theory of property provides an example of what an attempt to reconcile a liberal conception of the right to property with the equal right of individuals to use and develop their capacities by broadening the concept of property might look like. Such an approach has been advocated by C. B. Macpherson as the means of achieving the reconciliation of these two rights, both of which he considers to be essential aspirations of liberal democracy. Macpherson argues that broadening the concept of property is legitimate because the narrow concept of property as the individual right to exclude others from the use or benefit of something has become the paradigm of property for historical rather than logical reasons.[1] I argue below that although there is a sense in which Fichte appears to reconcile the right to property, understood as the right to exclude others from the use or benefit of something, with the equal right of individuals to use and develop their capacities, he also points to the limitations of the position advocated by Macpherson. Fichte does this by showing that although a broader conception of property may lead to the reconciliation of these two rights at the conceptual level, this reconciliation in turn demands reconciliation at the political level, which is no easy matter and will, in fact, require subordinating the right to exclude others from the use or benefit of something to the equal right of individuals to use and develop their capacities. In short, Fichte ends up presenting us with a hard choice between which of these rights is to be accorded priority, thereby showing himself to be prepared to pursue the full implications of his theory of property.

Thus, although the concept of property Fichte develops might be viewed as an attempt to reconcile certain rights which, according to Macpherson, represent essential aspirations of liberal democratic theory, and therefore need to be reconciled if the liberal democratic project is fully to succeed, Fichte's account as to how this concept of property can be realized, or applied, to use his own terminology, points to liberalism's inability to reconcile these rights. In this respect, a liberal interpretation of Fichte's theory of right turns out to ignore the critical potential that this theory has in relation to liberal ideology itself. This is especially the case when such a liberal interpretation contains an implicit acknowledgement of the idea expressed by Macpherson that liberal democracy aspires to reconcile the right to property, understood as the right to exclude others from the use or benefit of something, with the equal right of individuals to use and develop their capacities.

Frederick Neuhouser, for example, states that, 'even though Fichte's theory remains squarely within the liberal tradition, it at the same time provides a framework for defending many of the ideas espoused by socialist thinkers in the following century'.[2] As regards the assertion that Fichte's theory of right remains squarely within the liberal tradition, Neuhouser's previously mentioned claim that Fichte came to view individually owned property as essential to the realization

---

1 Cf. Macpherson, 'Liberal-Democracy and Property'.
2 Neuhouser, 'Introduction', xxviii.

of human subjectivity and as a central concern of a theory of right strongly suggests, in the absence of any indications to the contrary, that Neuhouser has in mind the right to exclude others from the use or benefit of something and the entitlement to dispose of it as one pleases. While this conception of property corresponds to the liberal understanding of property rights, when Neuhouser states that Fichte's theory of right provides a framework for defending ideas later espoused by socialist thinkers, he presumably has in mind the redistributive measures that Fichte proposes in the second part of the *Foundations of Natural Right*.

In this chapter, I show that this view of Fichte's theory of right greatly overestimates the extent to which Fichte's understanding of property corresponds to the liberal conception of property rights, and that it therefore represents a failure to gain a proper understanding of what exactly Fichte means by the term 'property'. This failure is especially problematic given the central role that the concept of property plays in Fichte's theory of right. Nor does it help to describe Fichte's position using the hybrid term 'liberal socialism', on the grounds that he reconciles such 'liberal' rights as the right to private property and the right to freedom of expression with such economic rights as the right to gainful employment.[3] The problem with this move is not only that it mistakenly equates Fichte's own understanding of property with the liberal right to private property, but also that it does not take seriously enough the extent to which Fichte limits the right to private property in favour of economic rights. Whereas when one does take seriously the extent to which he limits the right to private property in favour of economic rights, it becomes far from obvious that these two kinds of rights are reconciled in Fichte's theory of right.

In order to deal with the set of issues mentioned above, I must first outline Fichte's theory of property and its place within his theory of right, as it is presented in the *Foundations of Natural Right*, which falls into two main parts. The first part concerns the deduction of the concept of right and the demonstration of the possibility of applying this concept to the conditions of the sensible world, while the second part involves the actual application of the concept of right to the conditions of the sensible world. I also refer to the way in which Fichte seeks to develop the implications of his theory of property in *The Closed Commercial State*, though a fuller discussion of this widely

3 Nomer, 'Fichte and the Idea of Liberal Socialism', 53.

ignored work will be reserved for Chapters 2 and 3. I show that although it is possible to think of Fichte as reconciling the right to property, understood as the right to exclude others from the use or benefit of something, with the right to develop and use one's capacities at the conceptual level, he recognizes that definite limitations need to be placed on human freedom insofar as it consists in the freedom to appropriate parts of the world and external objects and to exclude others from the use or benefit of them, if the right to develop and use one's capacities is also to be realized by more than just a limited number of human beings. I also compare Fichte's theory of property to Locke's theory of property, so as to bring out the way in which Fichte consistently develops his insight into the fact that the right to property, understood as the right to exclude others from the use or benefit of something, may often violate the right of others to use and develop the set of capacities that he associates with the ideas of rationality and self-determination.

Fichte on property

As we have seen, Fichte identifies the concept of right with a relation in which human beings reciprocally limit their natural freedom. This act of self-limitation involves leaving open to others a sphere in which they may exercise free choice. The relation of right thus enables each person to distinguish himself from others by means of the different choices that he makes within this sphere, so as to become an individual distinct from others in ways that extend beyond the possession of certain merely natural differences, such as having different physical features or psychological characteristics from others. In this respect, the relation of right must be thought to constitute a condition of individuality and to make possible a specific form of self-determination, namely, the exercise of free choice. Right does not, therefore, simply amount to the imposition of limitations, albeit legitimate and necessary ones, on natural freedom: it also constitutes a positive condition of human agency.

In the *Foundations of Natural Right*, Fichte describes the type of human agency in question as containing two main elements. To begin with, there is 'the capacity to construct [*entwerfen*], through absolute sponta-neity, concepts of our possible efficacy [*Wirksamkeit*]',[4] that is to say, the

---

4 GA I / 3: 319; FNR: 9.

capacity freely to form the ends which direct one's actions. Yet if a person is to become conscious of his freedom, the following demand must also be met: that 'the object in experience that is thought of through the concept of the person's efficacy actually correspond to that concept; what is required, therefore, is that something in the world outside the rational individual follow from the thought of his activity'.[5] In other words, a person must also be able to realize his freely formed ends in the world, by turning, through his own actions, that which is merely thought into something that actually exists in space and time. For only in this way is the rational individual able to receive an external confirmation of his conception of himself as free and as having the ability to shape the world in accordance with the ends he has formed.

We shall see, however, that Fichte imposes extensive limitations on individual freedom of choice, so as to make law or right into a truly positive condition of human agency that guarantees all persons the genuine possibility of acting freely and effectively in the world. Although the way in which right is held to guarantee persons a sphere of activity in which they are free to act, and to constitute a condition of individuality, makes it tempting to identify the kind of political order that Fichte has in mind with a liberal one, Fichte's account of what the relation of right ultimately requires will, in fact, turn out to suggest that there are some significant problems with such a liberal interpretation of his theory of right. For this kind of interpretation will be shown to neglect the way in which Fichte treats the concept of property, which is itself a further determination of the concept of right, as a concept that needs to be applied to the conditions of the sensible world, with the process of its application leading to a fuller understanding of this concept.

Fichte introduces the concept of property in the third main division of the first part of the *Foundations of Natural Right*. This division concerns the systematic application of the concept of right, and Fichte refers to it as the doctrine of right (*Rechtslehre*), thereby indicating that this section of the work is concerned with explicating the basic principles of right insofar as they concern relations between persons in the sensible world. Fichte here develops the concept of right by deriving various principles of right from this concept after having deduced it as a condition of self-consciousness and having demonstrated the possibility of applying it in the previous two divisions of the first part of the *Foundations of Natural Right*. However, since Fichte is concerned only

5 GA I / 3: 319f.; FNR: 9.

with these principles of right in abstraction from their relation to actual experience, his application of the concept of right continues even at this stage to represent a merely formal element in his theory of right. Among the principles of right that Fichte identifies are certain original rights (*Urrechte*), which 'are contained in the mere concept of the person as such'.[6] Since Fichte uses the term 'person' to designate the type of being that 'posits' itself by exclusively ascribing to itself a sphere of freedom and by choosing freely within this sphere, an original right can be understood to express a condition of such agency. There are, according to Fichte, two main original rights: the right to 'the continued existence of the absolute freedom and inviolability of the body', and the right to 'the continued existence of our free influence within the entire sensible world'.[7] Fichte's initial justification of the right to property falls under the second of these original rights, since it turns on the idea that our free influence in the sensible world depends on the latter exhibiting certain regularities, not only with respect to the laws of nature, which are in any case unchangeable, but also with respect to the positions in space and time of the objects that we employ in order to realize our ends.

On the face of it, Fichte's account of original rights suggests the possibility of a liberal reading of his political philosophy. For what we appear to have is a set of rights that are not to be violated on the grounds that to do so would prevent individuals from acting freely within the limits set by the demand that in acting freely they do not themselves violate the right of others to do the same, whereas everyone has a right to all other actions which do not make 'the freedom and personality of another impossible'.[8] It should also be noted that there is no reference to the actual content of the ends that persons may pursue, apart from the demand that these ends must not themselves lead to any violations of right. In this respect, the principles of right do not seek to specify a particular, exclusive conception of the good life; they are instead restricted to identifying the conditions that would allow individuals to pursue their own conceptions of the good life insofar as their doing so remains compatible with the right of others to do the same. The end of right is, in short, that of guaranteeing individual liberty. Since liberal political theory has traditionally sought to avoid advocating an exclusive conception of the good life and has

6 GA I / 3: 390; FNR: 87.   7 GA I / 3: 409; FNR: 108.   8 GA I / 3: 390; FNR: 86f.

restricted itself to the same task that, as it stands, appears to motivate Fichte's theory of right, one might concede that this theory does indeed invite a liberal interpretation.

Then there is the way in which Fichte grounds the right to property on the idea that the world in which one acts must exhibit sufficient regularity and predictability to allow a person to form ends and to realize them in the sensible world. This approach evokes the idea of the right to property understood as the right to exclude others from the use or benefit of something, which implies viewing property as something that a person has an exclusive right to dispose of as he pleases. The apparent compatibility of the original right to property with the liberal right to private property means that it is not surprising that Neuhouser, who seeks to cast Fichte primarily as a liberal thinker, should refer to the theory of original rights in order to support his liberal reading of Fichte's *Foundations of Natural Right*, deliberately going no further than Fichte's account of these original rights, thereby restricting himself to the first part of this work.[9] To go no further than this, however, amounts to ignoring not only Fichte's attack on the formalism of other theories of natural right, which he reiterates in his account of original rights, but also his strictures concerning the idea of original rights.

Fichte refers to the idea of an original right as 'a mere *fiction*', and he even goes so far as to claim that there 'is no condition in which original rights exist; and no original rights of human beings'.[10] He makes such claims because the idea of original rights involves abstracting from the relations of free individuals to each other; whereas it is only within the context of such relations that it makes any real sense to talk about rights. This is partly a conceptual issue: Fichte points out that although an individual may have power over an external object, this does not by itself amount to a right to this object unless another person stands in some kind of relation to the same object.[11] In other words, the right to an object consists in both a relation to an object and a relation to another person by means of this same object, with one person being

---

9 Cf. Neuhouser, 'Fichte and the Relationship between Right and Morality', 167.
10 GA I / 3: 403f.; FNR: 102.
11 GA I / 3: 360; FNR: 51. Fichte is not himself always consistent on this point, however. For example, he speaks of a person who is thought of as being isolated in the world as having the right, as opposed to the power, to extend his freedom as far as he wills and can; a right which Fichte describes as 'the right to take possession of the entire sensible world' (GA I / 3: 412; FNR: 111).

in some way obligated to respect another person's claim to the object in question. In the case of a person's power over an object, however, no form of obligation can be thought to arise, because it makes no sense whatsoever to think of the object itself as being obligated to respect a person's claim to it.[12] Obligations can, in short, arise only between human beings, so that we cannot speak of rights in abstraction from the relations existing between human beings. Once a relation to others is taken to be constitutive of what it means to talk about rights, questions arise concerning the extent to which original rights, which abstract from such relations, can be thought of at all; and the way in which Fichte develops the concept of property in the course of his application of the concept of right serves to illustrate this point.

Given the way in which the right to something implies a relation to other persons, Fichte argues that the extent of a person's freedom in relation to another person's freedom must be founded on consent, for only in this way, it seems, can conflict be avoided by transforming the relation between independent persons into a rightful one based on obligation rather than physical force. This consent consists in each person declaring what he takes to be his and in his reaching an agreement with others on this matter, as well as on the conventions that are to govern all future acts of appropriation. Only in this way, according to Fichte, does possession, which signifies merely the power over an object at a given time, become property, in which case there also exists the right to exclude others from the use or benefit of something. Yet this process of mutual declaration and recognition of the extent to which each person's freedom extends itself gives rise to the problem as to what is to happen given the rational fear that one party may fail to honour the terms of any agreements thus made. Fichte's ultimate solution to this problem is the institution of a state authority equipped with coercive powers. This means that for him 'there is no *natural right* [*Naturrecht*] at all in the sense often given to that term, i.e. there can be no rightful [*rechtliches*] relation between human beings except within a commonwealth [*in einem gemeinen Wesen*] and under positive laws'.[13]

---

12 Something similar might be said of a situation in which one person has power over another person by means of physical force, as indeed Rousseau recognizes when he makes a distinction between relations based on force and those based on genuine consent in the first book of *The Social Contract*. Cf. Rousseau, 'Du contract social; ou, principes du droit politique', in *Œuvres complètes*, vol. III, 351ff.; The Social Contract *and Other Later Political Writings*, 41ff.

13 GA I / 3: 432; FNR: 132.

This claim should not, however, be understood as advocating some form of legal positivism, whereby right turns out to be nothing more than that which the state declares it to be in the form of positive laws.[14] For we shall see that Fichte clearly retains some notion of natural law or right, in the sense of the existence of certain normative constraints that can be identified by the use of human reason, and in the light of which the legitimacy of positive laws can be judged. The claim in question nevertheless tells us that original rights are of a fictional nature not only in the sense that they involve abstracting, for theoretical purposes, from the determinate relations existing between human beings that must be taken into consideration if the concept of right is to be fully applied, but also in the sense that once these relations are taken into consideration, such original rights turn out to presuppose, insofar as their actuality is concerned, a number of other things, including the existence of certain institutions.

It is in this respect that Fichte provides a negative answer to the question as to whether 'a genuine doctrine of natural right is possible, by which we mean a science of the relation of right between persons outside the state and without positive law'.[15] Moreover, Fichte's account of the problems that arise in relation to the original right to property introduced in the first part of the *Foundations of Natural Right* represents a clear attempt to justify this negative answer to the question as to whether there could be a genuine doctrine of natural right. For these problems, which all concern the possibility of conflict in relation to individual claims regarding ownership of parts of the world or of the objects within it, require modifying our understanding of the right to property, so as to allow for its full application to the conditions of the sensible world, which include the potentially conflict-ridden relations of free persons to each other. Although in Fichte's account of original rights there is no indication whatsoever that the right to property does not amount to the right both to exclude others from the use or benefit of something and to dispose of it as one pleases, it need not, therefore, be seen as an inconsistency on his part when he comes to limit the right to property understood in this way in the second part of the *Foundations of Natural Right*, which concerns the

---

14 Such an understanding of Fichte's position is suggested by the claim that rather than proving the existence of a form of right that constrains the actions of the state, Fichte deduces the necessity of a state which first posits right. Cf. Braun, *Freiheit, Gleichheit, Eigentum*, 15.

15 GA I / 3: 395; FNR: 92.

application of the principles of right established in the first part of this work to the conditions of the sensible world.

In the second part of the *Foundations of Natural Right*, the themes of mutual declaration and recognition of property rights found in the first part of this work resurface in Fichte's account of the civil contract (*Staatsbürgervertrag*), which concerns the act whereby individuals consent to the establishment of state authority. For Fichte, the object of this contract is 'exclusive' property, by which he means something that not only exhibits the regularity and stability that allow a person both to form ends and to realize them in the sensible world, but also, unlike light or air, say, allows itself to be divided up and its boundaries or limits clearly marked.[16] Prior to the civil contract, individuals have an equal right to such property, in the sense that the limits of a person's original rights can be legitimately determined only by means of consent; whereas any limits on the possession of parts of the world or the objects within it based on physical force cannot give rise to any lasting obligation to recognize the property of others, since everything here merely depends on who happens to be in the best position to coerce others at any given moment in time. Although the idea that property rights must be based on consent does not by itself rule out the possibility of thinking of property in terms of something from whose use or benefit one has the right to exclude others and which one has the right to dispose of as one pleases, in his account of the civil contract Fichte speaks of property 'in the broadest sense of the word', by which he means 'a person's rights to free action in the sensible world in general'.[17] We shall shortly discover the reason behind this move and its importance for a proper understanding of Fichte's theory of property.

In the first part of the civil contract, the citizens' property contract, persons agree among themselves concerning their respective rights and freedoms. This can be interpreted as meaning that they enter into a contract with each other concerning the extent of both their free actions in the sensible world and that which serves as a means in relation to these actions. Such agreement involves the declaration of what each person takes these rights and freedoms to be and the agreement of others to recognize what each person has declared to be his property; an agreement which can be honoured simply by one person

16 GA I / 4: 5; FNR: 165.
17 GA I / 4: 8; FNR: 168.

limiting his freedom in relation to the property of others. The second part of the civil contract, the protection contract, consists in the parties to the citizens' property contract agreeing to protect each other's property. Yet, in the absence of any firm guarantee that the terms of this contract will be honoured, a third contract becomes necessary, the unification contract, whereby a protective power, in the form of state authority, is established. Each person contributes towards the maintenance of this protective power and in this way fulfils his obligation to protect the property of others. Having given his account of the civil contract, Fichte goes on to say more about what the property contract, which forms the first stage of the civil contract, actually involves. It is here that he elaborates on what he means by property 'in the broadest sense of the word'. As we shall see, although Fichte does not dispense altogether with the idea of original rights, nor with the notion of exclusive property, he introduces some important qualifications with respect to these ideas, so as to show how the concept of right can be fully applied to the conditions of the sensible world.

For Fichte, the first part of the civil contract, the property contract, grounds the relations of right that exist between individuals in the state, and it thus forms the foundation of civil legislation. This stage of the civil contract shows how, with regard to the state's function, Fichte appears to be in basic agreement with an earlier representative of the modern natural law tradition such as Locke, insofar as the latter states that political power includes the right of making laws 'for the Regulating and Preserving of Property, and of employing the force of the Community, in the Execution of such Laws'.[18] Moreover, both Fichte and Locke operate with a conception of property that does not restrict the latter to land and goods, which is why Fichte speaks of property 'in the broadest sense of the word'. In Locke's case, this is evident from his claim that men join in society with others 'for the mutual *Preservation* of their Lives, Liberties and Estates, which I call by the general Name, *Property*'.[19] For property is here identified with three different things: the continued existence of oneself as a natural being; the various rights that one has in relation to other individuals and in relation to society as a whole; and the land and goods that one owns. How exactly is Fichte to be seen as operating with a similarly broad conception of property?

18 Locke, *Two Treatises of Government*, 268.
19 Locke, *Two Treatises of Government*, 350.

In his account of property in the second part of the *Foundations of Natural Right*, Fichte claims in accordance with the outcome of the property contract that each individual is allocated a sphere containing certain objects for the exercise of his freedom. This is in line with the idea of an original right to property to the extent that Fichte identifies this right with the continued existence of our free influence within the entire sensible world, which he thinks can only be guaranteed by each person reaching an agreement with all other persons concerning the extent of his and their freedom and rights and, ultimately, by the establishment of state authority. Fichte's description of the outcome of the property contract is also compatible with his claim that the object of the property contract is 'a particular activity'.[20] This claim already signals that Fichte does not necessarily mean by exclusive property parts of the world or the objects within it; and it may therefore strike one as strange if one has been assuming all along, on the basis of Fichte's initial presentation of the right to property in his account of original rights, that he equates property with land and goods understood as objects from whose use or benefit an individual has the right to exclude others and which he may dispose of as he pleases. Such an assumption, however, is not warranted by Fichte's description of exclusive property as something that possesses the regularity and predictability that allow an individual to form ends and to seek to realize them in the sensible world, as well as being something that can be divided up and its boundaries or limits clearly marked. For, as we shall see, Fichte thinks that particular activities can be characterized in such a way as to meet these requirements.

Fichte in fact understands property to be, broadly speaking, something external to a person which constitutes a condition of this person's being able to act freely and effectively in the sensible world, though we shall encounter below an important exception to this general conception of property. When it is understood in this way, property may involve the secure possession of material objects and parts of the world, but it may equally include the right to undertake a certain activity, which Fichte clearly considers to be a more fundamental property right than the right to exclude others from the use or benefit of parts of the world or the objects within it and to dispose of them as one pleases. In this respect, Fichte's talk of a 'sphere' in which an individual can exercise free choice is to be viewed as partly

20 GA I / 4: 20; FNR: 184.

metaphorical. Indeed, when it comes to the identification of property with land, which might be thought to correspond most closely to the idea of a sphere within which one acts, Fichte castigates this view of property, claiming that it is based on the idea that property consists in the exclusive possession of a thing. Historically, this view of property has, Fichte argues, made the nobility, as the owners of the largest amount of land, into the only true owners of property and the only citizens who form a state; and against this view of property, which has given rise to such injustices, he defines 'the first and original' form of property as 'an exclusive right to a determinate free activity'.[21] The precise sense in which this right to a determinate free activity for Fichte constitutes a more fundamental form of property than the right to land and goods, which he holds to be only conditional forms of property, can be explained with reference to the way in which he proceeds to link this understanding of property as the right to a particular activity to a right that he takes to be the most basic of all rights: the right to be able to live from one's labour.

Fichte argues for this right on the grounds that all activity is subordinate to the single one of being able to live. He bases this claim on the fact that human agency aims to bring about certain states of affairs and therefore has an essential relation to the future, together with the fact that human freedom is inextricably linked to the continued existence of a person's own body, because 'the free being – as appearance – is identical with its body',[22] in the sense that his body constitutes the means by which a person interacts with the world and other human beings. In short, the capacity to form ends and to seek to realize them in the world, as a form of activity that is necessarily oriented towards the future, depends on a person's ability to preserve himself, which in turn depends on having the means to live. This essential link between a person's agency and his continued existence as a natural being finds immediate expression in a physical feeling, the feeling of pain occasioned by hunger and thirst, leading Fichte to claim that 'the need for nourishment alone is the original impetus – and its satisfaction the ultimate end – of the state and of all human life and conduct'.[23] For Fichte, the end of being able to live is thus to be understood as the condition of all other ends, in the sense that a person's continued

21 GA I / 7: 85.
22 GA I / 3: 405; FNR: 103.
23 GA I / 4: 21; FNR: 185.

existence as a natural being is the ultimate condition of his being able
to act effectively and freely in the world. The end of being able to live is,
therefore, an end that all persons *qua* natural beings must be thought
to share, even insofar as they are also free and rational beings. In this
way, self-preservation is viewed not merely as a matter of preserving
oneself as a living organism, but also, and more essentially, as the
necessary means of preserving one's own will, that is, one's capacity
to be self-determining.[24]

As we shall see, this understanding of the right to be able to live from
one's labour as the most basic object of the property contract leads
Fichte to introduce a set of limitations on the freedom to own and
dispose freely of other forms of property. This apparent shift in his
theory of property should not, however, be viewed as an inconsistency
on Fichte's part, given his theory of original rights, which lends itself
to being understood in terms of the modern liberal conception of
property as the right to exclude others from the use or benefit of something and to dispose of it as one pleases.[25] Rather, the concept of
property, and with it the concept of right, has become more determinate
by means of its application to the conditions of the sensible world, which
include the biological conditions of human existence as well as the
possibility of conflict between individual human beings in their attempts
to satisfy these conditions. We therefore need to pay close attention to
this process of application, if we are to grasp properly what Fichte means
by the term 'property' in the *Foundations of Natural Right.*

The most fundamental form of property is, then, the right to be able to
live, which Fichte accordingly describes as 'the absolute, inalienable property of all human beings'.[26] As something that is essentially related to
oneself, in the sense of constituting a condition of one's capacity to be self-
determining, this is a form of property that cannot be regarded as external

---

24 Cf. Siep, *Praktische Philosophie im Deutschen Idealismus,* 36f.
25 The concept of property that Fichte employs in the section on original rights has been
cited as an example of the way in which he remains tied to the liberal tradition of
thinking about rights, whereas in the later parts of the *Foundations of Natural Right* he is
said to develop a less individualistic conception of property. Cf. Verweyen, *Recht und
Sittlichkeit in J. G. Fichtes Gesellschaftslehre,* 102ff. This view of the matter fails, in my view, to
recognize the way in which Fichte's theory of property involves a process, whereby the
concept of right and the concept of property both become ever less formal or abstract,
with the more concrete understanding of these concepts that we gain by means of their
application to the conditions of the sensible world representing a more adequate
knowledge of what they actually require.
26 GA I / 4: 22; FNR: 185.

to oneself, as is the case with any parts of the world or objects within it that a person may own. It is therefore something that a person cannot alienate without at the same time renouncing his humanity, which for Fichte consists in the capacity to be self-determining. For this reason, the right to be able to live from one's labour is not something that a person could be reasonably expected to renounce on entering into the civil contract with others; rather, it is, above all other forms of property, the 'property' that this contract is designed to protect.[27] It is, in fact, the only form of property that a person can be said legitimately to possess on entering into the civil contract, whereas the right to all other forms of property must be established by means of consent. In this respect, the right to be able to live from one's labour looks very much like a natural right, that is to say, a right which, in the eyes of reason, an individual human being must be thought to possess even outside the state and in the absence of positive laws.

Given the existence of such an inalienable right, the property contract would be rendered invalid in the case of any person who turned out to be unable to live from his labour after he had entered into the civil contract. This person would be then no longer obliged to recognize the property of others, as Fichte himself points out.[28] We may assume, moreover, that, as a result of this, the person in question would be at liberty to do all that he considers to be necessary to secure the means to live. We should accordingly interpret Fichte's claim that there is no natural right except within a commonwealth and under positive laws as meaning that only the right to property, understood as the right to be able to live from one's labour, but not the right to exclude others from the use or benefit of something, which depends on consent, is a right which human beings would have even in the state of nature, though this right can itself become fully actual only in a commonwealth and under positive laws. Fichte himself suggests such an interpretation when he claims that 'the state itself becomes the human being's natural condition [*Naturstand*], and its laws ought to be nothing other than natural right realized'.[29]

---

27 Fichte can be seen in this way to make explicit the idea of what human beings would in fact be able to consent to on entering into the social contract, so that his theory of right can be taken to represent the most consistent expression of the social contract tradition in political thought, rather than a departure from this tradition. Cf. Frischmann, 'Die Herausbildung des Sozialstaatsdenkens im neuzeitlichen Kontraktualismus von Hobbes bis Fichte'.

28 GA I / 4: 22; FNR: 185f.

29 GA I / 3: 432; FNR: 133.

In order to prevent property rights from becoming destabilized by the way in which someone who is unable to live from his labour would no longer be obliged to respect the property of others, the government must take steps to ensure that each person is actually able to live from his labour, which may require taking part of the property of others and making it available to the person who is unable to live from his labour. Although Fichte suggests that such redistributive measures may simply amount to some form of welfare provision, when he speaks of others as having to subsidize (*beisteuern*) a person who is unable to live from his labour,[30] the way in which his theory of right aims to guarantee the status of persons as self-determining beings, which demands that they are granted the possibility of realizing their freely formed ends in the sensible world, implies that this would represent a far from satisfactory solution. What is ideally required is instead a redistribution of resources that would allow each person to be able to live by means of his own activity, that is to say, from his own labour. Indeed, all the concrete proposals that Fichte makes point in this direction. Although any redistribution of resources should obviously not be done in such a way as to prevent the person from whom property is taken from being able to live from his labour, this does not rule out the possibility of redistributing property in a way that prevents a person from being able to enjoy living from his labour on the same scale as before.

This possibility by itself suggests that although Fichte thinks that individual persons will have an exclusive right to property in the form of the land and goods they need in order to be able to live from their labour, they may be nevertheless required to give up at least some of this property should the need arise. They cannot, therefore, be said to have the unlimited right to dispose of this property as they please, even if they have the right to exclude others from the use or benefit of it, though only to the extent that this is necessary for them to be able to live from their labour. For this reason, Fichte holds the central role of the state to be not only to protect property, but also to allocate it to individuals in the shape of the right to perform a certain occupation and the right to the objects or parts of the world needed to do so. This dual function of the state with regard to the right to property explains Fichte's claim that the proper determination (*Bestimmung*) of the state is first to give to each person that which is his, that is, to allocate him his property, and only then to protect the latter.[31]

---

30 GA I / 4: 23; FNR: 186.   31 GA I / 7: 53.

To return to the question as to how Fichte might be thought to operate with a broad conception of property similar to Locke's, it can now be said that he does so because he develops a theory of property that treats the right to be able to live from one's labour as the most basic form of property, while this right incorporates other rights. These other rights include the right to self-preservation and the right to the opportunity to act freely and effectively in the sensible world, together with the right to possess the necessary means of achieving this end, which may include land and goods. Fichte's theory of property is thus designed to explain how human beings living together in society can secure the most basic condition of their being able to use and develop their capacities by acting freely and effectively in the sensible world. Fichte's concept of property also includes the notion of property as the right to exclude others from the use or benefit of something, though not necessarily the right to dispose of this property as one pleases, because each person's property, in the sense of an individual's right to a certain activity and all that is required to engage successfully in this activity, can be considered to be an exclusive one.

There are consequently some grounds for thinking that Fichte's theory of property reconciles the right to exclude others from the use or benefit of something with the equal right of individuals to use and develop their capacities, with both of these rights deriving from a single relation, which is the relation of right. Fichte's theory of property is not, however, reducible to the modern liberal notion of property as the right to exclude others from the use or benefit of something and to dispose of it as one pleases. For Fichte clearly considers the right to be able to live from one's labour to be the most basic form of property, and guaranteeing this right, as indicated above, for him requires measures that appear to undermine the idea of an exclusive and unlimited right to exclude others from the use or benefit of something and to dispose of it as one pleases. The question as to whether Fichte's reconciliation of these two rights is really compatible with a liberal understanding of property rights is, therefore, surely a pertinent one to ask.

To begin addressing this question, it should first be pointed out that Fichte's theory of property, as he himself recognizes, justifies the exclusive right to the use or benefit of something only to the extent that such exclusive possession of a thing is necessary in order for a person to be able to live from his labour. It consequently does not entail the continued exclusion of others from the use or benefit of something if others could use it or benefit from it without violating another person's right to be able to live from his labour. What Fichte has to say about land as a form of property, particularly the property rights of the agriculturalist (*Landbauer*), provides a good example of this kind of limitation on property rights.

On the one hand, as we might have expected given Fichte's account of original rights, the agriculturalist's exclusive right to property is grounded on the idea that nature must exhibit a predictability that derives from its remaining exactly the same as the agriculturalist has previously known it to be. This is not to say that Fichte denies that natural objects undergo change according to certain natural laws. The agriculturalist must be nevertheless able to cultivate such objects in accordance with his knowledge of these laws, whereas human interference with these objects would threaten to introduce unforeseen factors that might prevent him from being able to do so. On the other hand, Fichte explicitly rejects the idea that the right to exclude a person from a piece of land in order to be able to cultivate it amounts to an exclusive right to a piece of land, in the sense of the permanent right to dispose of this piece of land as one pleases and to exclude others unconditionally from its use or benefit. For someone who can use this same piece of land without interfering with the agriculturalist's activity should be allowed to do so. Fichte here cites the example of a miner digging beneath land that has already been parcelled out; and he argues that the miner should be allowed to do this as long as his activity does not cause the field on which the agriculturalist works to become unsafe or to cave in.[32]

Fichte claims, moreover, that only the products of the earth, or its accidents as he otherwise calls them, are the agriculturalist's absolute property, by which he can be taken to mean things from whose use or benefit the agriculturalist has the right to exclude others, and which he may dispose of as he pleases. Whereas the land itself, or the substance, is something that the populace (*die Gemeine*) have saved for the purpose of future division should such a division prove necessary.[33] This clearly implies that land cannot become private property but must instead be held in common in case it should become necessary to redistribute it with the aim of ensuring that each and every person is able to live from his labour. Therefore, although a person may be granted an exclusive right to use a piece of land, this right is not to be understood as the

---

32 GA I / 4: 26; FNR: 190.   33 GA I / 4: 27; FNR: 191.

right to dispose of this land as he pleases, nor as a permanent right to the possession of this land. Fichte himself mentions an example of the limited sense in which there can be a property right to land, when he claims that a redistribution of land will be necessary if an agriculturalist is not able to earn a living by labouring on the land that is currently available to him.[34] Although this problem could be solved by making previously unused land available to this agriculturalist, it could conceivably also require taking land from other agriculturalists, or from any other persons, who do not need it as badly as this agriculturalist needs it. In the case of land, all that can be justified in terms of right is, therefore, the exclusive right to a particular use of land.[35] This suggests that, in order to ensure that each and every person is able to live from his labour, the state may be forced to undertake redistributive measures on such a frequent basis that the right to property, understood as the right to exclude others from the use or benefit of something, would be rendered highly unstable. Given the fundamental role that private property plays in a liberal social and political order, this potential instability appears very difficult indeed to reconcile with the idea that Fichte's theory of right is essentially concerned with justifying such a social and political order.

The radical nature of this particular limitation on property rights can be brought out by comparing Fichte's position to that of Rousseau on the issue of property rights. Although Rousseau at one point describes the state as the master of all its members' goods once they have entered into the social contract, which serves as the basis of all rights within the state, he appears to suggest that the right of the first occupant may determine what property can be considered to be rightfully a person's own even before the right to property has been established by means of the social contract, though he subjects the right of the first occupant to the following conditions. A piece of land must not have been previously occupied by anyone else; one should occupy only as much land as one needs to subsist; and one must have taken possession of this land by means of labour and cultivation (*culture*).[36] In the first part of the *Foundations of Natural Right*, Fichte also appears to recognize a right of the first occupant, as long as this is a rule that persons have agreed upon.[37] Yet from what has been said above

34 GA I / 4: 26; FNR: 190.   35 GA I / 7: 86.
36 Rousseau, 'Du contract social', 365f.; The Social Contract *and Other Later Political Writings*, 54f.
37 GA I / 3: 420f.; FNR: 119f.

concerning the property contract and all that it implies, it seems that for him the state cannot ultimately consider such conventions to be binding on its actions when it comes to discharging its responsibility of guaranteeing that each and every person is able to live from his labour. This in turn means that not even labouring on and cultivating a piece of previously ownerless land can found a legal right to exclude others from the use or benefit of this piece of land, let alone a right to dispose of it as one pleases. In this respect, Fichte develops more forcefully than Rousseau himself does the implications of his claim that, regardless of the way in which land is acquired, 'the right every individual has over his own land is always subordinate to the right the community has over everyone'.[38]

Fichte removes the ambiguity that still attaches to Rousseau's account of property rights by making land into something which cannot be privately owned but is instead to be distributed by the state according to individual need. Fichte in this way retains Rousseau's demand that one should occupy only as much land as one needs to subsist, while rejecting his suggestion, however vague, that there can be property rights in land prior to the social contract and its establishment of a general will. This point is made more explicitly in the 1812 *Rechtslehre*, in which Fichte makes a distinction between the form of right and the content of right when discussing the property contract. While concluding such a property contract is by itself enough to fulfil the merely formal condition that relations between human beings should be based on agreement rather than on force, it leaves a second condition unsatisfied. This is the condition that the property contract should have a determinate content, rather than its content being a matter of arbitrariness or chance. Thus, while each party to the property contract may have possessions (*Besizthum*), though not property (*Eigenthum*), prior to entering into the property contract, the actual result of this contract may differ depending on whether or not both of the above-mentioned conditions are met. If the formal condition alone is met, each person will keep what he already possesses, if this happened to be his aim on entering into the property contract, at the same time as what he possesses becomes property through its being given the form of right, which it previously lacked. However, when the property contract is also concerned with the issue as to whether or not its content

38 Rousseau, 'Du contract social', 367; The Social Contract *and Other Later Political Writings*, 56.

is a rightful one, which for Fichte it must be, a person's claim legitimately to possess something may be called into question, and a new
division of what people possessed prior to their entering into the
property contract may turn out to be necessary.[39] Fichte's theory of
property and his understanding of the state's role in relation to property
rights suggest, moreover, that such a new division of what people possess
within the state need not be thought of as something that happens only
once. Rather, further divisions may well prove to be necessary, and it is
the state's responsibility to ensure that they take place.

Moreover, Fichte appears to hold the view that there is not to be
any private ownership of certain other objects as well as parts of the
world. This relates to the way in which he makes a particular activity,
that is, the particular occupation that enables a person to live from his
labour, into the object of the property contract, so that the particular
act whereby a person consents to the property contract is to be
identified with a public declaration of his entry into a particular
occupation.[40] In the light of this claim, an analogy with Fichte's
views on land can be pointed to, since the government may need to
redistribute other resources (e.g. tools) in order to guarantee that
each and every person is able to pursue the particular occupation into
which he has entered, as long as the person who currently possesses
these resources does not need them in order to be able to live from his
labour. This suggests that for Fichte there can be no real private
ownership of other resources as well as land that turn out to be
necessary in relation to the end of being able to live from one's
labour; and that it is the state, in the name of the community, that
must decide how these resources are allocated. Attributing such views
to Fichte in any case amounts to a reasonable interpretation of the
following claim that he makes: 'Each person possesses property in
objects only insofar as he needs such property to pursue his occupation'.[41] It is consequently possible to attribute to Fichte the claim that
the means of production must be under common (i.e. collective)
control, even though he does not explicitly make such a claim.

Another example of the limitations that Fichte places on the right to
property is to be found in the case of the agriculturalist's right to
alienate the products of the land. Although Fichte describes these

39 GA II / 13: 208.
40 GA I / 4: 9; FNR: 170.
41 GA I / 4: 23; FNR: 187.

products, if not the land itself, as the agriculturalist's absolute property, he argues that a producer, which is what he classes an agriculturalist to be, is under an obligation to sell his products and that there must be a maximum price at which he is allowed to do so.[42] This leads Fichte to state that money is the only true form of absolute property over which the state has no rights. In other words, the money paid to someone for his products and goods, rather than these products or goods themselves, turns out to be the only form of property from whose use or benefit one truly has the right to exclude others, and which one has the right to dispose of as one pleases. By money Fichte here means the money paid by the state for the products and goods it needs to those who have cultivated or produced them, and which is left over once a person has fulfilled his obligations to the state by paying his taxes. Presumably, the idea here is that this money can be a person's absolute property in the sense identified above because his possession of it has no bearing on the right of others to be able to live, since the conditions of guaranteeing this right have already been satisfied by other means, including taxation and by ensuring that people have the resources they need in order to be able to live from their labour. The possession of this money allows a person to purchase various goods for his private use that are likewise to be classed as absolute property;[43] and we must therefore assume that a person also has the right to exclude others from the use or benefit of these goods and to dispose of them as he pleases.

Yet even here Fichte imposes limitations on the right to dispose of such absolute property as one pleases, in line with his ultimate concern that everyone should be able to live from his labour. He claims, for example, that 'a person who buys property must be obligated to use it, and must be in a position to be able to use it'.[44] Fichte also claims in relation to the alienation of property that the seller 'is not the absolute owner of his money, because it is his only means of subsistence, and he is responsible to the state for being able to provide for his own livelihood'.[45] In other words, the state has the right to make sure that a person does not recklessly dispose of his property, thereby depriving himself of the means to live.

Such restrictions appear to confirm that the only form of property that is absolutely guaranteed to persons is, in effect, their inalienable

42 GA I / 4: 40; FNR: 205.   43 GA I / 4: 43; FNR: 209.
44 GA I / 4: 56; FNR: 223.   45 GA I / 4: 56; FNR: 223.

right to be able to live from their labour. As we have seen, the state's task of guaranteeing this right rules out the private ownership of land and, to a large extent at least, the means of production, because the state may need to redistribute these resources without any regard for the manner in which they were previously acquired. The only constraint on such redistributive acts would be that they should not prevent the person from whom the resources are taken from being able to live from his labour. Thus, although Fichte's theory of property includes the right to the exclusive use of something, this right is not an absolute one, because it applies only as long as the object in question is needed for a person to be able to live from his labour. Fichte does allow for one form of absolute property, namely, money and that which a person can buy with it. Yet even here a person's freedom to dispose of his property as he pleases is subject to limitations which are by no means in any obvious sense compatible with the main principles of liberalism.

Fichte's theory of property is, however, compatible with the idea of right as that which guarantees the possibility of free agency in the sensible world. Indeed, Fichte thinks of his conception of property and the ways in which the state protects it as guaranteeing that a fundamental condition of a person's free agency in the sensible world, the continued existence of his body, is met in the case of each and every finite rational being. A problem admittedly arises if the possibility of free agency is in some way associated with the freedom to dispose of one's property as one pleases. Although this idea is arguably essential to economic liberalism and also to political liberalism, insofar as the right to dispose of one's property as one pleases is linked to the right of individuals to pursue their own conceptions of the good life, the extensive limitations that Fichte places on property rights need not be viewed as at odds with his understanding of right as that which guarantees a person's status as a self-determining being. For other forms of agency, such as meaningful work and creative expression, may still be possible in the face of these limitations on property rights. Also, it is far from clear that political orders other than a liberal one, such as a socialist one, by their very nature exclude the possibility of such private rights as freedom of expression and limited property rights, in the shape of money and personal belongings from whose use or benefit one has the right to exclude others, and which one may dispose of as one pleases. On the other hand, although political liberalism allows for some redistributive measures, Fichte's theory of property leads him to impose what must, from a liberal standpoint, be regarded as intolerable limitations on human freedom. This becomes especially evident when Fichte attempts to work out the implications of his claim that the state is to be given the roles of allocating individuals the right to perform an occupation and of ensuring that each and every person is in the position to live from his labour in *The Closed Commercial State*, which, as I show in the next section, forms an integral part of his more comprehensive theory of right.

From what has been said above, it is clear that Fichte thinks of himself as restricting freedom of choice in order to safeguard the freedom of all the citizens of the state, in the sense of providing them with the basic conditions of being able to use and develop their capacities by means of their own self-activity. This is shown by the way in which he adopts the position that state intervention will be required not only to protect existing property rights, but also to make sure that resources are distributed in such a way as to guarantee each and every person the means to live, thus securing the most basic condition of any person's being able to act freely and effectively in the world. In this way, restrictions on human freedom, specifically the freedom to appropriate parts of the world and its products, are held to stem from the need to secure the more general and fundamental conditions of human agency. Fichte develops a consistent position, given his view of right as both a positive and negative condition of human agency, as I hope to make clear below, by relating his theory of property more closely to the theory of property offered by Locke. I have already had reason to compare Locke's theory of property with Fichte's theory of it. However, I have so far concentrated on their similarities, whereas I shall now indicate some important differences between them.

Property and freedom

In an attempt to situate Fichte within the modern natural law tradition, Ludwig Siep claims that the way in which Fichte deduces the concept of right as a condition of self-consciousness, thereby tracing this concept and the obligations to which it gives rise back to self-consciousness as an indubitable foundation, places him in the 'Cartesian' tradition in modern natural law theory, of which Locke is said to be the main representative.[46] Siep classes Locke as belonging to this tradition in

---

46 Siep, *Praktische Philosophie im Deutschen Idealismus*, 19.

modern natural law theory because in his moral philosophy, as presented in the *Essay Concerning Human Understanding*, he derives the norms governing human actions from an indubitable, intuitive knowledge of one's own existence and the implicit, demonstrable knowledge of the existence of God that this knowledge of one's own existence contains. Locke does this by showing how knowledge of the divine law to strive for true and lasting happiness results from these two forms of knowledge. This divine law and Locke's analysis of the will then form the basis of his natural law theory, as presented in *The Second Treatise of Government*.[47] I here leave aside the question as to whether or not it is truly accurate to describe Fichte's position as a Cartesian one, to argue instead that the subject-centred approach which Siep ascribes to Locke helps draw attention to an important difference between Locke's theory of property and Fichte's theory of property.

Siep also claims that Fichte can be seen to incorporate another model found in the modern natural law tradition into his deduction of the concept of right. The model in question is this time associated with Hobbes, and it is identified as the encounter between independent individuals and the consequences of such an encounter for the individual consciousness.[48] This is a reference to the intersubjective dimension of Fichte's theory of right, as exemplified by the idea of a 'summons' in § 3 of the *Foundations of Natural Right*. By relating this intersubjective aspect of Fichte's theory of right, which implies the potential for conflict, to his conception of property rights, I show that he takes into account, far more than Locke does, the way in which property rights may restrict freedom, when they are understood primarily in terms of the right to exclude others from the use or benefit of something and to dispose of it as one pleases. In this way, Fichte demonstrates that a conceptual solution to the problem as to how the right to property, understood as the right to exclude others from the use or benefit of something, and the equal right to develop and use one's capacities are to be reconciled cannot be separated from the question of a political solution to this problem.

As we already know, the summons mentioned above consists in one human being summoning another human being to act freely, which is done by the first human being limiting his activity in relation to the second one. It is not my intention here to discuss Fichte's theory of the

---

47 Siep, *Praktische Philosophie im Deutschen Idealismus*, 19f.
48 Cf. Siep, *Praktische Philosophie im Deutschen Idealismus*, 29.

summons in further detail, apart from mentioning one problem to which it gives rise, since this problem is highly relevant to his theory of property insofar as it can be usefully compared to Locke's theory of property. The problem in question arises in connection with Fichte's understanding of the relation of right as a relation based on mutual recognition, with each human being summoning other human beings while equally being the object of a summons. This invites the question as to how a community of human beings standing in relations of right to each other originally arose. Although Fichte seeks to explain the possibility of a condition of right in terms of a process, when he identifies the summons to engage in free activity with a series of actions, which he calls upbringing (*Erziehung*),[49] rather than with a single act, we are still confronted with the question as to the origin of the kind of community within which such a process of upbringing itself became possible. This is because Fichte needs to explain how the first members of this community of human beings standing in relations of right to each other achieved a representation of their rationality and freedom, thereby becoming capable of 'summoning' others to think of themselves as essentially free and rational beings. The deduction of the concept of right offered by Fichte appears, in short, to end in an infinite regress.

Fichte shows an awareness of this problem when he is led to consider the question as to who brought up the first human couple; and he disposes of this question by referring to the wisdom of the Genesis account of the care that God took of Adam and Eve.[50] Fichte's appeal to the authority of biblical narrative is consequently to be understood as a retreat to the realm of myth motivated by the need to explain the possibility of a condition of right. This appeal to myth is made necessary by the way in which Fichte seeks to deduce the concept of right as a condition of self-consciousness, thereby demonstrating its necessity. We can, however, to some extent understand Fichte's theory of property, which constitutes an attempt on his part to determine further the concept of right, in abstraction from this ambitious transcendental project of grounding the concept of right in the conditions of self-consciousness, allowing us to treat this theory as independent of any mythic account of the origins of right.

It is arguably a different matter in the case of Locke's account of property in Chapter 5 of *The Second Treatise of Government*, however,

49 GA I / 3: 347; FNR: 38.   50 GA I / 3: 347f.; FNR: 38.

because Locke explains the legitimacy of private property in terms of its origin in a pre-political condition, where that with which a man 'mixes' his labour becomes rightfully his, despite the fact that God gave the world to mankind in common. If we bear in mind Marx's suggestion that theories of primitive accumulation can be placed on a par with a religious doctrine such as original sin,[51] Locke's appeal to a pre-political condition to explain the legitimacy of private property appears to share much in common with Fichte's recourse to the myth of the Garden of Eden to explain the origins of a condition of right. Yet, whereas Locke's theory of property, particularly his justification of private property, depends on an account of its origins, Fichte's theory of property does not, as long as it is not considered to depend on his attempt to deduce the concept of right as a condition of self-consciousness, since it does not rest on any claims concerning the historical origins of property rights. Indeed, we have seen that Fichte introduces the idea of a right of the first occupant only to go on to undermine the notion of such a right, by according the state the function of allocating property rights in land, which he considers to be of a purely conditional nature.

Locke's justification of property rights is based on the idea that the earth and its fruits can only be of benefit to humankind when they have been appropriated, with the act of appropriation giving rise to the right to exclude others from the use or benefit of that which has been appropriated. This act of appropriation occurs through a man's 'mixing' his labour with parts of the earth or its products, that is to say, by his labouring to make them useful, which may simply amount to gathering the fruits of the earth. Although property is here identified with land and goods, the extended meaning that Locke gives to the term 'property' noted earlier plays a vital role in his argument. This is because Locke's argument depends on the idea that by mixing his labour with something, a person joins something that was originally independent of him to something that is already his own, namely, his labour. A person owns his labour in the sense that he is his own person, whose movements and mental activity in relation to objects constitute his labour. In this way, one's body and labour, as well as land and goods, are classed as property. Since all of these forms of property have a role to play in Locke's argument for the right to property, even though he appears to reduce property to land and goods, this argument must be

---

51 Cf. Marx, *Capital*, vol. 1, 873.

thought to depend on the extended meaning that he gives to the term 'property'. For this reason, although the type of property whose legitimacy Locke seeks to establish appears to conform to current linguistic usage more than the extended meaning that both he and Fichte give to the term 'property', the way in which Locke restricts the meaning of this term, while justifying property rights in terms of a broader conception of property, gives his theory of property a rather tendentious appearance, inviting the claim that historical rather than logical reasons are here at work.

Locke sets limits to the extent to which parts of the earth and its products may be rightfully appropriated, however: the conditions that 'enough, and as good' should be left for others and that what is appropriated should not be allowed to spoil before it can be enjoyed. Yet Locke removes the second limitation, by claiming that money, which does not spoil, can be exchanged for useful but perishable goods as and when necessary.[52] This opens up the possibility of regarding acts of unlimited appropriation as legitimate, since the invention of money and people's tacit agreement to its use give rise to the right to larger possessions, by allowing people to sell the products of their land and labour that they cannot themselves use before these products perish, thus enabling them to retain the value of these things. Locke accordingly claims that a scarcity of land results from the invention of money and its use, because there arises an increasing demand for land driven by the fact that money can be made from what is produced on it; and it is this new condition of scarcity that is said by him to have led men to consent to having their property regulated by law. Locke claims, moreover, that in consenting to the use of money, men have consented to its consequences, including the 'disproportionate and unequal Possession of the Earth'.[53] Yet even in political society the legitimacy of the property that one owns must still be thought to be grounded on acts of primitive accumulation, since when money was introduced, its initial use must have been to facilitate the exchange of goods that were already the property of one or more persons, so that any later wealth

---

52 C. B. Macpherson claims that Locke removes the limitations that he places on the amount of property that may be appropriated so as to justify an emerging free market system of economic relations. Cf. Macpherson, *The Political Theory of Possessive Individualism*. It is not my intention here to examine this wider claim, which underlies Macpherson's thesis that historical rather than logical reasons are at work in Locke's theory of property.

53 Locke, *Two Treatises of Government*, 301f.

ultimately needs to be explained in terms of its origins in acts of appropriation that took place in the state of nature. The problems with Locke's justification of property rights, which appears to reduce the right to property to the right to exclude others from the use or benefit of something and to dispose of it as one pleases, despite the broader conception of property with which he otherwise operates, can be more clearly brought out by comparing his position to Fichte's theory of right and the place that he assigns to property in this theory.

Locke's attempt to justify private property provides evidence of the way in which his theory of natural law can be characterized as being based on a subject-centred standpoint. This is because his justification of property rights focuses on the idea of property as the relation between an isolated subject and an object, even though the role of labour in his theory of primitive accumulation makes this relation into something more than a purely contemplative one on the part of the subject. The impression that property relations are, for Locke, essentially those between an isolated subject and an object is heightened by his insistence on the fact that in the state of nature, prior to the invention and introduction of money, individuals will have no incentive to increase their property beyond what they can use, so that enough is always left over for others. For, in this way, Locke, who appears to assume a lack of scarcity in the state of nature, minimizes the potential for conflict between individuals aiming to secure their own self-preservation, thereby suppressing the idea that the process of primitive accumulation might have been, to quote Marx, 'anything but idyllic'.[54] Moreover, Locke attempts to render the unequal division of the world and its products that arises with the introduction of money unproblematic and to lend it legitimacy, thus making any redistribution of property appear unjust, by basing it on the idea of consent. It is, in fact, only with the introduction of money and the transition to political society that in Locke's view unequal possession of the earth and its products becomes so great and, from the standpoint of natural law, unjust, that consent becomes necessary to legitimize such a state of affairs. By introducing the notion of consent, Locke begins to base property rights explicitly on relations between human beings as mediated by objects, as opposed to relations between isolated human beings and objects. Yet this consent to the introduction of money takes place against the background of a pre-existing set of property rights established in the state of nature by means

54 Marx, *Capital*, vol. 1, 874.

of acts of appropriation in which an individual mixes his labour with something, so that we once again encounter a relation between an apparently isolated subject and an object as the ultimate basis of property rights.

It is, in any case, questionable that all individuals would have really consented to such a state of affairs, and some of the attempts made to defend Locke against the claim that he seeks to justify acts of unlimited appropriation serve to illustrate this problem. On the one hand, it has been claimed in Locke's defence that the government must regulate property in political society in accordance with the unconditional natural rights that he identifies, including the right to the material possessions necessary in order to preserve oneself.[55] This argument relates to Locke's first proviso that 'enough, and as good' should be left for others, which appears to make his theory of property more compatible with Fichte's demand that each person must be able to live from his labour. On this reading, the government becomes the guarantor of the condition that 'enough, and as good' is left for others.

It can be argued, however, that this reading fails to pay sufficient attention to Locke's claim that in consenting to the introduction of money, men have also consented to its consequences, which may include considerable inequalities with respect to the amount of property that individuals own. It also leaves space for the claim that the fact that some people may own no property at all involves no injustice, as long as they can still physically survive, even though this means that these people are deprived of an important means of being able to develop and realize their capacities. Locke's own acceptance of such a state of affairs is suggested by his comparison between the conditions enjoyed by a king of one of the nations of America and an English day labourer: 'And a King of a large and fruitful Territory there feeds, lodges, and is clad worse than a day Labourer in *England*'.[56] For the main point here seems to be that someone whose only property is his own labour has no grounds to complain about the inequalities brought about by the introduction of private property and money, since he is better off in such a condition than someone living in a society in which neither private property nor money exists, even though he lacks other forms of property, including certain goods that may constitute the necessary means of being able to develop and realize his capacities.

55 Cf. Tully, *A Discourse on Property*.   56 Locke, *Two Treatises of Government*, 297.

This has prompted criticism of Locke's attempt to justify inequality by means of the idea of consent to the consequences of the introduction of money. This criticism is tempered, however, by the argument that although individuals may have consented to inequality with respect to the rightful possession of goods, they would never have consented to dependence, so that Locke's position should be more properly understood as entailing the claim that even in political society acts of appropriation must at least leave all persons able to preserve and govern themselves.[57] Given the fact that this attempt to defend Locke against the claim that he seeks to justify acts of unlimited appropriation amounts to attributing to him a position that he should have adopted, rather than one which he did in fact adopt, Locke's theory of property here assumes an essentially ambiguous character.

This ambiguity becomes especially evident if one recalls that Locke's theory of the right to property is not only of a negative kind, as it would be if property rights were viewed as simply imposing limits on the natural freedom of others by excluding them from the use or benefit of the rightful property of others, but also of a positive kind, since property rights are held to be conditions of human agency. The claim that persons should be left enough to enable them to govern themselves provides an example of the positive aspect of Locke's conception of property rights, because it points to the importance of the idea of self-determination in the shape of the act of governing oneself; an act which, one might add, allows individuals to use and develop the capacities associated with the idea of them as essentially free and rational beings. The effective exercise of the right to self-determination will arguably require that existing property rights do not render individuals entirely dependent on others nor deprive them of the necessary means of using and developing their capacities. Locke's acceptance of the inequalities that arise in the wake of the introduction of money suggests, however, that, as in the case of the English day labourer, these conditions of the realization of the right to self-determination can be legitimately ignored, as long as the physical survival of all the members of society is ensured. Fichte's theory of property, which accords primacy to the right to be able to live from one's labour and makes other forms of property conditional in relation to this end, is far more consistent and unambiguous in this respect.

---

57 Cf. Simmons, *The Lockean Theory of Rights.*

We have seen that Fichte views property rights as being of an essentially intersubjective nature, because they consist in a relation of free and rational subjects to each other, though one that is mediated by objects, so that property rights contain the ever-present potential for conflict between human beings in relation to these objects. Fichte consequently claims that there could be no talk of property in the case of a man living alone on an inaccessible island, since this concept would have no application; the right to property instead arises only when there are several people, who may come into conflict with each other through the 'active expression of their power'.[58] In this way, Fichte is led to characterize property relations primarily as relations of persons to each other as mediated by objects, rather than as relations of isolated subjects to objects,[59] and this in turn allows him to do full justice to the potential for conflict contained in the idea of property rights. Moreover, although the relation of right is one in which individuals limit their natural freedom in relation to each other, the question arises as to what it means for individuals to do this, and how, in those cases when a person fails to limit his freedom in relation to others in the appropriate way, violations of right are to be prevented or punished.

When the right to property is understood primarily in terms of its function of enabling human beings to act freely and effectively in the world, this potential for conflict allows us to think of acts of unlimited appropriation, whether it be of parts of the world or of other resources, as constituting violations of right, on the grounds that they adversely affect the capacity of others to act freely and effectively in the world. As we have seen, Fichte argues that the redistribution of property is legitimate when it is undertaken to ensure that everyone is able to live from his labour, since being able to live is the most basic condition of a person's capacity to act freely and effectively in the sensible world. To deny the legitimacy of such redistributive acts in the name of a right to unlimited appropriation would consequently for him amount to the acceptance of actions that can be considered to be on a par with other violations of right, such as attacks on one's own person, even though acts of unlimited appropriation may not, in

58 GA I / 7: 86f.
59 It is therefore highly misleading to place Fichte in a tradition that allegedly begins with Locke and ends with Hegel, on the basis that all three thinkers derive the right to property from the fact that consciousness grasps objects in the world. Cf. Lampert, 'Locke, Fichte, and Hegel on the Right to Property', 40. For this suggests that Fichte conceives of property rights primarily in terms of the relation of a subject to an object.

fact, be motivated by the intention to harm the interests of any particular person or group of persons.[60]

We are now in a better position to understand Fichte's reasons for developing even further the theory of property that we find in the *Foundations of Natural Right* with respect to its economic implications in *The Closed Commercial State*, in which the right to property is described as 'the exclusive right to actions, and by no means to things',[61] and in which we find the previously mentioned description of the state's function as that of first giving each person what is his and only then protecting his property. *The Closed Commercial State* represents an attempt on Fichte's part to explain in more detail how the state is able to perform this function. In this work, Fichte makes a distinction between the rational state (*Vernunftstaat*) and actual existing states. While the rational state is associated with the question as to what is right, in the case of an actual state we are presented with the question as to the extent to which the principles of the rational state can be put into practice given existing conditions. Fichte then associates politics with the science of governing (*Regierungswissenschaft*) an existing state insofar as this is possible in accordance with the principles of the rational state. This form of politics would therefore need to be seen as being 'in the middle between the given state and the rational state: it would describe the continuous line, by means of which the former transforms itself into the latter, and ended in pure political right [*das reine Staatsrecht*]'.[62] Politics is thus concerned with the question as to how the principles of pure political right can be applied to empirically determined states, which may differ from each other in a number of important respects. *The Closed Commercial State* represents a contribution to this

---

60 In this respect, Fichte might be seen to provide a possible argument against a defence of free market capitalism that has been offered in more recent times. I here have in mind Hayek's view of the free market as an example of a spontaneous order which has not been brought about intentionally by anyone. Hayek argues that it makes no sense to call the unintended consequences of such an order unjust, since this term can only be applied to the actions of individuals or the concerted actions of the members of a collective body which are consciously designed to bring about a particular effect. Cf. Hayek, *Law, Legislation and Liberty, vol. II: The Mirage of Social Justice.* Fichte suggests that the inequalities generated by such a spontaneous order would nevertheless have to be regarded as unjust from the standpoint of those adversely affected by them, irrespective of whether or not these inequalities were intended, simply because these people cannot reasonably be expected to renounce their natural freedom in favour of a condition in which they turn out to be severely disadvantaged in relation to others.

61 GA I / 7: 54f.

62 GA I / 7: 51.

political task, because it provides a theory of a state that has been transformed in accordance with the principles that are constitutive of the
rational state. In other words, *The Closed Commercial State* represents
the final, necessary stage in the full and systematic application of the
concept of right that begins in the *Foundations of Natural Right*, insofar
as it is possible for philosophy to perform such a task. This work
must therefore be regarded as forming an integral part of Fichte's theory
of right.

The distinction between the rational state and actual existing states
points to an intermediate stage between the normative level and the
empirical level. This is the stage at which a theory of a state that has
been transformed in accordance with the demands that arise at the
normative level needs to be developed. Fichte thus suggests that philosophy ought not to be satisfied with having outlined the normative
principles of the rational state; it must also provide an account as to
how these principles are to be fully applied. In other words, philosophy
has the task of seeking a political solution, as well as a purely conceptual
one, to the problems connected with the concept of right, for otherwise it would remain a merely formal science. Fichte therefore considers himself to be obliged to provide a political solution, in the sense
indicated above, to the problem of property rights; a problem which
for him ultimately requires subordinating the right to property, understood as the right to exclude others from the use or benefit of something, to the right to exercise and use one's capacities by acting freely
and effectively in the world.

We may, of course, doubt whether *The Closed Commercial State* can
be really said to provide this political solution when, as we shall see, it
involves the imposition of extensive limitations on individual free
choice and assigns to the state a function that we may doubt it is
capable of performing without giving rise to other forms of injustice.
The failure of this work to provide such a political solution nevertheless serves to illustrate that even if we assume that a reconciliation
of the right to exclude others from the use or benefit of something
with the right to exercise and use one's capacities is possible at the
conceptual level, it will be a much harder task to achieve this reconciliation at the political level, at which the concept of property
needs, as Fichte would say, to be applied. Moreover, when Fichte
subordinates the right to property, understood as the right to
exclude others from the use or benefit of something, to the equal
right of individuals to use and develop their capacities, whose most

basic condition is that they are able to live from their labour, and then attempts to work out the implications of his theory of property at a more concrete level, he at least adopts a consistent position and demonstrates a refusal on his part to be satisfied with a merely conceptual solution to the problems raised by his theory of right.

For this reason Fichte deserves, I believe, to be classed as one of the most important theorists of both property rights and distributive justice in the history of political thought; whereas in the case of distributive justice, it has been claimed that the concept of distributive justice in its modern sense of a duty on the part of the state to direct or supervise the distribution of property first receives a clear formulation in Rawls's *A Theory of Justice*.[63] I hope to have shown that this judgement needs to be revised in favour of the claim that it is Fichte, not Rawls, who first provides us with a clear formulation of the concept of distributive justice in its modern sense, by seeking to show what would be required for the concept of property, as he understands it, to be realized in the sensible world. I now intend to show how Fichte's theory of property and the measures he introduces in order to explain the possibility of its realization in the sensible world point to a strong link between his political philosophy and the radical phase of the French Revolution, as exemplified by some of the main ideas associated with the revolutionary figure of Gracchus Babeuf, who sought to re-radicalize the Revolution after the fall of the Jacobins. My discussion of this topic once again demonstrates the problematic nature of a liberal interpretation of Fichte's political philosophy. It will also allow me to say something more about the economic proposals that Fichte sets out in *The Closed Commercial State*.

63 Cf. Fleischacker, *A Short History of Distributive Justice*.

2

APPLYING THE CONCEPT
OF RIGHT: FICHTE AND BABEUF

In her book *Fichte's Sozialismus und sein Verhältnis zur Marx'schen Doktrin*, published in 1900, Marianne Weber not only speaks of Fichte's socialism but also claims that the latter has its only real precursor in the ideas of the French revolutionary Gracchus Babeuf. Weber goes so far as to claim that the analogies between Fichte's and Babeuf's ideas suggest that Fichte may have known of Babeuf's communist theories and the failed revolutionary conspiracy known as the Conspiracy of the Equals, which took place in Paris in 1796 in an attempt to overthrow the government of the Directory and implement radical economic and social measures, and of which Babeuf was a leading member.[1] In 1914, Xavier Léon likewise stated that the analogies between some of Fichte's ideas and those of Babeuf provide strong grounds for thinking that Fichte was familiar with Babeuf's main ideas and the events of the Conspiracy of the Equals when he came to write *The Closed Commercial State*, which was published in 1800.[2]

Fichte could have become aware of Babeuf's views through the reports on the Conspiracy of the Equals given in the journal *Minerva. Journal historischen und politischen Inhalts* in 1796–97 and in the newspapers, consisting mainly of letters written by Germans living in Paris, entitled *La France en 1796* and *La France en 1797*, while in 1795, Fichte may have been able to acquire copies of Babeuf's own journal, the *Tribun du Peuple*, through Swiss friends.[3] However, in the absence of any direct proof that Fichte was acquainted with Babeuf's theories, the claim that Babeuf influenced the theory of right that Fichte

---

1 Cf. Weber, *Fichte's Sozialismus und sein Verhältnis zur Marx'schen Doktrin*, 18.
2 Cf. Léon, 'Le socialisme de Fichte d'après l'état commercial fermé', 201ff.
3 Cf. Buhr, *Revolution und Philosophie*, 78 and 149 n. 13; Léon, 'Le socialisme de Fichte d'après l'état commercial fermé', 204ff.

constructed in his 1796/97 *Foundations of Natural Right* and further developed with respect to its economic implications in *The Closed Commercial State* remains unsubstantiated. As we shall see, the proposals found in *The Closed Commercial State* to a large extent involve simply developing certain features of the theory of property that Fichte sets out in the earlier *Foundations of Natural Right*, which, given the proximity of its dates of publication to the events connected with the Conspiracy of the Equals, appears unlikely to have been directly influenced by these events. Although this does not rule out the possibility that Fichte later became familiar with some of these ideas, which then influenced the economic proposals found in *The Closed Commercial State*, the similarities between Babeuf's and Fichte's views can in any case be explained in terms of their having a common source of inspiration, such as Rousseau or the social utopias of the last decades of the eighteenth century.[4] Moreover, even the relation of Fichte's political philosophy to the radical phase of the French Revolution has been disputed, let alone its relation to a later radical figure such as Babeuf, who attempted to revive this radical phase. I shall therefore begin this chapter with some remarks on Fichte's relation to the French Revolution in general and its radical phase in particular.

Fichte and the French Revolution

One of Fichte's earliest published writings was his *Contribution towards Correcting the Public's Judgement of the French Revolution*, which appeared in 1793. This work represents a defence of the French Revolution written at a time when enthusiasm for the latter was already beginning to wane in Germany in the wake of such events as the executions of Louis XVI and the Girondins, although many German intellectuals had initially welcomed the Revolution as an attack on absolutism and as the victory of reason. The *Contribution towards Correcting the Public's Judgement of the French Revolution* is concerned with demonstrating the legitimacy of the Revolution. It does so with reference to a contract theory of the state, and by developing the implications of the claim that, since they can only be legitimately subject to laws that they have laid upon themselves, individuals have an inalienable right to annul unilaterally any contract they have entered into. This means that

---

4 Cf. Buhr, *Revolution und Philosophie*, 79.

people have an inalienable right to change the constitution of the state, which must be based on consent, because, for Fichte, only a civil society (*bürgerliche Gesellschaft*) founded on a contract made between its members is a truly rightful one, whereas all existing constitutions can be criticized for being based on the right of the stronger.[5] This claim recalls Fichte's theory of right developed in the *Foundations of Natural Right*, insofar as right is held to be based on consent as opposed to physical force.

The *Contribution towards Correcting the Public's Judgement of the French Revolution* also contains scathing criticisms of the absolute monarchs of the Europe of Fichte's own time, together with criticisms of feudalism and the privileges enjoyed by the nobility and the officials of the established Church. Yet none of these criticisms points in any obvious sense to developments connected with the radical phase of the French Revolution in particular, since even the earliest stages of this historical event were characterized by a concerted attack on feudal institutions and traditional privileges, including those of the Catholic Church, and by an attempt to limit the monarch's powers. In this respect, if German Jacobinism is identified with support for the radical phase of the French Revolution, it appears correct to state that such a position cannot be detected in the *Contribution towards Correcting the Public's Judgement of the French Revolution*, which contains only a defence of the 'moderate' Revolution of 1789.[6]

There is no firm evidence, then, on the basis of which a direct link might be made between the *Contribution towards Correcting the Public's Judgement of the French Revolution* and the radical phase that the French Revolution had entered by the time Fichte wrote this work, as if, for example, one were to maintain that Fichte was motivated to write this work by his sympathy for the ideas and aspirations that characterized this new phase of the French Revolution. However, this does not exclude the possibility that Fichte later came to develop a theory of right which can be considered to be in harmony with some of the central ideas that subsequently found expression in the radical phase of the French Revolution. Martial Guéroult, for example, notes a change in the theoretical basis of Fichte's support for the French Revolution, when he claims that Fichte remained loyal to the latter while coming to reject the individualism found in the *Contribution towards Correcting the Public's Judgement of the French Revolution*, which made the state into a

5 GA I / 1: 236.   6 Cf. La Vopa, *Fichte*, 83f.

highly precarious form of association, in favour of a more collectivist form of association that represents a kind of socialism. Moreover, Guéroult cites the change that Fichte's theory of property underwent as providing a clear indication of this shift in his grounds for supporting the French Revolution.[7]

The interpretation of Fichte's Jena theory of the state and society I develop in Chapter 4 supports the idea of a shift to a more collectivist form of association, though I also show that Fichte's separation of right from morality demonstrates an awareness on his part of how individualistic and collectivist viewpoints may coexist in relative independence of each other in the modern state. It is also true that *The Closed Commercial State*, which is based on the theory of property that Fichte had developed in the *Foundations of Natural Right*, contains what might be termed collectivist elements. The theory of property that Fichte develops in the *Contribution towards Correcting the Public's Judgement of the French Revolution* nevertheless suggests that this shift to a more collectivist form of association, insofar as it concerns the nature of property rights, may be seen as the result of a process of internal development. It does not, therefore, need to be explained in terms of Fichte's personal attitude to specific developments that took place in revolutionary France in the years preceding the development of his theory of right, as it is presented in the *Foundations of Natural Right* and *The Closed Commercial State*.

In the *Contribution towards Correcting the Public's Judgement of the French Revolution*, Fichte puts forward a theory of property that seeks to explain the legitimate acquisition of property in terms of two main ideas. The first of these ideas is that human beings have a natural right to use objects for their own purposes, while the second idea is that the formation of objects which have not been previously subjected to the formative activity of other human beings gives rise to an exclusive right to these objects, leading Fichte to identify the concept of property itself with this right to objects.[8] This theory of property exhibits certain similarities with Locke's theory as to how a person's labour founds the exclusive right to an object. It also clearly differs from the one set out in the *Foundations of Natural Right*, because it explains property rights in terms of their origin in the formation of previously ownerless objects. It thus appears to assert the validity of a right of the first occupant and, more generally, of acts of primitive accumulation.

7 Cf. Guéroult, 'Fichte et la Révolution française', 221f.
8 GA I / 1: 267.

Such a theory of property makes it difficult to explain how property acquired in the relevant manner can be legitimately redistributed by the state at a later point in time; whereas the theory of property that Fichte develops in the *Foundations of Natural Right* demands and seeks to legitimize redistributive acts on the part of the state, and therefore dispenses altogether with any attempt to explain property rights in terms of their origin in acts of primitive accumulation. The demand for such redistributive measures requires the existence of the state because only it, according to Fichte, has the power to implement these measures, which may require coercing individuals into giving up some of their property to others. In the *Contribution towards Correcting the Public's Judgement of the French Revolution*, by contrast, when arguing for the right to property Fichte claims that the moral law (*Sittengesez*), which in this work is made into the ultimate criterion of natural right, absolutely forbids one human being to disturb the free agency (*Wirkung*) of another human being. This moral prohibition thus gives rise to the right to exclude others from the use of a previously ownerless object that one has formed in some way.[9] This implies that human beings have certain natural rights, specifically the natural right to property, in the state of nature, that is, prior to the establishment of state authority. We may assume, therefore, that these rights are ones that the state is not entitled to violate by redistributing property, even if this were to prove necessary when it came to meeting the needs of other human beings. The differences between this position and the one that Fichte adopts in the *Foundations of Natural Right* are obvious.

Another major difference between Fichte's earlier and later theories of property again concerns the claim made in the *Contribution towards Correcting the Public's Judgement of the French Revolution* that the formation of an object founds an exclusive right to this object. This claim raises the question as to whether the right in question extends to the material object itself or only to the form that has been given to it. Fichte disposes of this question by making a distinction between the right to appropriate an object (*Zueignungsrecht*) and the right to property (*Eigenthumsrecht*). He argues that the former right pertains to the raw material which, since it has not been formed by human activity, cannot be the property of any one person nor even of the state. The establishment of the right to property by means of the act of forming an object in accordance with one's own ends means, however, that it becomes no

9 GA I / 1: 266f.

longer possible to separate the material from the form it has been given except in thought.[10]

When applied to landed property in particular, this distinction implies that every human being originally has the right to appropriate the whole earth, leading Fichte to suggest that acts of unlimited appropriation can, in principle, be held to be legitimate, as long as they are based on the formation of objects, although such factors as the limits of human strength and the actions of others will restrict the amount of property that any one person can actually own. Fichte appears explicitly to draw this conclusion when he states that 'he who works more may possess more, and he who does not work rightfully possesses nothing at all'.[11] This viewpoint is difficult to reconcile with Fichte's theory of property in the *Foundations of Natural Right*, insofar as the right of every person to be able to live from his labour imposes limits on the amount of property that any one person living in community with others may legitimately own. Fichte's distinction between the right to appropriate objects and the right to property also implies that the state cannot itself own land, understood as raw material that can be worked on, unless it were itself to form the land and thus become its rightful owner, which presents us with a rather implausible scenario; whereas in the *Foundations of Natural Right*, Fichte clearly advocates state ownership of land. There are, then, some fundamental differences between Fichte's earlier and later theories of property rights. These differences invite the question as to how we are to explain the shift from the earlier conception of property rights to the later one. I suggest below that this shift can be explained in terms of the fact that while the basic intention behind both theories of property is the same, the problems presented by the earlier theory of property in relation to this basic intention led Fichte to dispense with his earlier 'individualistic' theory of property and to develop an alternative one, which contains more collectivist elements that exhibit certain striking similarities with some of the main ideas associated with the revolutionary movement known as Babouvism.

The impression that Fichte adopts an individualistic model of property in the *Contribution towards Correcting the Public's Judgement of the French Revolution* is heightened by the way in which he advocates a free market with respect to land and that which can be produced

10 GA I / 1: 268f.
11 GA I / 1: 269.

on it.[12] A free market in land is, by contrast, something that Fichte must be seen to reject in the *Foundations of Natural Right*, when he asserts the need for state ownership of land; while, as we shall shortly see, he explicitly argues against a free market in goods in *The Closed Commercial State*. Fichte's proposal of a free market in land and the goods produced on it needs, however, to be placed in its proper context. Fichte advocates a free market in land and its products with the intention of preventing the existing owners of land from becoming the exclusive owners of the nation's wealth, which, if they were to become less extravagant, he considers to be a real possibility. If a free market in land and goods were established, land which is currently owned by one person would in time come to be divided among several people, or so Fichte claims, with the result that it would become more productive than it now is. Fichte clearly regards this development as being to the advantage of those who do not currently possess any land, since it will allow these people, who are in fact those who work the hardest, to escape the miserable conditions that he goes on to describe in graphic detail.[13] It would do so, moreover, by allowing them to live by means of their own labour and in a way that avoids making them dependent on the will of another person. In short, these persons would be able to lead a more dignified form of life that accords more fully with the human essence, which is freedom. In this respect, we encounter what is, in effect, the same basic intention that motivates the theory of property which Fichte sets out in the *Foundations of Natural Right*. We should not, therefore, overemphasize the differences between Fichte's earlier and later theories of property insofar as the basic intention behind them is concerned.

An element of continuity is also to be found in Fichte's radical contractualism in the *Contribution towards Correcting the Public's Judgement of the French Revolution*, which, as previously mentioned, involves the idea that each individual has the right unilaterally to annul any contract he has entered into. This claim is designed to justify the idea that those who are disadvantaged by existing social

12 GA I / 1: 319.
13 Witness, for example, Fichte's criticism of his contemporaries' pity for a queen who has no fresh linen, as opposed to their acceptance as natural of the privations suffered by 'another mother, who has also given birth to healthy children for the fatherland, whom she, wrapped in rags herself, sees wandering around naked in front of her, while, on account of a lack of a food and drink [*Unterhalt*], in her own breasts the source of nourishment, which the youngest child demands with a feeble whimpering, has dried up' (GA I / 1: 320).

and political arrangements, particularly feudal ones, have the right to reject these arrangements and to seek better conditions. A clear example of this is provided by Fichte's complaints concerning arrangements in which people suffer the disadvantage of having no choice but to buy goods or services from people whom existing social and political arrangements favour, by giving them the exclusive right to provide these goods or services, so that 'we cannot bargain with them, they prevent all competition; they offer us their services at as high a price as they want, and we can do nothing else but pay'.[14] Here again the clear implication is that a free market in goods would benefit those who are the victims of these existing arrangements.

Nor should the contractual terms in which Fichte describes the relation of worker to employer, and the way in which he treats a person's powers, including his labour, as a form of property, be viewed as signalling his acceptance and support of the idea that labour is itself simply a commodity like any other commodity. Rather, Fichte is suggesting that people who are propertyless in the modern sense of the term nevertheless have some property, and thus a source of dignity, in the capacities and skills that they own. This interpretation is supported by Fichte's claim with respect to the property that human beings have in themselves that originally 'we are ourselves our property. No one is our master [*Herr*], and no one can become it', with property here being understood as a person's physical and mental powers.[15] Fichte links this idea to the optimistic assumption that the ownership of these powers will, under the right conditions, result in the ownership of things,[16] that is to say, in property rights in the modern sense of the term. Moreover, in the *Contribution towards Correcting the Public's Judgement of the French Revolution,* Fichte already maintains that the right to live is an inalienable human right.[17] This is, of course, the very same right that the theory of right developed in the *Foundations of Natural Right* seeks to guarantee, so as to enable individuals to enjoy an independent and dignified existence. The difference is that in the later work the aim in question leads Fichte to reject his earlier claims that the formation of objects grounds a right to property and that free competition will be in the interests of those people who are disadvantaged by existing social and political arrangements.

The problems occasioned by the idea that the formation of an object grounds an exclusive right to this object in relation to the

14 GA I / 1: 303.   15 GA I / 1: 266.   16 GA I / 1: 315.   17 GA I / 1: 315.

basic intention behind Fichte's theory of property in the *Contri-bution towards Correcting the Public's Judgement of the French Revolution* help explain why he came to offer a different theory of property in the *Foundations of Natural Right*. To begin with, as indicated above, the earlier theory of property, which contains both the idea that the formation of an object grounds an exclusive right to this object and the demand for a free market in land and its products, aims to improve the conditions of those disadvantaged by existing social and political arrangements, particularly the arrangements that char-acterize feudalism. It must do so, moreover, without reproducing the injustice of these arrangements. This raises the question as to how exactly both the idea that the formation of objects grounds a prop-erty right to them and Fichte's support of a free market in land and its products point to the successful realization of this end. The answer to this question is, I think, that feudal property relations are, in Fichte's view, illegitimate because property rights are here undeserved, in the sense that they are not the result of a person's own activity. This answer is suggested by Fichte's claim that if the privileged party in such relations no longer had recourse to the property he has inherited without having worked for it, he would have to work whether he wanted to or not.[18] What is required, therefore, is a process whereby property rights are generated by means of a process that depends on an individual's labour and this requirement appears to be met by basing property rights on the formation of objects.

This approach raises considerable problems, however, both in itself and in relation to the end of guaranteeing everyone an independent and dignified existence. For a start, given the existence of feudal property rights, how would it be possible to return land and other material objects to the point at which they once again became raw material waiting to be formed by human beings? Yet this is something that would surely need to happen if the right to property were to be conclusively established on the basis of an act of formation that precedes any other such act in relation to a specific object. It is probably his awareness of this problem that leads Fichte to identify two other legitimate ways of gaining an exclusive right to something. He is driven to identify these alternative ways of establish-ing property rights by the prospect that in time there may no longer exist any ownerless (that is, unformed) parts of the world or objects, which a

18 GA I / 1: 319.

person might subject to his own formative activity so as to establish a property right to them. Yet both these ways of establishing property rights appear to run counter to Fichte's aim of explaining how those who are disadvantaged by existing social and political arrangements may come to improve their situation by entering into a new contract, whose terms would, we must assume, more closely correspond to the proposals concerning property rights that Fichte himself outlines in the *Contribution towards Correcting the Public's Judgement of the French Revolution*.

The first alternative means of establishing an exclusive right to something that Fichte identifies is that of inheritance. Fichte initially allows that the first person to come upon the property of a deceased person may establish a right to the now ownerless object by taking possession of it. He goes on to argue, however, for the rightful nature of paternal inheritance, on the grounds that people would agree to restrict themselves to this form of inheritance, so as to avoid the effort and the conflict associated with a form of inheritance in which the first person who came across a deceased person's property would have a right to the latter.[19] The second means of establishing a property right without forming raw material that is ownerless is by means of a labour contract, whereby someone who lacks any property in the modern sense of the term agrees to work upon objects that are already the property of someone else and to receive in return some form of recompense, which becomes his rightful property.[20]

In the first case, Fichte's acceptance of paternal inheritance means that he fails to show why we must regard the existing distribution of property as unjust. For if the property that a person, particularly a feudal lord, has inherited is one that originally became the property of one of his ancestor's through the act of forming raw material that no one else had previously formed, the person in question would be able to claim to have a perfectly legitimate right to this property, irrespective of its consequences in relation to other human beings, even though this right was not established by means of his own self-activity. While in the second case, if a person without property in the modern sense of the term cannot find a property owner willing to enter into a contract with him concerning the use of his labour, there would appear to be no cause for complaint, even when the consequences may be dire for the

19 GA I / 1: 274f.
20 GA I / 1: 275.

person concerned, since the unwillingness of others to enter into a contract with him might deprive him of the means of subsistence and thus of the right to live. In the one case, Fichte fails to show that existing feudal property relations are inherently unjust; indeed, he himself provides grounds for defending them. In the other case, his radical contractualism results in a failure to explain how the inalienable right to live can be guaranteed in such a way as to depend on a person's self-activity, thereby allowing a person to enjoy a more dignified form of life than is possible under feudalism for those people who are disadvantaged by existing social and political arrangements. Given such problems with his theory of property in relation to the basic intention behind it, it is not surprising that Fichte should have come to modify his views on property and to reject the idea that the basis of property rights is to be located in acts of primitive accumulation.[21] The changes in Fichte's theory of property do not, therefore, need to be explained in terms of his attitude towards particular phases of the French Revolution.

Although my explanation of Fichte's changing views on property points to the difficulties involved in seeking to explain certain shifts in his social and political philosophy in terms of his personal reaction to different phases of the French Revolution, Fichte's attempt in the *Foundations of Natural Right* and *The Closed Commercial State* to provide a more compelling account of how the basic intention behind his various accounts of property rights might be realized, leads him to address more explicitly such social questions as that of the right of existence. This in turn opens the way for drawing certain parallels between his social and political philosophy and the revolutionary democratic dictatorship of the Jacobins,[22] even though the theory of property that Fichte sets out in the earlier *Contribution towards Correcting the*

21 Another problem is that Fichte's appeal to the idea of an act of original appropriation in which the formation of objects becomes the source of property rights ultimately appears to rest on a right of the stronger, since the extent to which any individual will be able to form raw material and, in so doing, establish a property right to certain objects will depend on such factors as physical strength. This approach conflicts with Fichte's claim that only a civil society founded on a contract made between its members is a truly rightful one, as well as with the way in which he criticizes existing constitutions for being based on the right of the stronger.
22 For a classic example of this approach, see Buhr, *Revolution und Philosophie.* Buhr also seeks to establish parallels between the *Contribution towards Correcting the Public's Judgement of the French Revolution* and the radical phase of the French Revolution, most notably, those between Fichte's and Robespierre's justifications of the use of revolutionary violence.

Public's Judgement of the French Revolution can be said at most to reflect his sympathy for the main ideas and aspirations behind the 'moderate' Revolution of 1789. For it is not difficult to find public statements from the radical phase of the French Revolution that appear to be in perfect harmony with the way in which Fichte subordinates the right to property, understood as the right to exclude others from the use or benefit of something and to dispose of it as one pleases, to the right to be able to live from one's labour. The views expressed by Robespierre in a speech to the National Convention on 2 December 1792 are a case in point:

> What is the first object of society? It is to maintain the imprescriptible rights of man. What is the first of these rights? The right to exist.
>
> The first social law is therefore the one that guarantees all members of society the means to live; all the others are subordinate to that law. Property has been instituted and guaranteed only in order to reinforce it; it is primarily in order to live that one has property. It is not true that property can ever be in opposition to human subsistence.[23]

It is worth mentioning here that the kind of liberal interpretation of the *Foundations of Natural Right* which stresses the role of original rights in this work invites, by contrast, a comparison of these rights with the Declaration of the Rights of Man drafted by the National Assembly in 1789,[24] whose second article states that the aim of every political association is the maintenance of the natural and imprescriptible rights of man, which are identified as those of liberty, property, security and resistance to oppression.[25] The theory of right that Fichte developed in the *Foundations of Natural Right*, especially insofar as it concerns the concept of property, appears to go beyond such statements when it asserts the right of existence and the demand that the state should guarantee individuals the means to live. Although these aspects of Fichte's theory of right do not find their corresponding expression, at least not explicitly so, in the 1789 Declaration of the Rights of Man, they do find expression in the 1793 'Jacobin' constitution. For this constitution's declaration of the rights of man and the citizen contains, as its twenty-first article, the statements, that public assistance

23 Robespierre, 'Sur les subsistances', in *Œuvres de Maximilien Robespierre*, vol. IX, 112.
24 Cf. Neuhouser, 'Introduction', xi.
25 Le but de toute association politique est la conservation des droits naturels et imprescriptibles de l'homme. Ces droits sont la liberté, la propriété, la sûreté et la résistance à l'oppression.

is a sacred debt and that society owes its citizens a living, either by providing them with work or by providing those unable to work with the means of subsistence.[26]

Consequently, there do appear, after all, to be some grounds for claiming that Fichte developed a theory of right that was in certain significant respects in harmony with the radical phase of the French Revolution. This should not, however, be understood as equivalent to the claim that Fichte thought of himself as a German Jacobin. In my view, the available biographical material relating to Fichte's personal views on the French Revolution is simply not enough to decide this issue either way. Indeed, Fichte's personal views on the French Revolution are not well-documented at all, though in a letter from 1795 Fichte explicitly associates his philosophical system with the French Revolution, comparing the way in which his 'system of freedom' removes the bonds imposed by the idea of things in themselves and external influences to the way in which the French nation tears away the external chains binding human beings. Fichte even goes so far as to link the development of his philosophical system to his writing of his defence of the French Revolution in the *Contribution towards Correcting the Public's Judgement of the French Revolution*, and to compare the French people's struggle for political freedom with his own struggles both with himself and with prejudice in the years during which he developed this system.[27]

Although this letter provides evidence of Fichte's continuing support for the French Revolution and his conviction of its legitimacy in the face of the events associated with the period of the Revolution known as the Terror, it does not tell us anything specific about the views that Fichte may have held concerning particular phases or tendencies within the French Revolution. The same goes, to give another example, for a letter from 1798, in which Fichte states that it is simply doing him justice to call him an admirer of political freedom and the nation which promises to spread it, by which he clearly means the French Republic.[28] There is also the problem of defining Jacobinism itself. One recent attempt to do so characterizes Jacobinism as a fairly unified phenomenon that nevertheless contained various tendencies

---

26 Les secours publics sont une dette sacrée. La société doit la subsistance aux citoyens malheureux, soit en leur procurant du travail, soit en assurant les moyens d'exister à ceux qui sont hors d'état de travailler.
27 GA III / 2: 298.
28 GA III / 3: 138.

within itself, of which the two main ones were the concern to defend private rights and a concern for the public good, with the failure of Jacobinism, that is to say, its descent into state-sponsored terrorism, being explicable in terms of its inability to reconcile these two concerns.[29] Despite the collectivist nature of the economic proposals that Fichte makes in *The Closed Commercial State* on the basis of his theory of property, property rights are nevertheless for him still essentially private rights, in the sense that they concern an individual's right to be able to live from his labour, and they are, therefore, ultimately based on self-interest. However, we shall see in due course that Fichte's theory of right also leaves room for a concern for the common good. In this respect, it appears possible to relate Fichte's social and political philosophy to the characterization of Jacobinism mentioned above, irrespective of the difficulties involved in any attempt to establish whether or not Fichte might have classed himself as a German Jacobin.

Parallels between Fichte's theory of property, as set out in the *Foundations of Natural Right* and *The Closed Commercial State*, and the radical phase of the French Revolution can also be exhibited by identifying some of the ways in which this theory articulates certain ideas that are, in essence, the same as those put forward by Babeuf, who, although at one time critical of the Jacobins, came to advocate a return to the 'Jacobin' constitution of 1793 as a preliminary stage in the attainment of absolute equality, claiming that this constitution represented 'the true law of the French nation'.[30] In this respect, we can speak of elements of Babouvism in the theory of right that Fichte developed in the *Foundations of Natural Right* and *The Closed Commercial State*, even though it appears impossible to establish firmly the existence of any direct form of influence.

To this extent, earlier interpreters of Fichte's political and economic thought, such as Weber and Léon, appear to be justified in linking Fichte's ideas to those of Babeuf. Such a link has some important implications when it comes to assessing the viability of the more recent tendency to interpret Fichte's political philosophy as being compatible with modern day liberalism, or at least with some of its central tenets. For, given the clear parallels between Fichte's theory of right and some of the main ideas associated with a radical proto-communist thinker such as Babeuf that I identify, it makes more sense to think of the type

29 Cf. Higonnet, *Goodness beyond Virtue.*
30 Quoted in Thomson, *The Babeuf Plot*, 34.

of political order that Fichte has in mind as some kind of socialist one, as Weber and Léon do, for whom liberalism had not become the dominant political ideology, to which Fichte's thought had to be made to conform. I shall be led, nevertheless, to point to some essential differences between Fichte's theory of right and the revolutionary movement known as Babouvism. One of these differences relates to a topic that will be discussed in more detail in Chapter 4 and will form a central theme of Chapter 5, in which I discuss the *Addresses to the German Nation*. The topic in question concerns Fichte's conception of society as an ethical community, rather than a legal and political one, and the position that he believes the scholar ought to occupy within this ethical community. This difference does not, however, in any way point to the need for a liberal interpretation of Fichte's social and political philosophy but rather speaks against it.

Fichte and Babeuf

On the strength of what has already been said concerning Fichte's views on property, a number of parallels can be drawn between his theory of right and some of the main ideas associated with Babeuf. For if we turn to the so-called *Analyse de la doctrine de Babeuf*,[31] a manifesto that, as far as is known, was not written by Babeuf himself, but was, we may assume, endorsed by him, we encounter a number of claims that are essentially compatible with some of the central features of Fichte's theory of right.

To begin with, there is the claim made in the *Analyse de la doctrine de Babeuf* that nature has given every man an equal right to the enjoyment of all wealth. This is compatible with Fichte's claim that at the level of original rights, where individuals are considered in abstraction from their relations to each other, the concept of an original right is 'infinite' with respect to its quantity, because what is at issue here 'is only that the person is to be free in general, but not the extent to which he is to be free'.[32] In other words, at the level of original rights, human beings have an equal right to extend their spheres of activity as far as they possibly can, because the imposition of legitimate limits on the exercise of original rights can only be based on consent, with each person limiting his freedom so that it may coexist with the freedom of others.

---

31 The main articles of this manifesto are given in Thomson, *The Babeuf Plot*, 33f.
32 GA I / 3: 404; FNR: 102f.

Fichte thus appears to hold the view that prior to the institution of the state by means of a civil contract, no one can legitimately claim to possess a right to a greater part of the world or to the objects within it than others, in the sense that in the absence of any limitations based on consent, everyone has an equal right to extend his sphere of activity as far as he possibly can, which will ultimately depend on such factors as physical power.

Yet even when Fichte introduces constraints on the extent to which any one person can appropriate objects and parts of the world, which are the ultimate sources of wealth, these constraints are themselves of an egalitarian kind in two important respects. First of all, they apply to everyone and secondly, and more positively, they serve to guarantee each and every person the possibility of being able to live from his labour. As well as demanding that a person is guaranteed a particular activity by means of which he is able to live, each person must also be provided with the resources, and in this sense 'wealth', that this activity requires in order to be performed successfully. Moreover, as Fichte makes clear in *The Closed Commercial State*, by being able to live from one's labour, he means not only being able to subsist but also being able to live as agreeably as possible, given the conditions of the state in which one lives, together with the fact that one will be living alongside a certain number of other persons who enjoy the same right.[33] We can therefore speak of people as having the equal right to the enjoyment of all wealth even in the more literal sense of the term. As we shall see, in *The Closed Commercial State*, Fichte develops a theory as to how a certain number of persons living together can live from their labour in as agreeable a manner as possible based on the idea that they will to some extent have to cooperate with each other. In this respect, the intention behind this work is, broadly speaking, compatible with another Babouvist doctrine, namely, that the aim of society is not only to defend natural equality but also to increase, by the cooperation of all, the enjoyment of all wealth.

Other similarities between Fichte's theory of right and the doctrines set out in the *Analyse de la doctrine de Babeuf* concern the need to work and the nature of work. Fichte makes the point that since the state is obliged to guarantee that each person is able to live from his labour, each person is correspondingly obliged to work, so that just as 'there ought to be no poor people in a rational state, so too . . . there ought to

<hr />

33 GA I / 7: 55.

be no idlers in it, either'.[34] In the *Analyse de la doctrine de Babeuf*, it is likewise stated that human beings have the duty to work, and that abstaining from work constitutes a crime. In short, for both Fichte and Babeuf, the benefits that come from living in a just society impose corresponding obligations on a person. This in turn relates to the Babouvist doctrine that labour and enjoyment ought to be in common, so that oppression exists 'when one man exhausts himself working and wants for everything, while another wallows in abundance without doing anything'.[35] Fichte can be seen to express a similar sentiment concerning the limits to which any one person should be made to work in the following passage, in which he castigates exploitative labour practices:

> It is not merely a pious wish but an essential demand of right and their vocation that human beings live on the earth as easily, as freely, as commandingly over nature, in as genuinely human a way as nature allows. A human being is to work; but not as a beast of burden does, falling asleep under its burden, and being roused to carry the same burden again after only the shortest rest of its exhausted powers. He is to work without fear, with pleasure and joy, and to have time left over in which to raise his mind and eyes to heaven, which he was formed to behold.[36]

The idea of a fair distribution of labour and enjoyment in fact came to play an increasingly significant role in Fichte's thoughts on property, as is shown by his 1812 *Rechtslehre*, which adheres closely to the theory of property that Fichte developed during his Jena period. Fichte thinks that a problem arises with his earlier theory of property and its application on account of the way in which human freedom is ultimately subordinated to the law of necessity in both a natural and a legal sense. In the first case, this is because the use of freedom is reduced to that of working to satisfy the basic needs of life; while, in the second case, necessity takes the form of the contributions that a person is obliged to make towards maintaining the state as a coercive power. Yet the whole point of a person's entering into the contract which institutes a condition of right was to have his freedom

---

34 GA I / 4: 23; FNR: 186f. In a similar vein, Fichte states that, 'Everyone must work and has, if he works, enough to live on: there are no vagabonds (*Chevaliers d'industrie*), for they are not tolerated anywhere within the state' (GA I / 4: 92; FNR: 262f.).

35 Quoted in Thomson, *The Babeuf Plot*, 33.

36 GA I / 7: 71.

guaranteed. In order to remove this contradiction, Fichte argues that the state must guarantee that each and every person, after he has satisfied his basic needs and has fulfilled his duties as a citizen, has freedom left over in which he can freely form his own ends.[37] This leads Fichte to identify the absolute right to property (*absolute Eigenthumsrecht*) with 'free leisure for arbitrary ends' (*freie Muße zu beliebigen Zweken*).[38]

The growing importance that Fichte attaches to leisure lies behind his claim that the amount of leisure a state enables its citizens to enjoy defines how rich or poor it is. It also helps explain his identification of the final end of the state as that of guaranteeing its citizens leisure, which means that all must be done to reduce the means to it (that is, work), by the introduction of such measures as a division of labour.[39] This implies that any gains in productivity which result from the introduction of a division of labour should be used to free up more leisure time, as opposed to the hours of work being allowed to remain the same while the number of goods in circulation and levels of consumption increase. For Fichte, the citizens of the state must, in short, be guaranteed not only freedom from any illegitimate inference on the part of others in relation to their own bodies and the property they need in order to be able to live, but also the highest possible degree of freedom from work. Fichte thus comes to view leisure as an object of distributive justice and one of the state's main tasks as distributing it equally among its citizens. This innovation should not surprise us, given the way in which he considers guaranteeing people the most basic conditions of free and effective human agency to be the main function of right. We can accordingly think of Fichte as holding the view that a condition in which some people enjoyed considerable periods of leisure while others were made to work long hours would be a highly unjust one.

Given the way in which Fichte treats the absolute and inalienable right to be able to live from one's labour as fundamental to his theory of right, and the fact that this right demands that resources are distributed in such a way as to allow each and every person to live from his labour and to enjoy as much leisure as possible, it appears that he would also have to agree with the Babouvist doctrine that it is a crime

---

37 GA II / 13: 223f.
38 GA II / 13: 229.
39 GA II / 13: 230.

for any one person to appropriate to himself the wealth of the earth or of human industry. Indeed, consistency demands treating any act that would prevent the state from being able to guarantee the right of each and every person to be able to live from his labour and to enjoy a sufficient amount of leisure, including acts of unlimited appropriation or any attempts to thwart the redistributive measures that the state needs to undertake, as a violation of right. This becomes evident if we turn to Fichte's deduction of the right of coercion (*Zwangsrecht*) in the *Foundations of Natural Right*.

In the first part of the *Foundations of Natural Right*, Fichte introduces the right of coercion as the solution to certain problems that arise in connection with the attempts undertaken by two persons to determine between themselves the extent of their rights, particularly their property rights. The recognition of each other's rights that results from this process of mutual determination is highly unstable, because it presupposes that each person can trust the other person to stick to any agreements they have made between themselves, not only at the moment at which an agreement is made or immediately afterwards, but also with respect to all future actions covered by the same agreement. This means that, on the one hand, the '*possibility of a relation of right between persons in the sphere of natural right is conditioned by mutual honesty and trust*',[40] and, on the other hand, that any violation of an agreement made between persons may result in the disappearance of these preconditions of right, by serving to undermine the trust and mutual honesty on which agreements are based.

In addition to this problem, Fichte invokes the Hobbesian problem of the rational suspicion of the sincerity and constancy of another person's declarations, which, even to begin with, makes the establishment of a condition of mutual honesty and trust impossible, when he makes the following claim: 'As soon as one of them thinks that such insincerity or change is possible, he can no longer rest easy but must always be on his guard and prepared for war; he thereby puts the other (who might have still been sincere about the agreement) into a similar position, arousing the other's distrust as well'.[41] Here the problem of knowing what others really intend and the mere thought of the possible violation of an agreement made with another person, rather than any actual violation of this agreement, are enough to undermine the

40 GA I / 3: 424; FNR: 124.
41 GA I / 3: 424; FNR: 124.

basis of the provisional relation of right established between two persons by means of their attempts mutually to determine the extent to which their rights extend.

In the face of these problems, 'a rightful state of affairs ... once again becomes impossible; and the concept of right still seems to be empty and devoid of all application'.[42] This failure to apply the concept of right leads Fichte to introduce the idea of a law that ultimately leaves a person free to act, since right deals with rational beings that are free and it must therefore operate in a manner that is essentially different to how natural laws operate, while annulling any action that constitutes a freely willed violation of right, by producing the opposite of what the agent intended. Rather than any particular intention, Fichte here appears to have in mind the fact that any person who acts is seeking, whether consciously or not, to give expression to his freedom. Yet in violating the relation of right through his actions, this same person becomes subject to a law that deprives him of his freedom by means of the legal sanctions attached to it. A person who wishes to avoid losing his freedom consequently has an incentive not to become subject to such a law. The law in question needs to be further determined and applied, however, and it is on this basis that Fichte deduces a commonwealth with positive laws as the only type of community in which people can have rights.

The way in which the state, rather than agreements freely made by individuals among themselves, comes to determine how far actual rights extend, means that we must think of the moment of consent, which is what distinguishes relations of right from relations based on force alone, as having to be introduced in another way. This is the point of the civil contract, in which persons freely renounce their natural freedom, by agreeing to the establishment of a protective power, which then decides on how property is to be distributed. As we have seen, this contract is grounded on the property contract, in which property is understood to be most fundamentally the right to be able to live from one's labour. If this right is not guaranteed by the state, the latter will lose its legitimacy in relation to any person who, through no fault of his own, is unable to live from his labour; and to avoid this possibility, the state will need to redistribute property. In this way, Fichte's theory of property serves to fill out the abstract account of the right of coercion and the state given in the first part of the *Foundations of Natural Right*, by

42 GA I / 3: 423; FNR: 123.

indicating the kinds of laws and measures concerning property that the state will need to introduce and enforce, so as to fulfil its function. Given the state's function of guaranteeing each and every person the right to live from his labour, it seems that among such laws and measures we must include ones that aim to prevent or to punish acts of resistance committed in connection with the state's attempt to redistribute property, or any other acts which undermine the state's attempts to guarantee this right. The conclusion that, in terms of his theory of right, such acts must be held to constitute violations of right and must be accordingly subjected to coercion is drawn by Fichte himself, when he claims, in relation to the state's task of redistributing property, that 'the poor (those, of course, who have entered into the civil contract) have an absolute right of coercion to such assistance'.[43]

Thus, while the account of distributive justice found in Fichte's theory of property already points to the compatibility of his theory of right with the Babouvist doctrine that in a true society there should be neither rich nor poor people, when it is taken together with his theory of the right of coercion, it also turns out to be compatible with the further claim associated with Babeuf that the rich who will not give up what they do not need to help the needy are enemies of the people. This raises the question as to whether there could, in fact, ever be any rich people in a state in which there should not, according to Fichte, be any poor people; for the absence of any poor people within a state might possibly require a division of resources and wealth that would make the existence of a class of rich people impossible. Fichte, however, never offers a clear statement as to how far his egalitarianism is meant to extend. He instead restricts himself to remarking that in the ideal state no one can become overly rich and no one can sink into poverty.[44] This provides a rare example of a failure on Fichte's part to seek to develop the full implications of his theory of property, by applying the concept of right to the conditions of the sensible world.

On top of the close relationship between Fichte's theory of right and the particular Babouvist doctrines mentioned above, another link between Fichte's theory of right and some of the main ideas associated with Babeuf concerns the way in which Babeuf and his fellow conspirators can be characterized in general terms as dreaming of 'a communist society without private property and with the collective administration

43 GA I / 4: 23; FNR: 186.
44 GA I / 7: 68.

of the production and distribution of goods'.[45] As regards communism, we have seen that Fichte clearly rejects the idea that land can be privately owned and that there is some firm evidence that he thinks this is also true of the means of production. To this extent, Fichte's theory of right appears to open the way for a limited form of communism, even though it allows for private property in the form of money and any personal belongings that can be purchased by means of it. Then, in *The Closed Commercial State*, Fichte offers a fully worked out theory concerning the collective administration of the production and distribution of goods which he thinks is necessary to guarantee each and every person's right to be able to live from his labour.

The first book of this work develops in more detail certain ideas already contained in the second part of the *Foundations of Natural Right*, so that, as previously indicated, the proposals found in *The Closed Commercial State* are to be seen as forming part of Fichte's extended attempt to apply the concept of right to the conditions of the sensible world. Fichte begins by distinguishing between two main forms of activity by means of which life is sustained and made more agreeable: the growing or cultivation of natural products and working upon natural products for some further end. A set of people dedicated to one of these forms of activity constitutes an estate (*Stand*), which itself divides into various subgroups, with each estate possessing the exclusive right to engage in the form of activity associated with it. In the present case, this means that we have one estate, that of the producers (*Producenten*), which has the exclusive right to grow, catch, raise or cultivate natural products, and another estate, whose members Fichte calls artists (*Künstler*), which has the exclusive right to work upon these products in accordance with some end. The members of these two estates agree to restrict themselves to their respective spheres of activity and, more positively, to exchange their products, so as to guarantee each other the means both to live from their labour and to live as agreeably as possible. In order that the exchange of natural products and finished articles can take place with maximum efficiency and the minimum waste of time, a third estate with the exclusive right to engage in the specific activity of exchanging goods becomes necessary. This is the estate of merchants (*Kaufleute*), whose members are obliged to buy the natural products and finished articles of the other estates and to sell the members of these estates the goods they need,

---

45 Rose, *Gracchus Babeuf*, 232.

while the members of these other estates are obliged to sell their natural products and finished articles to the merchants and to buy what they need from them. The introduction of an estate of merchants does not signal the move to any form of free market economy. The merchants are obliged to sell what they buy from the members of the other estates and are to be punished by the state if they should attempt to hold back goods so as to increase their value. It is not surprising, then, that Fichte later came to class the merchants as state officials.[46] Goods are, moreover, to be bought and sold at fixed prices, in line with a theory of value whose basic measure is grain, considered in its relation to the amount of time it is able to nourish a person.

The state oversees the whole process of production and exchange, so as to ensure not only that the various estates honour the agreements they have made with each other, but also that there are enough natural products and finished articles available to satisfy the needs of all the citizens. In other words, the state makes sure that the levels of production and consumption remain in harmony with each other. The planning of the economy thus requires guaranteeing that there is a sufficient number of natural products and finished articles available to satisfy people's basic needs and, once this condition is satisfied, that there is also a sufficient amount of them available to ensure that everyone is given the possibility of living as agreeably as possible. The number of persons in each estate is accordingly determined by the number of producers needed, given such factors as the fertility of the land and the state of agricultural technology, with the number of people belonging to the other estates depending on how many non-producers can be supported by the existing number of producers. As Fichte himself puts it: 'There may not be more artists than can live off the products of the land. A barren earth does not allow for luxury. In that case, the people must learn to live within limits'.[47] The need to control the number of people belonging to each estate leads Fichte to argue that a person who intends to enter an occupation must make his intention known to the government, which will then either grant or refuse the person in question the right to do so.

The state must also prevent too many natural products and finished articles becoming available, because this would render invalid its calculations concerning the value of the natural products and finished

46 GA II / 13: 247.
47 GA I / 4: 39; FNR: 204.

articles in circulation at any given time. Since the total sum of money in circulation at any given time is meant to represent the total amount of goods in circulation at the same time, any failure to calculate correctly the number of goods available would, in fact, completely undermine the state's monetary system and its regulation of the price of goods. It is to prevent any unpredictable elements from undermining the state's careful planning of the economy that Fichte proposes banning and making impossible any trade on the part of the citizens with foreigners. Instead, the state alone will conduct foreign trade until the time comes when it has made itself economically self-sufficient and thus able to sever all commercial links with other states. Similar proposals to these last ones were put forward by Babeuf.[48]

Although Fichte may have developed his theory of a closed commercial state in the absence of any knowledge of Babeuf's ideas, this theory clearly involves the collective administration of the production and distribution of goods in the name of the people. In fact, while the *Analyse de la doctrine de Babeuf* represents an incomplete version of Babeuf's own views, because it contains no hint of the collectivist form of economic organization outlined by him in the *Tribun du Peuple*,[49] the theory of a planned economy that Fichte develops in *The Closed Commercial State* finds a clear echo in the following description of the economic plans developed by Babeuf himself in 1795, before the Conspiracy of the Equals:

> The tasks assigned to the government of 'the association' thus included the regulation of production in industry according to a rational calculation of present and future need. It would assign a fixed output to each producer, determine the number of workers to be employed in a particular craft, and exercise a control over the number of young men allowed to enter any craft or profession. By dint of such planning the evil effects of competition could be avoided and industry conducted more efficiently.[50]

In the light of this close connection between Babeuf's and Fichte's economic theories, as far as their basic intentions and character are concerned, the claim that Fichte's economic theories stopped well short of Babeuf's 'communitarian alternative' to a free market amounts to an overstatement to say the least; especially when this

48 Cf. Léon, 'Le socialisme de Fichte d'après l'état commercial fermé', 203f.
49 Cf. Rose, *Gracchus Babeuf*, 231.
50 Rose, *Gracchus Babeuf*, 193.

conclusion is based on the argument that while Babeuf left no room for private property, Fichte allows for a form of property that '*was* private in a real sense', despite the restrictions that he imposes on the individual's right to dispose of his property as he pleases.[51] For although this claim is true to the extent that Fichte's account of the role of money in the state involves the idea of a limited form of private property, it is nevertheless his account of the concept of property in the *Foundations of Natural Right* and its further application in *The Closed Commercial State* that are the ultimate sources of those features noted above that link Fichte's theory of right to some of the main ideas associated with Babeuf. To use Fichte's theory of property as a means of firmly distinguishing his views from those of Babeuf also downplays to an unjustifiable degree the extent to which his theory of right does not allow for the existence of private property. As we have seen, the limitations that Fichte imposes on the right to property represent by far the main thrust of his theory of property. This is not to say, however, that there are no fundamental differences between Fichte's theory of right and the doctrines associated with the revolutionary movement known as Babouvism.

One such difference concerns the fact that the Conspiracy of the Equals aimed at the overthrow of the existing government and the establishment of a provisional revolutionary government, whereas Fichte appears to advocate in *The Closed Commercial State* a process of approximation to his ideal, rational state. This is evident from the short introduction to this work, in which, as previously mentioned, Fichte makes a distinction between the rational state and actual existing states. According to Fichte, the divide between the *a priori*, normative level and the empirical level is not one that can be suddenly overcome by destroying an existing constitution without placing human beings in a barbaric condition. Therefore, what is required instead is to allow the ideal, rational state to develop out of the existing state, in the sense that the latter is gradually made to conform to the former. The question thus becomes not what is right, as with the rational state, but the extent to which the introduction of that which is right is achievable given the conditions in which an existing state finds itself. *The Closed Commercial State* itself aims to provide the statesman with a model as to how economic relations in the existing state must be shaped if it is to be made to conform to the rational state. It is then up to the statesman to

---

51 La Vopa, *Fichte*, 320f.

APPLYING THE CONCEPT OF RIGHT: FICHTE AND BABEUF 81

try to introduce this model should conditions prove favourable enough in the case of the particular state of which he is himself a member.

On this basis, another stage in the application of the concept of right can be identified, though this time one concerning which philosophy can provide some guidance but which it cannot itself undertake: the stage of shaping a given historically situated legal and political community in accordance with the principles of the rational state. The philosopher and statesman are in this way viewed as being engaged in a common project, which Fichte thinks removes the need for revolutionary action; and it is therefore not surprising to find him dedicating *The Closed Commercial State* to the Prussian Minister of Trade and Finance Karl August von Struensee. It has, in fact, been suggested that Fichte thought of the conditions in Prussia, where he had moved in the wake of the Atheism Controversy, as being favourable to the introduction of the proposals outlined in *The Closed Commercial State*, since the question of economic reform was already a major issue of the day, to which von Struensee had made his own contribution. In this respect, far from being utopian in nature, *The Closed Commercial State* can be seen to represent an original solution to contemporary economic problems.[52] This gradualism and dependence on the introduction of changes by the existing authorities are, however, far removed from the plans hatched by Babeuf and his comrades in the Conspiracy of the Equals with the intention of preparing the way for the introduction of their economic and political proposals, as the following description of these plans shows:

> The conspirators seem to have seen the conspiracy as involving three stages. Firstly, there would be the Day of the People, accompanied by an orgy of primitive popular justice, of slaughter, revenge and looting. This would usher in a return to a rigorous version of Robespierre's revolutionary government, which would prepare, within as short a time as possible, the triumph of the principles of pure democracy and pure communism, and establish the reign of *le bonheur commun*.[53]

The fundamental difference between Fichte's gradualism and the revolutionary violence associated with the Conspiracy of the Equals relates to another significant difference between Fichte's and Babeuf's views, which this time concerns certain limits to Fichte's egalitarianism that do not apply in the case of Babeuf.

52 Cf. Léon, 'Le socialisme de Fichte d'après l'état commercial fermé', 47f.
53 Rose, *Gracchus Babeuf*, 242.

As is clear from what has been said above concerning how an existing state is to be transformed in accordance with the principles of the
rational state, Fichte accords the philosopher an important role in this
process, which is that of seeking to guide the actions of the statesman.
The view that the philosopher has a privileged role to play in society
also finds expression in Fichte's doctrine of ethical duties set out in
The System of Ethics, published in 1798. Both this doctrine of ethical
duties itself and the role assigned to the philosopher within it are
highly relevant to Fichte's separation of right from morality, which
I look at in more detail in Chapter 4, as well as to the role that he
accords to virtue in his *Addresses to the German Nation*, which I consider
in Chapter 5. In the next section, I concentrate on showing how
Fichte's theory of a society in which particular ethical duties derive
from one's membership of an estate, and, in particular, his views on the
philosopher's place within society, point to the existence of another
fundamental difference between his standpoint and the kind of absolute egalitarianism associated with Babeuf. This difference does not,
however, invite a liberal interpretation of Fichte's social and political
philosophy, but rather speaks against such an interpretation, because
it suggests that Fichte operates with the type of traditional view of
society which, historically, liberalism helped to undermine.

Fichte's traditionalism

In the doctrine of ethical duties that he sets out in *The System of Ethics*,
Fichte claims that the achievement of the 'end of reason' requires a
division of labour, whereby different individuals become responsible
for the different tasks that need to be accomplished in order to achieve
this end. This arrangement in turn requires the establishment of different estates (*Stände*).[54] These estates are based on either natural or
artificial relations. The ones based on the former type of relation are
those of the members of the family to each other, while Fichte uses the
term 'profession' (*Beruf*) to designate the second type of estate.[55] The
professions themselves subdivide into those that involve acting immediately upon the community of rational beings and those that involve
acting upon nature for the sake of this community.[56] The members of

---

54 GA I / 5: 232; SE: 247.
55 GA I / 5: 286f.; SE: 310.
56 GA I / 5: 300; SE: 325.

the first set of professions, which Fichte refers to as the 'higher' ones, act immediately upon the community of rational beings because their object is a person's intellect in the case of the scholar, a person's moral sense in the case of the cleric, and his aesthetic sense in the case of the artist. This set of professions also includes the state official, whose task is to ensure that legal relationships between human beings are guaranteed. The members of the second set of professions, which Fichte refers to as the 'lower' ones, direct nature or else gather or tend its products (farmers, miners, fishermen, hunters etc.), fashion the raw materials that nature provides (craftsmen, artisans and factory workers), or facilitate the exchange of objects (merchants). In the case of this second set of professions, the formal correspondence between the structure of the division of the members of society into various professions and the division of the citizens into various estates found in Fichte's account of the workings of his closed commercial state is obvious.

In the first book of *The Closed Commercial State*, Fichte introduces the higher professions when he claims that persons must be appointed to administer the laws and maintain public order, together with others whose exclusive concern is with public education and those people charged with defending the nation from its internal and external enemies. As with the members of the lower professions, the members of the higher professions form estates that have the exclusive right to undertake a certain activity within the state, while renouncing the right to undertake other activities. In order that the members of these estates may themselves be able to live from their labour and have the opportunity to live as agreeably as possible, the other estates must provide them with natural products and finished articles in return for the administrative, educational and military services that the members of the higher professions provide within the state. Fichte here claims that the members of the higher professions exist for the sake of the members of the lower professions.[57] One way of interpreting this statement is that the members of the higher professions perform roles that are essential to guaranteeing the rights of the other members of society, including the right to be able to live from one's labour and such rights as the right to education. There would consequently be no need for the higher professions if the persons concerned with the economic activity of the state did not need to have their rights

---

57 GA I / 7: 58.

guaranteed. On the other hand, from the standpoint of morality and philosophy, the lower professions exist equally for the sake of the higher professions, by guaranteeing the satisfaction of their members' basic needs. This is evident from the following claim that Fichte makes in *The System of Ethics* concerning the lower classes of the people: 'Even if they are not the pinnacle of empirical humanity, they are surely the pillars of the same. How could the scholar do research, the teacher of the people teach, or the state official govern if they could not live in the first place?'[58]

In the present context, this last claim is highly significant because it can be related to another claim that is made in *The Closed Commercial State*. This is the claim that the person whose task is to engage in deep thought, which can be taken to mean the philosopher more than anyone else, requires a different form of nourishment and different conditions to those of the farmer (*Ackerbauer*), who is engaged in a mechanical, purely physical form of activity. For the latter it is, according to Fichte, no misfortune to have to satisfy his hunger with vegetables, and he has no need to wear fine, clean clothes except on holidays; whereas the person whose activity is to engage in deep thought, whether it relates to the higher arts or to science (*Wissenschaft*), requires a more varied and refreshing form of nourishment, together with surroundings that continually place before his eyes the purity and nobility that ought to reign within him.[59] This clearly suggests that for Fichte what it means to live as agreeably as possible is relative to one's station in life and the particular form of activity associated with it, with the philosopher providing a prime example of someone who requires better nourishment and conditions than a member of one of the lower professions. In stark contrast to this acceptance of some degree of inequality, Babeuf rejects outright the idea of any preferential treatment for those engaged in intellectual activity, when he claims in the *Tribun du Peuple* that the high standing attributed to this form of activity is the result of an ideological ploy on the part of intellectuals:

> There is absurdity and injustice in the pretended attribution of a greater recompense for whoever works at a task that demands a higher degree of intelligence and more application and stretching of the mind ... for this does not in any way extend the capacity of his

58 GA I / 5: 314; SE: 342.
59 GA I / 7: 67f.

stomach ... It is the intelligentsia [*les intelligens*] who have fixed such a high price for conceptions of their brains.[60]

Fichte's additional claim that the lower classes of the people ought to show respect (*Achtung*) for the scholar as a more highly cultivated human being, together with his claim that they even ought to exhibit a form of 'deference' (*Ehrerbietigkeit*) towards him,[61] thus also appear far removed from Babeuf's radical egalitarianism.

This fundamental difference between the revolutionary movement known as Babouvism and Fichte's theory of society by no means suggests a liberal interpretation of Fichte's social and political philosophy. The way in which Fichte makes what it means to live as agreeably as possible relative to one's station in life and the particular form of activity associated with it can be seen, in fact, to replace an objective measure for determining the distribution of goods with the historical fact of a traditional society of estates, each with its own distinctive mode of life.[62] In this respect, rather than pointing towards a liberal social and political order, Fichte appears to turn to the past for inspiration, and, more specifically, to the decaying social and political order with which he was himself most familiar and which, historically, the rise of liberalism, among other forces, helped destroy, by understanding individual human beings primarily as the bearers of certain basic rights deriving from their status as human beings as such, that is, in abstraction from any determinate social or political relations in which they might stand with other human beings. As we shall see in Chapters 4 and 5, this traditional conception of society, together with the role that Fichte accords to the scholar within it, have an important part to play in Fichte's social and political philosophy with respect to the question of the relation of right to morality and the role of the concept of virtue.

In his Jena theory of right, Fichte admittedly appears to regard individuals in abstraction from the traditional conception of society mentioned above when he separates right from morality and treats individuals primarily as the bearers of certain rights. In this respect, one might be tempted to speak of a liberal element in his political philosophy. In this chapter I have shown, however, that even here the revolutionary aspects of Fichte's theory of right, which centre on his theory of property and exhibit a number of clear parallels with some of

60 Rose, *Gracchus Babeuf,* 213.
61 GA I / 5: 315f.; SE: 343.
62 Cf. Weber, *Fichte's Sozialismus und sein Verhältnis zur Marx'schen Doktrin,* 42.

the central doctrines associated with the revolutionary movement known as Babouvism, present a serious challenge to any attempt to provide a liberal interpretation of his political philosophy without offering an extremely truncated account of it. Given his views on property it would, in fact, make more sense to interpret Fichte as a potential critic of liberalism, especially of its conception of property rights. In the next chapter, I show in relation to Kant's theory of cosmopolitan right that Fichte also succeeds in identifying problems with what can be seen as an attempt on Kant's part to stress the benefits of economic liberalism insofar as relations between different independent states are concerned; so that even if we might want to reject the specific economic proposals that Fichte sets out in *The Closed Commercial State*, it is still possible to appreciate the critical dimension of this work.

3

FICHTE'S REAPPRAISAL OF KANT'S
THEORY OF COSMOPOLITAN RIGHT

In the first few years after its publication in 1795, Kant's essay *Perpetual Peace* (*Zum ewigen Frieden*) provoked intense discussion in Germany, prompting figures associated with German Romanticism such as Friedrich Schlegel and Joseph Görres to write about it.[1] Fichte also wrote about Kant's essay, which deals with the rights of nations and cosmopolitan right while setting out to show how a lasting global peace might be possible, in the form of a review that appeared in 1796 in the *Philosophisches Journal einer Gesellschaft Teutscher Gelehrten*, at a time when Fichte was developing the theory of natural right that he eventually published as the *Foundations of Natural Right*. In the second part of this work, published in 1797, Fichte attempts to make his own contribution towards the main question with which Kant deals in *Perpetual Peace*, which is the question of the possibility of a peaceful global order subject to law. Fichte does this in the second appendix to the doctrine of natural right entitled, 'Outline of the right of nations and cosmopolitan right' (*Grundriss des Völker- und Weltbürgerrechts*).

As its title indicates, this appendix falls into two parts. One part concerns the rights that nations have in relation to each other in times of war and peace, while the other part concerns the idea of world citizenship and the rights that it entails. Thus, simply in terms of the topics it deals with, the second appendix to the doctrine of natural right already points to the influence of Kant's essay. In what follows, I concentrate on discussing Kant's and Fichte's views on the issue of cosmopolitan right and its relation to the idea of a lasting global peace. In so doing, I cast doubt on the claim that Kant's 'general cosmopolitan approach still remains convincing',[2] by showing that

1 Cf. Höffe, *Kant's Cosmopolitan Theory of Law and Peace*, 154ff.
2 Höffe, *Kant's Cosmopolitan Theory of Law and Peace*, xvii.

Fichte identifies a significant problem with Kant's cosmopolitanism. Fichte does this in his account of the relations of states to each other given in *The Closed Commercial State*, which was published in 1800, when he identifies a problem with which we are familiar today: the problem of one-sided relations of economic dependence between states.

In relation to the issue of cosmopolitan right, which for both Kant and Fichte is intimately connected with the question of the possibility of a lasting global peace, I show in the following section that, in the *Foundations of Natural Right*, Fichte adopts a position that broadly corresponds to the kind of cosmopolitanism that Kant advocates in his essay *Perpetual Peace* and in the section on cosmopolitan right found in the later *The Metaphysics of Morals* (*Die Metaphysik der Sitten*), which was published in 1797, the same year in which the second part of the *Foundations of Natural Right* containing Fichte's own views on this topic was published. Although Fichte's apparent indebtedness to Kant can be understood as an implicit acknowledgement on his part of the value of Kant's thoughts on the topic of cosmopolitan right, Fichte will be shown in *The Closed Commercial State* to reassess his earlier acceptance of Kant's cosmopolitanism, when he identifies the problem of one-sided forms of economic dependence; a problem that Kant fails to recognize, or, as I suggest, uncritically accepts as something given. Fichte's rejection of Kant's and, by implication, his own earlier cosmopolitanism, is of an especially radical nature, since the solution to the problem of one-sided forms of economic dependence that he proposes is that states should completely close themselves off economically from other states. This is not to say, however, that the theory of a closed commercial state which Fichte advocates represents a complete rejection of his own earlier cosmopolitanism and of any attempt to explain how a lasting global peace might be possible. Rather, *The Closed Commercial State* amounts to an attempt, though an ultimately implausible one, to explain how a lasting global peace might be attained by removing one-sided relations of economic dependence between states. This rather neglected text[3] will be thus shown to constitute an important contribution to the debate occasioned by Kant's essay *Perpetual*

---

3 Among the few works that deal at any length with this work are Weber, *Fichte's Sozialismus und sein Verhältnis zur Marx'schen Doktrin*; Léon, 'Le socialisme de Fichte d'après l'état commercial fermé'; Batscha, *Gesellschaft und Staat in der politischen Philosophie Fichtes*, 190ff.; and Verzar, *Das autonome Subjekt und der Vernunftstaat*. None of these works, however, seeks to relate *The Closed Commercial State* to Kant's theory of cosmopolitan right.

Peace, especially insofar as it reveals the limitations of Kant's theory of cosmopolitan right.

The Kantian cosmopolitanism of Fichte's
Foundations of Natural Right

In his account of cosmopolitan right in the *Foundations of Natural Right*, Fichte claims that private persons from one state 'may visit another state, either for business (*um ihrer Geschäfte willen*) or simply for pleasure, provided that the two states recognize one another and are on friendly terms'.[4] Such visits will take place according to the terms of the contracts made between states as outlined in the preceding section of the second appendix to the doctrine of natural right, which concerns the right of nations. This explanation of how cosmopolitan right is possible raises the question, however, as to what is to happen in accordance with principles of right when a foreigner enters a state's territory in the absence of any formal agreement between the state of which he is a citizen and the state which he enters. Fichte's theory of cosmopolitan right attempts to answer this question.

Since, for Fichte, the right to something as recognized within a particular legal and political community can be regarded as legitimate only if it somehow rests on agreement between human beings, a foreigner who enters the territory of a state of which he is not himself a citizen would appear to be devoid of any rights, as long as no prior agreement concerning the rights that he has exists between the state of which he is a citizen and the state which he enters. Fichte claims that there is, however, a right which precedes all positive rights established on the basis of agreement between human beings in the form of contracts, because it is itself the condition of the possibility of all contracts. The right in question is the 'original' human right of a person to expect others, in the absence of any evidence to the contrary, to proceed on the assumption that he is someone with whom it is possible to enter into rightful relations established on the basis of mutual consent. Fichte describes this right as 'the right to be able to acquire rights',[5] so as to bring out the way in which its status as an original human right derives from its being a condition of all further rights. To call that which is the possibility of all rights itself a right invites confusion, because it fails to

4 GA I / 4: 163; FNR: 332.
5 GA I / 4: 163; FNR: 333.

establish a clear conceptual distinction between that which is conditioned (that is, a particular right) and its condition, which is here the
possibility of entering into agreements with others in order to determine
the nature and the extent of the rights that one has in relation to them.
At the same time, the way in which Fichte develops the idea of the
possibility of being able to acquire rights provides some firm evidence
of his indebtedness to Kant's theory of cosmopolitan right.

Fichte thinks that the original human right that consists in the possibility of being able to acquire rights implies the existence of a more
specific right that again appears to exhibit the character of an original
right, since it does not have to be established by means of a contract
between human beings. This is 'the right of a mere *citizen of the world* [*das
Recht des bloßen* Weltbürgers]', which is the right 'to go about freely on the
earth and offer to establish rightful connections with others'.[6] As the
bearer of such a right, a person may freely enter the territory of a state
with which his own state has not established any kind of formal agreement concerning the positive rights that he is to have on entering this
foreign state. He may do so, moreover, with the expectation that he will
be given the opportunity to explain his reasons for entering the territory
of this state and for wanting to enter into communication with its
citizens; while the state he has entered has the equal right to refuse
him entry if it judges these reasons to be unsatisfactory.[7]

Kant's influence can be detected here especially if one accepts the
claim that his theory of cosmopolitan right affirms the right of a person
to enter into voluntary relations with the citizens of other states without
being treated in a hostile manner, while also allowing that a state
retains the right to refuse entry to this person, so that a foreigner
would appear to have 'universal visitor rights' but not 'the right to
hospitality'.[8] Terminologically this distinction between 'visitor' rights
and 'the right to hospitality' is slightly misleading, because in *Perpetual
Peace* Kant identifies hospitality with 'the right of a stranger not to
be treated with hostility when he arrives on someone else's territory',
which seems to correspond to the notion of visitor rights, while also
claiming that a stranger can be legitimately turned away as long as
this can be done without causing his death.[9] These statements

6 GA I / 4: 164; FNR: 333.
7 GA I / 4: 164; FNR: 333f.
8 Cf. Höffe, *Kant's Cosmopolitan Theory of Law and Peace*, 142.
9 Immanuel Kant, 'Zum ewigen Frieden', in *Kant's gesammelte Schriften*, vol. VIII, 357f. /
   Political Writings, 105f.

nevertheless show that Kant's account of cosmopolitan right in *Perpetual Peace* exhibits a formal agreement with Fichte's account of it in the *Foundations of Natural Right*, making it plausible to suggest that Fichte's reading of Kant's essay helped shape his own views on this topic. Yet, for all its emphasis on voluntary agreement, the conception of cosmopolitan right that Fichte appears to adopt from Kant does not completely rule out the possibility of justifying steps taken by the party that enters the territory of a foreign nation that might be deemed coercive, even though the right to refuse entry to a person or to persons wishing to enter the territory of a foreign nation has been linked to Kant's 'harsh reckoning' of the colonial policies of the European states of his own time.[10]

Kant makes statements that certainly point to a harsh assessment of the colonial policies of his own time, as in *Perpetual Peace* itself, when he speaks of 'the *inhospitable* conduct of the civilised states of our continent, especially the commercial states, the injustice which they display in *visiting* foreign countries and peoples (which in their case is the same as *conquering* them)'.[11] Although this statement expresses moral outrage, it does not by itself amount to a full account as to why exactly a state has the right to turn foreigners away in order to maintain its independence, even when the foreigner's intentions are ostensibly peaceful ones. Kant in fact stresses the validity of the right to hospitality, whereas he pays far less attention to explaining the equal right of states to turn foreigners away. For example, in the section on cosmopolitan right in the *Metaphysics of Morals*, Kant affirms the right to hospitality by stating that all the nations of the earth

> stand in a community of possible physical *interaction* (*commercium*), that is, in a thoroughgoing relation of each to all the others of *offering to engage in commerce* with any other, and each has a right to make this attempt without the other being authorized to behave toward it as an enemy because it has made this attempt.[12]

Kant then identifies this right with cosmopolitan right as such. Although Kant acknowledges that this right has been abused, he immediately emphasizes that 'this possible abuse cannot annul the

10 Höffe, *Kant's Cosmopolitan Theory of Law and Peace*, 141.
11 Kant, 'Zum ewigen Frieden', 358 / *Political Writings*, 106.
12 Kant, 'Die Metaphysik der Sitten', in *Kant's gesammelte Schriften*, vol. VI, 352 / *The Metaphysics of Morals*. The English translation contains the Akademie edition page numbers.

right of citizens of the world *to try to* establish community with all and, to this end, to *visit* all regions of the earth'.[13]

None of this by itself contradicts what Kant elsewhere has to say about the right to hospitality, and he is admittedly at pains to point out that cosmopolitan right does not entail a right to make a settlement on the land of another nation without this nation's consent, as expressed by means of a contract, though he does allow for settlement without consent if it does not encroach on anyone's 'use' of the land.[14] These limitations are ambiguous, however, for they do not deal adequately enough with such questions as the one concerning how exactly contracts can be considered to be freely made by peoples with no real conception of what it means to enter into a contract in the European understanding of the term, nor with the question as to how to determine the extent to which a piece of land can be regarded as already being used. The need to provide fuller answers to these questions becomes apparent when it is borne in mind that the British and the French employed both the idea of consent, either through concession or purchase, and the idea of settling on unoccupied land, to distinguish their mode of colonizing America from that of the Spanish, as if this mode of colonizing other lands represented a less iniquitous form of colonization.[15]

To this one might well respond that Kant would view any claim to a right to land based on deception or on the inability of one of the parties to a contract to understand the full implications of consenting to its terms as being morally no more legitimate than the seizure of land by physical force; and one might then seek to justify this claim with reference to certain features of Kant's moral philosophy. Yet, leaving aside the issue of the extent to which such an approach is valid, there is, as I intend to argue with reference to Fichte's *The Closed Commercial State*, at least one respect in which Kant fails to recognize, or else uncritically accepts, the possibility of an indirect form of coercion exercised by one state, or its representatives, on another state. This allows us to think of Kant's cosmopolitanism as having the potential to be used to justify the kinds of abuses that Kant himself otherwise condemns. This indirect form of coercion is based on unequal relations of economic power; and Kant's failure to question it cannot be so

---

13 Kant, 'Die Metaphysik der Sitten', 353.
14 Kant, 'Die Metaphysik der Sitten', 353.
15 Cf. Pagden, *Lords of all the World*, 82ff.

easily explained away with reference to his moral philosophy precisely because, as we shall see in due course, he appears to treat unequal relations of economic dependence not only as something given, but also as something morally acceptable, on the grounds that such relations do not violate the moral status of human beings. Fichte, by contrast, demonstrates in *The Closed Commercial State* a better understanding of the possibility of this indirect form of coercion and its consequences, leading him to reject his own earlier Kantian cosmopolitanism. Yet, in order to explain how it does so, we first need to look in more detail at the 'commerce' of which Kant speaks.

Although this commerce may include voluntary relations between the citizens of foreign states other than purely economic ones, such as cultural forms of exchange, Kant clearly views the establishment of economic relations between states as an increasingly important factor in human history. For example, in the Eighth Proposition of his essay *Idea for a Universal History* (*Idee zu einer allgemeinen Geschichte in weltbürgerlicher Absicht*), Kant argues that with the development of the human race as a whole, civil freedom (*bürgerliche Freiheit*) cannot be infringed without this having a negative effect on trade, industry and commerce, which would in turn lead to a decline in a state's power.[16] States are accordingly viewed as having a strong incentive for promoting this form of freedom, so as to maintain or increase their degree of overall power in relation to other states. Then, in *Perpetual Peace*, Kant points to the possible benefits of the development of economic relations between states with respect to the realization of global peace, when he puts forward the theory that after the arts of cultivating and utilizing natural products became possible with the establishment of landed property, trade between nations began, and that it was in this way that 'nations first entered into *peaceful relations* with one another, and thus achieved mutual understanding, community of interests and peaceful relations, even with the most distant of their fellows'.[17]

Thus, although Kant's emphasis on the alleged benefits of economic relations between states does not imply an absolute obligation on the part of a state to avail itself of these benefits, Kant must be seen to stress the benefits of commercial relations between states. This clearly implies that he would view an increase in such relations as being highly

---

16 Kant, 'Idee zu einer allgemeinen Geschichte in weltbürgerlicher Absicht', in *Kant's gesammelte Schriften*, vol. VIII, 27f. / *Political Writings*, 50.
17 Kant, 'Zum ewigen Frieden', 363f. / *Political Writings*, 110f.

desirable, since it would help promote the spread of civil liberties at the domestic level and, he assumes, the establishment of peaceful relations between states at the international level. Kant here appears to be advocating the kind of commerce instead of conquest theory put forward by other Enlightenment figures such as Diderot and the marquis de Mirabeau.[18] Fichte, by contrast, will be shown to recognize that commercial relations between states may not, in fact, be as voluntary in nature as these Enlightenment thinkers, including Kant, suppose them to be, and that although they may not be based on direct physical force, they can still involve an element of coercion.

In *The Closed Commercial State*, Fichte adopts a position that is far removed from Kant's views on the benefits of commerce, for he argues that commercial relations between states are to be completely avoided. Although Fichte can be seen in this way to renounce the model of cosmopolitan right that he himself adopts in the *Foundations of Natural Right*, his reappraisal of this earlier position will be shown in the next section to point to a particular problem with Kant's optimism concerning the benefits of increased commercial relations between states. This is the problem of one-sided forms of economic dependence with respect to the relation of one state to another state. Fichte's awareness of this problem is already hinted at in his review of Kant's essay *Perpetual Peace*, since he recognizes that should the stage be reached at which the European states of his own time have consumed all that their domestic productive capacities are able to provide, 'the commercial oppression of foreign nations and portions of the world [*die Unterdrückung fremder Völker und Welttheile im Handel*] opens up a constantly flowing and lucrative source of assistance'.[19] Yet it is only in *The Closed Commercial State* that Fichte develops more fully the implications of this idea in relation to the themes of cosmopolitan right and the possibility of a lasting global peace, while also attempting to sketch an alternative to the state of affairs that he alludes to in his review of Kant's essay.

Fichte's critique of Kant's theory of cosmopolitan right

In *The Closed Commercial State*, Fichte develops the theory of a state that is economically as well as politically independent and is thus in the position to ensure that each and every citizen is able to live from

18 Cf. Pagden, *Lords of all the World*, 178ff.
19 GA I / 3: 227; RRP: 320.

his labour, a demand which, as we already know, Fichte thinks he has justified in the *Foundations of Natural Right*. In the first book of *The Closed Commercial State*, Fichte sets out the basic economic conditions and relations that need to be established if the right of all persons to be able to live from their labour is to be guaranteed. As we have seen, these conditions and relations include the division of the citizens of the state into different estates, each of which involves a particular type of economic activity that is essential to the functioning of the state insofar as it aims to meet its citizens' basic needs, together with a planned economy designed to ensure that there is an adequate supply of goods available to satisfy people's needs. This planned economy in turn requires state supervision of the number of citizens belonging to each estate.

Since commercial relations with foreigners, who do not stand under the same laws as the citizens of the state and are therefore not subject to the same restrictions as they are, would introduce unforeseeable, incalculable factors that might threaten the carefully regulated economic life of the state, all such commercial relations must be forbidden and made impossible. The demand thus arises for the state to secure itself completely against any trade with foreign countries and from then on to form a separate commercial body (*Handelskörper*), just as it has already come to form a separate juridical and political body.[20] We here encounter what appears to be a clear rejection on Fichte's part of the Kantian cosmopolitanism and proposals for the attainment of a lasting global peace found in his own *Foundations of Natural Right*, in which he advocates the establishment of a federation of states as a preliminary stage on the road to a lasting global peace. Fichte's apparent indebtedness to Kant when it comes to this proposal needs to be brought out in order to show the extent to which *The Closed Commercial State* represents a departure from the position that he adopts in the *Foundations of Natural Right*.

In *Perpetual Peace*, Kant argues for the idea of a federation of free states or federation of peoples (*Völkerbund*) on the grounds that, in the absence of such a federation, nation states 'may be judged in the same way as individual men living in a state of nature, independent of external laws', so that, in order to preserve itself, each state 'can and ought to demand of others that they should enter along with it into a constitution, similar to the civil one, within which the rights of each could be secured'.[21] In the section on the right of nations in the *Foundations of Natural Right*, Fichte makes a similar point when he claims that every nation, as long as it has a government of some kind, 'has a right of coercion [*ein Zwangsrecht*] to demand recognition from the adjoining states'.[22] The condition of mutual recognition required by states that are otherwise independent of each other points to the need for a *Völkerbund*, which is a voluntary form of organization, in which each state recognizes the independence of the other member states. This federation of nations is not an end in itself, however; it is instead only the means to a higher end, namely, the establishment of perpetual peace (*der ewige Friede*).[23] In his essay *Perpetual Peace*, Kant likewise claims that a federation of states which have voluntarily committed themselves to preserving and securing each other's freedom has the potential to spread gradually further and further, so as to encompass all states and eventually lead to a lasting global peace.[24]

We can nevertheless note a difference in emphasis between Kant's and Fichte's positions on the idea of a federation of independent states, for in the *Foundations of Natural Right*, Fichte appears to be primarily concerned with the idea that states must fulfil the negative duty of recognizing each other's independence, whereas Kant suggests that states also have the positive duty towards each other of securing each other's independence. In the later *The Closed Commercial State*, Fichte's concern with the issue of a state's need to preserve its

21 Kant, 'Zum ewigen Frieden', 354 / *Political Writings*, 102.
22 GA I / 4: 154; FNR: 323. Kant is far more specific on this issue than is Fichte, who demands of a nation that may coerce others into recognizing it only that it has a government of some kind. For by a free state, Kant specifically means one that has a republican constitution founded on the following three principles: the freedom of all the members of society in virtue of their common humanity; the dependence of everyone upon a single common legislation; and legal equality. Kant contrasts this republican constitution with a democratic one in which the legislative and executive powers are not separated, so that the people both makes the laws to which it is subject and executes these same laws. By republicanism Kant thus means a constitution in which there is a separation of the executive and legislative powers, with executive power being exercised by the representatives of the people and not by the people itself. He claims that a republican constitution offers a better prospect of achieving a lasting global peace, because it requires that the citizens must give their consent as to whether or not war is to be declared, with such consent not being easily given, or so Kant alleges, because of the citizens' knowledge of the miseries of war, including the fact that they would themselves have to fund it. Cf. Kant, 'Zum ewigen Frieden', 349ff. / *Political Writings*, 99f.
23 GA I / 4: 162; FNR 331f.
24 Kant, 'Zum ewigen Frieden', 356 / *Political Writings*, 104.

independence differs even more noticeably from Kant's position, in the sense that Fichte makes a state's self-preservation depend entirely on this state itself, so that he appears not to place any faith whatsoever in the recognition of its independence accorded to it by other states. This leads Fichte to outline in the third and final book of *The Closed Commercial State* a series of measures that the state must itself undertake to preserve its independence, which essentially means closing itself off economically from other states.[25] To this extent, the idea of a federation of states becomes no longer necessary; a state must instead be responsible for securing its own independence, and this will demand making itself economically as well as politically independent. A state's membership of such a federation might even be considered to be a dangerous thing, because it could give rise to a sense of complacency on the part of a state, leading it to neglect taking the necessary steps towards preserving its independence.

Although it is not my intention here to discuss in detail the specific measures that Fichte proposes, I do intend to show how in the second book of *The Closed Commercial State* he succeeds in identifying an issue

---

25 The main measures that Fichte identifies as allowing an existing state gradually to close itself off economically from other states include that of developing the means of producing goods that previously had to be imported and discovering substitutes for raw materials that are not to be found in a particular country, as well as getting its citizens to do without the goods which these measures cannot serve to provide, especially when the goods in question are only needed to satisfy artificial, inessential needs. The state must also determine its 'natural frontiers', so as to gain access to all the natural products that are essential to its aim of attaining economic independence and self-sufficiency. Another essential measure the state must implement is to render any direct commercial transactions between its citizens and foreigners impossible, by taking out of circulation the necessary means of exchange, namely, an internationally recognized currency (*Weltgeld*), and replacing it with a currency that is recognized only within the closed commercial state itself and is the only valid currency within the latter (*Landesgeld*). The state then uses the internationally recognized currency that it has after it has closed itself off economically from the rest of the world, including that which it gains by exchanging the internationally recognized currency that its citizens possess for the new currency that now forms the only valid currency within the state, to buy the goods it needs from other countries while it is still in the process of developing the means of producing these goods itself or finding substitutes for them, or else gradually making its citizens dispense with these goods. The state uses this money also to fund such measures as taking over the role of honouring commitments previously made by its citizens with foreigners. Moreover, the internationally recognized money that it possesses can be used to tempt foreign experts to come and work for the state, and to develop its industries by purchasing machines from abroad. Finally, the state needs this money to help arm itself, so as to be in the position to resist any attacks by foreign forces while it is in the process of securing its natural frontiers.

concerning the idea of a state's economic independence which has certain implications with respect to the idea of its political independence. Fichte's identification of this issue allows us to think of him as providing a critical reappraisal of Kant's theory of cosmopolitan right insofar as economic relations between states, and not just between individual persons, are concerned. In this respect, although the economic isolation that Fichte advocates runs counter to the role that Kant accords to commerce in the historical process, which is that of making global peace more likely, it may in fact be seen to represent a response to a problem that arises in connection with the theory of cosmopolitan right that Fichte himself previously adopted, almost certainly under Kant's influence: the problem of one-sided forms of economic dependence.

In the second book of *The Closed Commercial State*, Fichte seeks to reconstruct the genesis of the condition of economic anarchy which he thinks characterizes the economic relations existing between the European states of his own time. Whereas the nations of the ancient world were sharply separated from each other, regarding each other as enemies and barbarians, the nations of the newly emerged Christian Europe considered themselves to be a single nation united by a common descent; a nation whose origins lay in the forests of Germany and in a shared religion. The importance of this shared allegiance to the Christian religion meant that even nations of non Germanic descent were able to become part of this single nation, by gradually adopting the same Germanic system of customs and concepts. Therefore, rather than viewing the European states of his own time as coming into being by means of the amalgamation and unification of a number of independent persons – as one might have expected given his contract theory of the state in the *Foundations of Natural Right* – Fichte understands these states to be the result of the separation and division of large masses of people, who were only weakly united by the limited forms of political organization and authority to which they were subject. This process of separation and division was aided by the revival of Roman law and the transference of the Roman concept of the Emperor to modern kings, since these developments led various peoples (*Völkerschaften*) to become distinguished from each other by means of their different constitutions. This process was aided also by the divisions brought about in the Christian Church by the Reformation.

On this basis, Fichte proceeds to argue that it is not surprising that some present day concepts and institutions should presuppose the previous interconnectedness of the states of Christian Europe, treating the latter as if it still existed. Fichte cites as a specific example of this phenomenon the way in which the trading system formed during the period of the unity of Christian Europe has essentially continued to operate until the present day. The system in question was one in which the members of each and every part of the great whole cultivated and produced that for which local conditions proved most favourable, and in which they were able to trade these goods anywhere in Christian Europe, with the prices of goods establishing themselves in the course of the process of trading these goods. This absence of economic regulation was the result of a lack of any common leader who could have introduced and upheld the regulation of the economy across the whole of Christian Europe.

In its original context, this lack of economic regulation was not particularly harmful, however, because of the undeveloped nature of the productive forces and the simple, modest needs of the people. Yet, once Christian Europe had divided itself into separate nations with their own constitutions, the continuance of this state of economic anarchy became, for reasons to be given below, extremely harmful. Whereas what should have happened, Fichte claims, is that the anarchy which characterized economic relations when Christian Europe formed a single whole should have been abolished by each state closing itself off economically from other states, in the same way as political anarchy was abolished by means of the formation of separate states with their own constitutions, legislatures and magistracies. Fichte can be here accused of offering a tendentious account of history that is designed to support his claim that states should close themselves off economically from other states, by showing that this measure is in line with the development of individual politically independent nations out of the greater whole previously formed by Christian Europe. He nevertheless proceeds to identify a feature of economic relations between states that goes some way towards justifying his rejection of his own earlier Kantian cosmopolitanism, since it shows that Kant's theory of cosmopolitan right fails to take sufficiently into account the problem of one-sided forms of economic dependence as a possible feature of the relations existing between politically independent states.

Fichte describes the emergence of separate, centrally controlled states in terms of the way in which the citizens who paid taxes came to form a single body represented by the concept of a government, whose aim was to maintain and further the common interest of these citizens, by employing the nation's wealth (*National Vermögen*), as derived from the taxes these citizens paid, in pursuit of this end. This leads Fichte to consider the possible relations between separate nations, each with its own national wealth; and he identifies three such relations. To begin with, a state may achieve a balance of trade, exporting goods of the same total value as those that it imports. This equilibrium allows the state in question to maintain its national wealth without having to raise taxes, though it is also unable to increase its wealth. The second relation is when a nation is able to produce more and better goods of the type that can satisfy the needs of the citizens of other nations than these nations are themselves capable of producing. This allows a nation to sell the goods that are surplus to its own requirements to foreign nations, making itself richer in the process, though only as long as it is able to maintain the same levels of production and the needs of the citizens of the foreign nations to which it sells its products remain the same. With its increased wealth, such a nation is able to buy goods that its citizens do not absolutely need from foreign nations, which are made to produce these goods in order to survive, and are thus prevented from producing goods aimed at satisfying the basic needs of their own citizens. These nations are, in short, reduced to working for another nation's pleasure.

The third type of relation, which is the one most relevant to the present topic, is basically this second type of relation as seen from the other side; for it is essentially this same relation viewed from the standpoint of a nation which has become dependent on a richer nation in the manner described above. The wealth of this economically weaker nation constantly diminishes on account of the unfavourable terms on which it is able to trade with other nations, leading to a corresponding loss of prosperity and power, and to such consequences as depopulation caused by its citizens' seeking to escape the condition of poverty which has arisen in the wake of this loss of prosperity and power. Fichte argues that a state may even end up selling its independence by continually accepting subsidies from another state, and he claims that, in so doing, the first state may make itself into little more than a province of the second state and into a means of satisfying the latter's arbitrary ends. Fichte, however, rejects the protectionist measures employed by the mercantilism of his own time as a solution to this problem, arguing that these measures amount to an attempt to shape existing conditions in one's own favour, and that they lead to a trade war which may result in actual wars motivated by commercial interests.[26] In Fichte's view, only the closure of the state with respect to all economic activity provides the solution to the problems caused by economic dependency, since only this measure can make a state genuinely independent and self-sufficient. Even if we reject this proposed solution to the problems associated with one-sided forms of economic dependence that Fichte identifies, the way in which his analysis of economic relations, however crude it may be from a modern perspective, allows him to identify these problems represents a great achievement, given his historical position. This becomes evident when we compare Fichte's awareness of the problems associated with one-sided forms of economic dependence with Kant's simple acceptance of the existence of such forms of dependence.

Kant on economic dependence

Kant regards commercial relations between the citizens of foreign nations and, by implication, those between states themselves as essentially voluntary ones, because they are not, or at least should not be, based on force. Commercial relations instead depend on the consent of both parties. Although the notion of consent is central to Kant's understanding of cosmopolitan right as the right to hospitality, the distinction between agreements based on consent and those based on force is arguably not precise enough to do justice to the problem of one-sided forms of economic dependence. For although both parties may agree to enter into commercial relations with each other, one party may, in fact, be in such a disadvantageous position in relation to the other party that the extent to which it can be truly said to enter freely into commercial relations with the latter becomes an open question. This is not to say that Kant did not recognize the existence of one-sided forms of economic dependence. Indeed, the problem with Kant's theory of cosmopolitan right currently under discussion can be seen as a result of his uncritical acceptance of such forms of dependence and their consequences. In this respect, Kant's neglect of the problem of one-sided forms of economic dependence, which is a problem that Fichte succeeds in identifying, is to be explained in terms of a fundamental feature of Kant's political philosophy, rather than in terms of a single oversight on his part.

---

26 For more on the mercantilism of Fichte's own time in relation to Germany in particular, see Léon, 'Le socialisme de Fichte d'après l'état commercial fermé', 33ff.

Kant's acceptance of one-sided forms of economic dependence is evident from the distinction he makes between active and passive citizenship. Kant makes being a citizen into the only qualification of a person's being fit to vote. Yet he restricts the right to vote, by which he means the right to vote on legislative matters, to active citizens, who possess the quality of being independent. Possession of the right to vote is thus made contingent on a person's fitness to vote, which Kant defines in terms of the notion of independence. The independence in question consists in being one's own master (*sein eigener Herr*), which for Kant amounts to having property by means of which one is able to support oneself. In addition to land, such property may include the products of one's labour, as in the case of artisans, or the possession of a skill, trade, art or science, as in the case of the members of a profession.[27] The kind of independence that Kant has in mind is consequently to be understood as primarily an economic form of independence. By contrast, those who lack property are regarded as being dependent on others and therefore unfit to vote.

Kant claims, however, that this dependence on the will of others, together with the inequality that it entails in political terms, is 'in no way opposed to their freedom and equality *as men*, who together make up a people'.[28] The political implications of this move can be illustrated with reference to the way in which Kant bases the civil state on the following three principles, which he claims are all of an *a priori* nature: the freedom of every member of society as a human being; the equality of each member of society with all others as a subject; and the independence of each member of the commonwealth as a citizen.[29] Although the first two principles, that of freedom and equality, which both derive from the moral status of human beings as ends in themselves, imply the extension of the status of citizen to all (male) adult members of the state, Kant's identification of active citizenship with the idea of economic independence limits the extent to which the status of citizen in the full sense of the term pertains to all members of the state.

Kant, in effect, grants certain human beings their freedom and equality while denying them full independence. He does, however, impose an important constraint on the sort of laws that the active

27 Immanuel Kant, 'Über den Gemeinspruch: Das mag in der Theorie richtig sein, taugt aber nicht für die Praxis', in *Kant's gesammelte Schriften*, vol. VIII, 295f. / *Political Writings*, 78.
28 Kant, 'Die Metaphysik der Sitten', 315.
29 Kant, 'Über den Gemeinspruch', 290 / *Political Writings*, 74.

citizens may legislate for all citizens, which is that 'these laws must still not be contrary to the natural laws of freedom and of the equality of everyone in the people corresponding to this freedom, namely that anyone can work his way up from this passive condition to an active one'.[30] Each citizen must, in other words, be able in principle to become a property owner and thus to qualify as an active citizen. Yet Kant might be said here to underestimate the difficulties involved in working one's way up from a passive to an active condition, not least because of the fact that political decisions clearly have some influence on the economic sphere, which means that passive citizens, who are deprived of political power, will lack an important means of shaping existing economic relations in such a way as to maximize their chances of becoming property owners; while the already active citizens may well have an interest in maintaining existing economic relations in their present form. Although Kant would surely argue that it would be wrong for the active citizens to pursue and consolidate their own interests in this way, considerable practical problems remain as a result of his distinction between active and passive citizenship. This may lead one to argue that justice demands that those without property are given a proper political voice, rather than having to depend entirely on the decisions made by others, even if these decisions are allegedly made on their behalf and in their best interests. After all, does this reliance on the judgement and fairness of others not itself constitute a form of dependence, which is the result of an economic form of dependence?

In the present context, it is of particular relevance that among the examples of people who are not sufficiently independent to qualify as active citizens, Kant includes persons who have only their labour to sell (for example, the 'woodcutter I hire to work in my yard') and tenant farmers, who do not own the land they cultivate.[31] For these particular examples all point to forms of economic dependence, whereby a person's ability to live from his own labour turns out to be dependent on another person's will. In the first case, this is because the relation of the wage labourer to his employer is one in which the latter is understood to own the labour of the former for a specific period of time that has been agreed upon by both parties. While in the second case, the tenant farmer's activity depends on the

---

30 Kant, 'Die Metaphysik der Sitten', 315.
31 Kant, 'Die Metaphysik der Sitten', 314f.

agreement of the landowner to lease him the land he cultivates, which again involves a contractual relation between them, and thus one that, for Kant, is based on consent.

These examples show that Kant clearly recognizes the reality of one-sided forms of economic dependence and that he appears to regard such forms of dependence as acceptable, since he allows them to determine the political status of the parties involved. This status is either that of an active citizen with the right to vote on the laws to which all members of the state are subject, or that of a passive citizen, who lacks this right and therefore becomes subject to laws that are not, strictly speaking, of his own making, but who nevertheless possesses the other attributes of citizenship that Kant identifies, including equal legal status in relation to all the other members of the state. This one-sided form of economic dependence in turn suggests the possibility of indirect forms of coercion, even though the examples of relations of economic dependence of which Kant speaks are held to be based on consent, such as the agreement to sell one's labour or to rent a piece of land for a particular period of time. This possibility can, in fact, be more clearly illustrated with reference to one possible explanation of Kant's distinction between active and passive citizens. The explanation in question relates to the issue of the right to vote on legislative issues affecting all the members of the commonwealth, which is the only type of voting with which Kant concerns himself.[32]

Although Kant does not explicitly make this point, I would suggest that he makes the right to vote on legislative issues affecting all members of the commonwealth rest on the condition of a person's being economically independent, because this independence helps guarantee that a person will not be made to vote in a particular way by another person with whom he stands in a relation of economic dependency.[33]

32 Although Kant appears to have in mind only the right to vote directly on legislative matters, rather than the right to vote for representatives who make laws on the people's behalf, the problem I suggest Kant has in mind would also apply in the case of voting for representatives, since it centres on the worry that those who lack true independence will be forced to vote in a certain way by others on whom they depend.
33 Another explanation of Kant's distinction between active and passive citizens, and the way in which it appears to involve an inconsistency on his part, is that his *a priori* construction of the concept and principles of right that determine the nature of civil society has become entangled with the predicate of independence as it has been traditionally applied to the citizen in a theory of a *societas civilis* that can be traced back to Aristotle, which involves a conception of the citizen as free in the sense of being both economically and legally independent. In this way, Kant, like the representatives of this earlier tradition, ends up treating existing relations of power as something given. Yet in

For example, an employer or landowner can be thought to be in the position to make voting in a particular way into a condition of hiring a person or leasing him the land he needs, so that, in order to support themselves, the persons concerned will need to vote in a way that does not necessarily reflect their own views and convictions. This problem could be solved by the holding of secret ballots, of course. Yet the idea of a secret ballot appears to conflict with one of the basic assumptions underlying Kant's views on politics and, we may assume, his views on the nature of such political processes as that of voting on legislative issues affecting all members of the commonwealth.

This is the condition of 'publicness' (*Publizität*), which demands that any proposal affecting the rights of other human beings must lend itself to being made public without thereby frustrating the purpose behind it. In other words, the proposal must be of such a kind that it does not need to be kept secret in order to succeed, because declaring it openly would be bound to arouse resistance on the part of those affected by it.[34] Such publicness will be demanded above all else in matters of legislation, since here 'each decides the same for all and all decide the same for each'.[35] However, in addition to the demand to make any proposed piece of legislation public, one might also demand that the process of voting itself is of a public nature, so that it can be known whether or not someone is supporting a proposed law because he has a personal interest in doing so that conflicts with the public interest; whereas such personal interests could be more easily concealed if the ballot was a secret one, so that in this respect the idea of a secret ballot turns out to fail the publicity test. In short, secret ballots can be seen to violate the spirit of the civil constitution, which demands

Kant's case a conflict arises between the *a priori* principles of freedom and, despite his designation of it as *a priori*, the *a posteriori* principle of independence, leading to difficulties in the definition of the concept of the citizen that were absent in the traditional theories of natural law. In short, Kant's account of the principles on which the modern state is based involves tensions that arise from his awareness of the principles that were coming to determine the nature of the modern state and citizenship in the wake of the French Revolution, namely, freedom and equality, and his failure, nevertheless, to make a complete break with traditional conceptions of citizenship, even though his association of independence with property goes some way towards doing this. Cf. Riedel, 'Die Aporie von Herrschaft und Vereinbarung in Kants Idee des Sozialvertrags'. As important and convincing as it is, this explanation does not preclude additional explanations such as the one that I put forward concerning the issue of voting and its relation to the notion of publicness.

34 Kant, 'Zum ewigen Frieden', 381 / *Political Writings*, 125f.
35 Kant, 'Die Metaphysik der Sitten', 314.

that the act of making laws for others as well as for oneself forms part of an entirely transparent process.

Understanding Kant's distinction between active and passive citizenship in this way provides an example of how Kant himself appears to recognize that one-sided forms of economic dependence have the potential to lead to indirect forms of coercion, which, in this case, consists in a person's being made to vote in a particular way. At the same time, Kant's identification of economic independence as a condition of the right to vote, even though it is designed to prevent an indirect form of coercion in the political sphere, signals an acceptance on his part of one-sided forms of economic dependence and their political implications. It is arguably Kant's uncritical acceptance of such relations that prevents him from considering solutions to the problems involved in the process of voting on legislative matters that would be more in line with the principles of equality and independence that underpin his political philosophy. I shall now indicate an analogy between this acceptance of one-sided forms of economic dependence and Kant's theory of cosmopolitan right.

When applied to the international stage, Kant's acceptance of one-sided forms of economic dependence, on the grounds that these forms of dependence do not affect a person's legal status and his status as equal in relation to all the other members of the state, gives rise to a problem analogous to the one presented by his distinction between passive and active citizens. This distinction, as mentioned above, appears to acknowledge that one-sided forms of economic dependence have the potential to lead to indirect forms of coercion, whereby the weaker party is forced to act in conformity with the wishes of the stronger party, without the latter needing to exercise any form of physical coercion, which would indeed be a violation of right and would be therefore punishable by law, as required by the equal legal standing that even passive citizens possess. The possibility of extending this notion of an indirect form of coercion based on relations of economic dependence to the international stage can be illustrated with reference to Kant's own essay *Perpetual Peace*, in which we encounter the demand that no state 'shall forcibly interfere in the constitution and government of another state' as one of the main articles aimed at establishing rightful relations and a condition of lasting peace between states.[36] This demand entails that the legal status and political

36 Kant, 'Zum ewigen Frieden', 346 / *Political Writings*, 96.

independence of economically weaker states must be guaranteed as much as that of economically stronger states under international law and within a *Völkerbund*, in the same way that every member of the state must be granted the status of passive citizen and the rights that he enjoys in virtue of this status must be guaranteed by the state. However, this formal equality does not by itself rule out the possibility of indirect forms of coercion based on one-sided relations of economic dependence that seek to bring about changes in the constitution or government of another state without resorting to the use of direct military force. In this way, an economically weak state may have its status as a free (i.e. independent) state guaranteed under international law, which consists in being granted formal legal equality in relation to other states, at the same time as it lacks the full independence that comes from being free of the kind of indirect form of coercion that may be exercised upon it by other, economically more powerful states.

It seems to me that Kant does not sufficiently acknowledge such a possibility in his theory of cosmopolitan right. Indeed, as I have suggested above, his failure to do so stems from his uncritical acceptance of one-sided forms of economic dependence. On the one hand, Kant clearly recognizes that such forms of economic dependence can give rise to indirect forms of coercion. On the other hand, he appears to accept that the contractual basis of these relations means that they are based on consent and are therefore not to be seen as the result of coercion, so that the relations in question can be regarded as legitimate ones. Yet it might be objected that the positions occupied by each party prior to any contract can be so unequal economically that the extent to which the weaker party agrees in any meaningful sense of the term to enter into a contract with the stronger party becomes highly debatable.

In this respect, when it comes to the relations between economically weak and economically strong states, we may well question the extent to which the 'commerce' between them can be held to be of a truly voluntary nature. Fichte, by contrast, recognizes the possibility of indirect forms of coercion based on economic power, and this allows him to adopt a more critical standpoint in relation to the idea of cosmopolitan right; one that amounts, moreover, to a reappraisal of his own earlier theory of cosmopolitan right. This invites the question as to whether Fichte's idea of a closed commercial state, which represents his solution to the problem of one-sided forms of economic dependence, provides a viable alternative to Kant's cosmopolitanism. I restrict myself below to giving one example as to why it clearly does not, given the fact that Fichte continues in *The Closed Commercial State* to seek a solution to a problem that both he and Kant link to the issue of cosmopolitan right: the question of the possibility of a lasting global peace.

The idea that Fichte understands *The Closed Commercial State* to constitute not only an economic theory designed to show how the inalienable right to be able to live from one's labour can be guaranteed, but also a contribution to the debate on the topics of cosmopolitanism and global peace occasioned by the publication of Kant's essay *Perpetual Peace*, is suggested by his discussion in this work of the need for a state to attain its natural frontiers,[37] whether by means of an increase or decrease in its territory. Fichte considers this measure to be necessary in relation to the end of achieving the self-sufficiency which is a precondition of a state's being able to close itself off economically from other states. Fichte argues that if a state has not attained its natural frontiers, it will exhibit the tendency to engage in wars of conquest, or will, at the very least, place itself in a condition of constant preparedness for war on account of its awareness, however dim, of lacking something that it needs, whether it be a fertile province or coal or salt mines. A state that has closed itself off economically from other states after having attained its natural frontiers will, by contrast, have nothing to gain from seeking to extend its territory.[38] Given its lack of any incentive to engage in wars of conquest and its renunciation, or so Fichte alleges, of any attempt to influence the political conditions in other states, which in turn reduces the prospect of its being attacked by them, a closed commercial state will need a standing army only insofar

---

37 Xavier Léon suggests that the French Revolutionary Georges Danton is the source of this idea of natural frontiers. Cf. Léon, 'Le socialisme de Fichte d'après l'état commercial fermé', 216. As the troops of the French Republic crossed into territories that were not part of France at the time, calls were made to incorporate them into the Republic. This included Belgium, where Danton, on mission to the armies of Belgium, made the following statement in January 1793: 'The limits of France are marked out by nature. We shall reach them at their four points: at the Ocean, at the Rhine, at the Alps, at the Pyrenees'. Quoted in Doyle, *The Oxford History of the French Revolution*, 200.

38 GA I / 7: 117ff. The severing of all commercial relations with foreign nations does not, however, preclude the possibility of other relations with the citizens of foreign states capable of fostering the idea of world citizenship. Fichte advocates, for example, the establishment of academies charged with introducing the treasures of foreign literature and exchanging them with domestic ones (GA I / 7: 141). He also advocates the exchange of products that can be produced in one country but not in another, but only on the condition that this process of exchange is conducted by the state and involves the direct exchange of the goods themselves (GA I / 7: 136).

as one is necessary to ensure peace and order within the state itself; while, in the unlikely event of its having to fight a defensive war, this could be done by arming all the citizens capable of bearing arms.[39] The closed commercial state is in this way held by Fichte to satisfy one of the preconditions of the establishment of a lasting global peace that Kant identifies in *Perpetual Peace*: the gradual abolition of standing armies.[40]

Fichte's proposal that a state must secure its natural frontiers before closing itself off economically from the rest of the world appears, however, to conflict with the idea of the establishment of a lasting global peace. For it is arguably more likely to lead to conflict between states over resources, with each state attempting to incorporate areas containing certain natural resources into its territory, while justifying its attempt to do so on the grounds that such areas belong within its natural frontiers. In this way, Fichte's proposal invites forms of economic imperialism, whereby one state seeks to invade another state for purely economic reasons; whereas his reappraisal of Kant's cosmopolitanism provides the basis for a critique of economic imperialism. The ominous nature of the link that Fichte establishes between the idea of the state and the idea of natural frontiers in relation to subsequent events in European history was already in 1900 remarked upon by Marianne Weber;[41] and, in the light of later events in European history, Fichte's views on natural frontiers are more likely than ever to be associated in people's minds with a pretext for wars of conquest rather than with the means of achieving a lasting global peace. Admittedly, Fichte himself was not blind to the possibility of acts of violence in connection with a state's attempt to attain its natural frontiers. Yet he appears to view such violence as a necessary evil in relation to the ultimate goal of achieving lasting global peace, as is evident from the following passage:

> From time immemorial it has been the privilege of the philosopher to sigh over war. The author does not like it any more than others do; but he believes himself to have insight into its inevitability given the present state of affairs, and he regards lamenting over what is inevitable as useless. If war is to end, the cause of war must be removed. Each state

---

39 GA I / 7: 138.
40 Kant, 'Zum ewigen Frieden', 345 / *Political Writings*, 94.
41 Cf. Weber, *Fichte's Sozialismus und sein Verhältnis zur Marx'schen Doktrin*, 65.

must attain what it aims to attain by means of war, and can only reasonably aim to attain: its natural frontiers.[42]

The fact nevertheless remains that the idea of natural frontiers is so vague and open to abuse that its appearance in a theory that purports to point the way towards the establishment of a lasting global peace has the effect of rendering this theory itself highly unconvincing. Yet this need not prevent us from regarding *The Closed Commercial State* as a significant reappraisal of the related idea of cosmopolitan right as it was developed by Kant in his essay *Perpetual Peace* and then adopted by Fichte himself in the *Foundations of Natural Right.* For Fichte is able to call into question Kant's rather optimistic assumptions concerning the mutual benefits of commercial relations between states, by pointing to the possibility of a one-sided form of economic dependence and the problems to which it may give rise.

In this respect, even if we acknowledge the possibility of the establishment of an international legal order capable of bringing about and sustaining a lasting global peace, or, more realistically perhaps, the desirability of such an order, and to view it, therefore, as something we should strive to realize, the idea of this global legal order may itself be thought to conceal another source of tension between states and of injustice. This source of tension and injustice is located in the indirect forms of coercion that are made possible by the existence of one-sided relations of dependence based on unequal economic power. Any attempt to develop the potential allegedly contained in Kant's theory of cosmopolitan right would therefore have to deal with this problem, or run the risk of condoning at the international level the kind of distinction found in Kant's theory of active and passive citizenship, insofar as an analogy can be drawn between this distinction and the relation of politically independent, but economically stronger and weaker, states to each other in a *Völkerbund.*

In alerting us to the existence of such a problem with Kant's theory of cosmopolitan right, Fichte again shows himself to be aware of the dangers of an overly formalistic approach. An attempt to avoid a merely formalistic approach can also be detected in Fichte's presentation of the issue of how a state, in which relations of right exist between human beings, is able not only to maintain itself but also to provide the basis for a potentially flourishing form of human society, as I show in the

---

42 GA I / 7: 118.

next chapter with reference to the concept of virtue, which plays a largely implicit, but nevertheless vital, role in Fichte's social and political philosophy. However, in order to understand Fichte's account of virtue, by which I have in mind a social or political form of virtue, we first need to understand his separation of right from morality and to appreciate the insights contained in this separation of right from morality.

4

THE RELATION OF RIGHT TO MORALITY
IN FICHTE'S JENA THEORY OF THE STATE
AND SOCIETY

A distinctive feature of Fichte's ethical and political philosophy from the period of his professorship at the University of Jena between 1794 and 1799 is the way in which he separates the juridical and political sphere of right from morality. In his 1796/97 *Foundations of Natural Right*, Fichte claims to have effected this separation by deducing the concept of right as a condition of self-consciousness, thereby making it independent of the moral law or law of ethics.[1] The originality of this approach can be brought out by comparing Fichte's position to that of some of Kant's other followers, who did derive the concept of right from the moral law. This was done by making the moral law into the rule of that which is morally commanded or forbidden, and by then identifying right with the sphere of possible actions that one has a right to perform because they are morally indifferent, in the sense that the moral law neither directly commands nor forbids them. This leaves each individual free to decide whether or not to perform these actions, none of which threatens to transgress the moral law.[2] Right is here characterized in terms of a permissive law, that is, a law that states which actions are permissible within the limits set by the moral law. Fichte himself adopted such a conception of right in his 1793 *Contribution towards Correcting the Public's Judgement of the French Revolution,* in which he characterizes a right as anything that the moral law does not expressly forbid one to do, and claims that whenever the moral law is silent, an individual's actions are left to the promptings of his own arbitrary will (*Willkühr*).[3] Yet Fichte

---

1 GA I / 3: 359; FNR: 50.
2 Cf. Kersting, 'Die Unabhängigkeit des Rechts von der Moral'.
3 GA I / 1: 220. Fichte also speaks of the right to do that without which it would be impossible for the moral law to be active in us. In other words, we have the right to do our duty, which means that no person is entitled to hinder another person from doing his

explicitly rejects this approach in the later *Foundations of Natural Right*, arguing that it is hard to see how a permissive law can be derived from a law that commands unconditionally, as the moral law does.[4]

In addition to the problem as to how a permissive law can be derived from a law that commands unconditionally, another explanation of Fichte's change in attitude with regard to the question of the relation of right to morality has been offered, which this time concerns his recognition of the impossibility of reducing the rational significance of right to its relation to the moral autonomy of the individual. The sphere of right must be seen instead to have its own distinctive end, which is the fostering of individuality, so that in this respect right and morality turn out to be concerned with two essentially distinct forms of self-determination: the capacity to exercise free choice and moral autonomy respectively.[5] This explanation of Fichte's separation of right from morality is, in any case, compatible with the alleged impossibility of deriving a permissive law from a law that commands unconditionally. We can therefore think of Fichte's separation of right from morality as being motivated by a number of reasons. Yet, as they stand, both of these explanations of Fichte's separation of right from morality appear to accept that this separation is an absolute one; whereas, in what follows, I show that Fichte suggests that there is an important link between right and morality and their respective forms of self-determination.

This becomes evident once we read his *Foundations of Natural Right* in the light of his 1798 *The System of Ethics*, in which Fichte offers a deduction of the moral law as a condition of self-consciousness. My discussion of this issue will in turn allow me to establish a connection between the state and society understood as an ethical, as opposed to legal and political, community, and to suggest that Fichte allows for a broader conception of the state than that of the legal and political order founded on self-interest that we encounter in the *Foundations of Natural Right*. This broader conception of the state is that of a unified

---

duty. In such cases, the corresponding right not to do one's duty does not exist, however, because one has an absolute obligation to do what the moral law commands. It is therefore only those actions concerning which the moral law is silent that form the possible objects of any contract and thus belong to the legal realm of right; and, since a person has a right either to perform or not to perform these actions, they remain a matter for his own arbitrary will.

4 GA I / 3: 324; FNR: 14.
5 Cf. Neuhouser, 'Fichte and the Relationship between Right and Morality'.

political community which incorporates within itself the economic, legal and ethical spheres of human existence. I argue, in fact, that we can think of the *Foundations of Natural Right* and *The System of Ethics* as forming parts of a single theory of the state and society, so that Fichte is, in effect, to be seen as working with two conceptions of the state during his Jena period: an amoral one, in which the state is identified exclusively with the juridical and political sphere of right, and a more ethical one, which incorporates the moral sphere, thus bringing right and morality into relation with each other. I do this by showing that although Fichte argues that right and morality are essentially separable from each other, he nevertheless implies the existence of a relation between them when it comes to the question of the possibility of a state that functions in a truly effective manner and has the potential to flourish.

I argue, however, that the firm conceptual distinction that Fichte makes between right and morality remains a valid one, because it acknowledges and brings to light the different dispositions that individuals may have towards the laws and institutions of the state and towards other persons. It is therefore in my view a mistake to criticize Fichte's separation of right from morality on the grounds that the egoism and distrust that for Fichte characterize right conflict with the way in which he makes a relation of mutual recognition into the ontological foundation of right, thereby suggesting a union of individuals that is more fundamental than the form of community achieved by means of the civil contract set out in the *Foundations of Natural Right*.[6] My interpretation of Fichte's account of the relation of right to morality suggests that this claim misses the point, because it fails to do justice to the way in which people's dispositions may vary when it comes to what actually motivates them to recognize others as legal persons and to recognize their property rights.

I also show that it is by no means clear that one should understand the relation of right, as Fichte presents it in his deduction of the concept of right in the *Foundations of Natural Right*, in essentially moral terms, despite such claims as the one that the subject who summons another subject 'has, in *his* choice, in the sphere of his freedom, taken my free choice into consideration, has purposively and intentionally left a sphere open for me'.[7] This claim does not make explicit what actually motivates

---

6 Cf. Robert R. Williams, 'Recognition, Right, and Social Contract', in Breazeale and Rockmore (eds.), *Rights, Bodies and Recognition*.

7 GA I / 3: 353; FNR: 44.

the person, who respects the freedom of another person by leaving open a 'sphere' for this person's exercise of free choice, to act in the way that he does; whereas, in other parts of the *Foundations of Natural Right*, Fichte seeks to explain the source of motivation in explicitly nonmoral terms. In this respect, to seek to ground right on an ethical relation risks devaluing Fichte's insight into the different dispositions that individuals may have towards the laws and institutions of the state and towards other people within society. The theory of the state and society that Fichte developed during the period of his professorship at the University of Jena is, in fact, a complex one, which suggests a number of reasons for avoiding any moralization of the concept of right, while also not ruling out the possibility of a relation between the concepts of right and morality. Indeed, Fichte points to the desirability, if not the necessity, of such a relation.

I begin this chapter by revisiting Fichte's theory of the civil contract given in the *Foundations of Natural Right*. This will allow me to say something more about the main ways in which Fichte separates right from morality beyond offering separate deductions of them as conditions of self-consciousness. I also relate Fichte's theory of right to Hegel's account of the 'state of necessity', so as to bring out the amoral conception of the state, together with its corresponding disposition, that we encounter in Fichte's *Foundations of Natural Right*. This is not to be understood as an attempt to turn Fichte into Hegel. Rather, Hegel will be seen to offer a powerful objection to the kind of contract theory of the state developed by Fichte; an objection which is best met, I suggest, by showing that Fichte's idea of a civil contract can be understood in metaphorical terms, and, more specifically, as highlighting a type of disposition that individuals may have towards state authority. Fichte's avoidance of any attempt to moralize the concept of right then turns out to throw light on the kind of disposition that Hegel associates with civil society understood as the state of necessity, while Hegel's account of the latter helps illustrate Fichte's amoral conception of the state.

Finally, I relate Fichte's theory of right to his theory of ethical duties as set out in *The System of Ethics*, insofar as these duties derive from a person's profession, with the aim of revealing the ways in which this theory of ethical duties implies a reciprocal relation between right and morality, despite the various ways in which Fichte otherwise separates them. It is here that I introduce the concept of virtue, which has a largely implicit, but nevertheless vital, role to play in Fichte's theory of right, although this is something we might not have expected, given his amoral conception of the state and the fact that the concept of virtue does appear to play a significant role even in his ethical theory. The type of virtue I have in mind is a social or political form of virtue, which provides the means of specifying more closely the relation that can be thought to exist between right and morality in Fichte's social and political philosophy. This relation between right and morality, however, does not demand the rejection of Fichte's separation of these concepts, even if it does in some respects point to the desirability of overcoming their separation.

The separation of right from morality

As we have seen, Fichte describes the concept of right as a relation in which human beings reciprocally limit their freedom. This act of self-limitation on the part of each person involves leaving open to others a sphere in which they may exercise free choice, thereby allowing each person to distinguish himself from others by means of the different choices that he makes within this sphere. In this respect, the relation of right constitutes a condition of individuality, which is itself a condition of self-consciousness for Fichte. There are consequently solid grounds for claiming that the end of the sphere of right is the fostering of individuality, and that right is concerned with a distinct form of self-determination, which is the capacity to exercise free choice.

We have also seen that Fichte's view of right as a relation between free and rational persons means that for him human beings have actual rights only in community with others. Fichte specifies the nature of such a community when he offers a deduction of a commonwealth with positive laws as the condition of being able to apply the right of coercion. Fichte sees the common will embodied in this commonwealth as being established by means of a civil contract. This contract serves to give a better idea of Fichte's amoral conception of the state, by making clearer some of the fundamental differences between right and morality, insofar as these differences concern the grounds which motivate a person's actions when it comes to recognizing others as legal persons together with their property rights.

The civil contract consists of various stages, with each new stage being a condition of the application of the previous stage. To begin with, there is the citizens' property contract, in which each individual reaches an agreement with all other individuals regarding each other's property rights. As we know, Fichte adopts a broad conception of property, which involves understanding property, in the first instance, to be the particular activity which enables a person to live from his labour. Since the most fundamental object of the property contract concerns a person's right to be able to live from his labour, this contract requires that people are in actual fact guaranteed the possibility of being able to live from their labour. The protection of property will accordingly require, if necessary, the redistribution of land and goods, because such objects may be needed in order for some individuals, who do not currently possess them, to be able to live from their labour. In the light of this conception of property, it becomes easier to understand Fichte's claim that the property contract involves all persons declaring to all other persons how they intend to make a livelihood, so that 'no one becomes a citizen *in general*, but each enters into a certain class [*Klasse*] of citizen at the same time that he enters into the state'.[8] The idea that a person enters into a certain class of citizen at the same time as he enters into the state will play an important role in my attempt to suggest a link between the spheres of right and morality, despite Fichte's separation of them. I must first, though, mention the various ways in which Fichte separates right from morality, beyond offering separate deductions of them as conditions of self-consciousness.

One way in which Fichte's contract theory of the state illustrates his separation of right from morality concerns the state's role, through its application and enforcement of law, of guaranteeing that persons are not made dependent on the good will of others, as they would be if the moral law alone determined the relation of one person to another person. As Fichte expresses it

> Each wills, and has the right to will, that the other undertake only those actions he would undertake if he had a thoroughly good will; whether or not such a will is actually present is beside the point. Each has a claim only to the other's *legality*, but by no means to his *morality*.[9]

In other words, from the standpoint of right, unlike that of morality, what essentially matters is that a person's external actions conform to the demands of right, irrespective of what actually motivates this person to act in conformity with these demands. The fact that right concerns external actions, while morality or ethics concerns inner

---

8 GA I / 4: 23; FNR: 187.
9 GA I / 3: 425; FNR: 125.

ones, already constitutes an essential difference between right and morality.[10] One important role played by the state is therefore to ensure that people's external actions are made to conform to the demands of right when the moral motivation for doing so may be lacking.

Another central aspect of Fichte's separation of right from morality that finds expression in his contract theory of the state concerns his insistence on the fact that right is simply a matter of logical consistency, so that it again does not depend on any moral considerations. This logical consistency concerns a form of instrumental reasoning, in which the willing of the appropriate means of achieving a certain end serves as the mark of what it is to think consistently. When it comes to a person's entering into the civil contract, the act of thinking consistently requires both that the conditions to which he subjects himself are consistent with the end that he intends to achieve by entering into this contract and that these conditions apply equally as much to others as to himself.[11] One does not, therefore, commit

10 As Fichte himself puts it, 'the concept of right concerns only what is expressed in the sensible world: whatever has no causality in the sensible world – but remains inside the mind instead – belongs before another tribunal, the tribunal of morality [*der Moral*]' (GA I / 3: 360; FNR: 51). Yet is it really possible to make such a clear distinction between the intentions behind an action, which Fichte here suggests belong to the moral sphere alone, and the sphere of right? For example, when external actions need to be judged in legal terms, part of this process will often involve asking what the intention behind the action was, so as to determine the extent to which it should be punished. Fichte himself distinguishes between violations of right that are a result of the wish for personal gain or the result of negligence and those which are the result of a formally bad will, which causes harm not in order to gain some advantage but simply for the sake of it. He claims, moreover, that in the last case at least a person's disposition (*Gesinnung*) must be taken into account, because such violations of right demand to be more severely punished (GA I / 4: 62f.; FNR: 230).

11 The idea that the conditions to which one subjects oneself should apply equally to others is an important feature of Rousseau's theory of the social contract, which may have been Fichte's main source of influence here. Rousseau claims that the social contract produces moral equality between human beings because each individual subjects himself to conditions that apply equally to all, so that no one has any interest in making the civil condition burdensome to others, and each person 'by giving himself to all, gives himself to no one'. Rousseau, 'Du contract social', 360f. / The Social Contract *and Other Later Political Writings*, 50. The idea behind this claim appears to be that the establishment of a just set of laws would remove any arbitrariness from the relations existing between human beings in the civil condition, in which all individuals would be equally subject to the laws of the collective body of which they are members, because these laws are universal in character and thus apply equally to all. This is taken to remove the possibility of the kind of dependence that comes from being subject to unequal conditions, that is to say, to ones that benefit some people at the expense of

oneself to protecting the property of others without having an absolute guarantee that one's own property will be protected by them in turn, since this would be inconsistent with respect to the end which one hopes to achieve by entering into the civil contract, namely, the end of securing one's own property. As Fichte himself puts it, 'each desires public security because he desires his own security'.[12]

The consistency (*Consequenz*) that Fichte has in mind rests on the rules of thinking in general as 'scientifically presented in general *logic*'.[13] Although he claims in the same paragraph, which belongs to the corollary of his deduction of the concept of right, that 'we are both *bound* [*gebunden*] and *obligated* [*verbunden*] to each other by our very existence',[14] Fichte need not be seen as introducing a specifically moral form of reasoning. For this claim can be interpreted in essentially nonmoral terms as meaning that the laws of thinking are ones to which all finite rational beings are subject. Thinking and acting in accordance with these laws demands entering into agreements with others that we are bound and obligated to keep only insofar as we wish to achieve the end of securing our lives and property. In this respect, Fichte's position is similar to Hobbes's, to the extent that the latter maintains that there are certain laws of nature, each of which is 'a Precept, or generall Rule, found out by Reason, by which a man is forbidden to do, that, which is destructive of his life, or taketh away the means of preserving the same; and to omit, that, by which he thinketh it may be best preserved'.[15] For leaving aside the question of the specific content of these laws of nature, their basis in human reason and the end at which they ultimately aim, that is, self-preservation, exhibit a formal agreement with the principles of right that Fichte identifies. Moreover, for both Fichte and Hobbes, it is ultimately inconsistent for a person to think that he can rely on others recognizing and adopting

others. I therefore take Rousseau to be claiming that although an individual makes himself dependent on the moral and collective body established by means of the social contract, in so doing he avoids making himself dependent on any particular individual or group of persons. This is why Rousseau maintains that the citizen's membership of this body 'guarantees him against all personal dependence'. Rousseau, 'Du contract social', 364 / The Social Contract *and Other Later Political Writings*, 53. Civil freedom is thus understood in terms of a person's independence of the arbitrary wills of other human beings, but not as absolute independence.

12 GA I / 3: 436; FNR: 137.
13 GA I / 3: 355; FNR: 45.
14 GA I / 3: 354; FNR: 45.
15 Hobbes, *Leviathan*, 91.

the principles of reason that instruct them to enter into agreements with others so as to preserve their own lives, or to honour any agreements should they decide to enter into them. As Hobbes vividly expresses it, 'Covenants, without the Sword, are but Words, and of no strength to secure a man at all'.[16] The end of securing one's life and property consequently demands the establishment of a state authority able to enforce and maintain a condition of right in which human beings are bound, under the threat of coercion, to fulfil their obligations towards each other; a state authority that is consented to by rational individuals who are capable of thinking consistently.

The terms of the civil contract therefore need to be compatible with the demand to think consistently. This is why Fichte is led to introduce two more stages to the civil contract in addition to the property contract. These are the protection contract and the unification contract. The protection contract consists in each person promising to help protect everyone else's property against any possible violations of it by a third party. However, since there is no guarantee that others will protect one's property when the need to do so arises, Fichte introduces the unification contract, which consists in the establishment of a protective power that can enforce the recognition of property rights, and towards the maintenance of which each individual on entering the state agrees to contribute. This again demands logical consistency, because one must accept that if the end towards which the civil contract is designed to serve as the means (that is, the protection of property) is to be realized, then one must, like everyone else, honour its terms or face the legal sanctions to which one has oneself consented with the intention of securing one's own property. A certain individual might nevertheless feel that it is his moral duty to protect the property of others, irrespective of whether other people would protect his own property should the need to do so arise. Yet, in the case of right, which is concerned with external actions and does not count on the existence of a good will in others, a person's thinking would be inconsistent with respect to the end of securing his property if he agreed to protect and recognize the property of others in the absence of any guarantee that others would act in the same way in relation to his property. This person's thinking would be inconsistent, however, only if he wills the end in question.

---

16 Hobbes, *Leviathan*, 117.

This brings me to another distinction between right and morality: the unconditional nature of the latter, that is, its absolute validity regardless of whatever any particular individual just happens to think or will, and the conditional nature of the former. Fichte implies that right is of a merely conditional nature when he expresses the view that although one must enter into the civil contract with others if one wants to secure one's property, there is nothing to prevent someone from renouncing this end or the necessary means of achieving it. All that could be said against such a person is that in willing the end of having and securing his property but not the means of achieving this end, he would be thinking and acting inconsistently. While in renouncing this end altogether, a person would be thinking inconsistently in the sense that the end of having and securing property, which for Fichte essentially means being able to live from one's labour, is one that all finite rational beings can be expected to adopt.

The conditional nature of right finds expression in Fichte's theory of the civil contract in the way in which he treats the act of entering into this contract as an optional matter, thereby suggesting that each state is ultimately based on an actual contract and, consequently, on each of its member's having actually consented to enter into it. Right is also conditional in the sense that each individual person is obliged to act in conformity with its demands only on the condition that all others do the same. This is why Fichte speaks of the law of right (*das Rechtsgesez*) as being directed at everyone, whereas the moral law, which commands unconditionally, is directed at me alone.[17] In other words, my duty to obey the moral law does not depend on what others do, since I ought to do my duty irrespective of what other people may or may not do; whereas my obligation to act in accordance with principles of right depends on the actions of others, because there would be no reason or obligation on my part to act in accordance with these principles if other people did not subject themselves to the same conditions as those to which I subject myself.

By means of his separation of right from morality, insofar as it concerns the grounds which may motivate individuals to act in conformity with the demands of right, Fichte presents us with a form of recognition of the legal personality and property of others that is based on self-interest and is guaranteed by state authority. This is not to say that some individuals will not recognize other individuals as persons

17 GA II / 13: 206.

and respect their property rights on purely ethical grounds. Yet, as Fichte realistically points out, this is not something that can be reasonably relied upon. In the next section, I show that the amoral conception of the state that arises on the basis of Fichte's separation of right from morality also finds expression in Hegel's characterization of modern civil society as the 'state of necessity' (*Notstaat*).[18] Fichte himself uses the term *Nothstaat* to refer to an existing state insofar as it constitutes the condition of the development of the just and rational state, but is not yet itself this just and rational state; hence the translation of *Nothstaat* as 'makeshift state', which stresses its temporary nature.[19] Hegel's theory of civil society suggests, however, that this term can also be translated as 'state of necessity' in the case of the *Foundations of Natural Right*, because his conception of civil society corresponds in a number of important respects to the amoral conception of the state found in this work.

On the other hand, Hegel criticizes contract theories of the state for ultimately making opinion and the arbitrary will (*Willkür*) into the basis of the state.[20] As I point out below, this line of criticism is already developed in Hegel's theory of civil society, which contains a powerful objection to the kind of contract theory of the state offered by Fichte. Yet, rather than seeking to defend Fichte's theory of the civil contract

---

18 In some of the writings from his own Jena period, Hegel was highly critical of Fichte's theory of right. Cf. Hegel, 'Die Differenz des Fichte'schen und Schelling'schen Systems der Philosophie', in *Werke*, vol. II / *The Difference between Fichte's and Schelling's Systems of Philosophy*; and 'Über die wissenschaftlichen Behandlungsarten des Naturrechts, seine Stelle in der praktischen Philosophie und sein Verhältnis zu den positiven Rechtswissenschaften', in *Werke*, vol. II / 'On the Scientific Ways of Treating Natural Law, on its Place in Practical Philosophy, and its Relation to the Positive Sciences of Right'. It has been pointed out, however, that at a later stage in his Jena period and thereafter, Hegel came to incorporate some central aspects of the modern natural law tradition into his philosophy of right, and that this change was in part the result of a reengagement with Fichte's writings. Cf. Riedel, *Between Tradition and Revolution*, 76ff. Some important features of Hegel's theory of civil society, such as the idea of the 'state of necessity', might be regarded as results of this reengagement. Robert R. Williams notes the resemblance between Fichte's state and Hegel's idea of civil society as the 'state of necessity'. Cf. Williams, 'The Displacement of Recognition by Coercion in Fichte's *Grundlage des Naturrechts*', 61. He fails, however, to acknowledge that this connection can be thought to have a positive dimension, because he restricts himself to Hegel's early criticisms of Fichte, and he does not, therefore, take sufficiently into account the way in which civil society came to form a constitutive, and thus essential, moment of the theory of modern ethical life that Hegel developed in his own philosophy of right.
19 GA I / 5: 215; SE: 226.
20 Hegel, 'Grundlinien der Philosophie des Rechts', in *Werke*, vol. VII / *Foundations of the Philosophy of Right*, § 258 *Anmerkung*.

in the face of this powerful objection, which I regard, in fact, as compelling, I show that Fichte's theory of the amoral state can be reinterpreted in largely noncontractual terms, with the idea of a civil contract being ultimately reduced to something that has a merely metaphorical and regulative role to play in Fichte's political philosophy. This move nevertheless allows the voluntarism characteristic of contract theories of the state and the insights contained in the separation of right from morality to be retained. My discussion of these issues will in turn lead me to argue that a positive link between right and morality can be discovered in the theory of the state and society that Fichte developed during his Jena period. This link relates specifically to the claim made by Fichte cited above that each citizen enters into a certain class of citizen at the same time that he enters into the state. The various ways in which Fichte separates right and morality listed above should not, therefore, mislead us into thinking that he denies that there is any relation whatsoever between these two concepts. On the contrary, I argue that the concept of virtue provides the means of illustrating and understanding a relation that Fichte himself suggests must be thought to exist between right and morality.

The state of necessity

In his theory of ethical life (*Sittlichkeit*), Hegel locates civil society (*die bürgerliche Gesellschaft*) between the family and the political state. He describes it as a condition in which selfish ends are, with respect to their actualization, conditioned by universality, in the sense that any attempt to realize these ends will take place within a system of mutual dependence, which he calls the system of needs.[21] This is because each individual is, on the one hand, dependent on others, who produce or supply the means of satisfying his natural and artificial needs, while, on the other hand, other people may be dependent on this same individual for the satisfaction of their needs. Since human beings are caught up in this condition of mutual dependence, we can speak of them as being subject to necessity. As we shall see below, it is this aspect of the 'state of necessity' that forms the basis of the powerful objection to contract theories of the state that Hegel offers.

---

21 Hegel, 'Grundlinien der Philosophie des Rechts' / *Foundations of the Philosophy of Right*, §§ 189–208.

A set of laws and institutions arises on the basis of the condition of mutual dependence which characterizes civil society. These laws and institutions aim to guarantee basic rights and to ensure that society functions effectively and in everyone's interests. In particular, they seek to guarantee the inviolability of a person's body and property rights, while also being concerned with the welfare of the citizens of the state and with such tasks as that of maintaining society's infrastructure. Hegel accordingly describes civil society as a condition in which the individual's subsistence, welfare and 'rightful existence' (*rechtliches Dasein*) are inextricably tied up with the subsistence, welfare and rights of all, and are actual and secure only within this context; and it is this form of society that he calls the 'state of necessity' or the 'external' state.[22] To this extent, the state of necessity can be thought to correspond closely to the amoral conception of the state found in Fichte's *Foundations of Natural Right*. For this conception of the state is essentially that of a protective power whose task is to secure property, which for Fichte ultimately means guaranteeing that each and every person is able to live from his labour, so that the state's functions include ones relating to an individual's subsistence and welfare as well as to his legal existence. As we have seen, such a protective power is necessary because there is no guarantee that individuals will act in accordance with the demands of morality in relation to each other. Insofar as its primary function is held to be that of a protective power, Fichte's amoral conception of the state fits well the description of the state of necessity given by one of Hegel's followers, Eduard Gans, in his own lectures on the philosophy of right held in 1832/33, about a year after Hegel's death:

> Some people say that the state is a state which guarantees security [*ein Sicherheitsstaat*]; it does not actually have to exist; but human beings are simply so immoral, hence state of necessity [*Nothstaat*]. They conceive of it as nothing else than civil society, which has the task of safeguarding the separate interests of individuals. The state is a limitation on natural freedom. Human beings must sacrifice a part of their freedom and power in order to preserve the remaining part of it.[23]

The way in which the state functions to guarantee the rights and welfare of individual human beings helps explain why Hegel calls it

22 Hegel, 'Grundlinien der Philosophie des Rechts' / *Foundations of the Philosophy of Right*, § 183.
23 Gans, *Naturrecht und Universalrechtsgeschichte*, 94.

the 'external' state. For this view of the state suggests that the existence of the state is an essentially contingent matter, with its ultimate basis being located in the allegedly immoral nature of human beings and in their deciding to sacrifice part of their natural freedom in order to preserve it, in the form of a set of rights that they enjoy in relation to other persons and in relation to the state itself. The state is therefore external to individuals in the sense that it is not thought by them to stand in an essential relation to their own wills; the individual's relation to the state is instead one that is based on opinions concerning human nature and what it would be in one's own best interests to do. Fichte's contract theory of the state gives expression to this element of apparent contingency, which Fichte himself stresses in the following passage, when he claims that the kind of absolute obligation associated with morality does not exist in the case of right:

> Now in the doctrine of right there is no talk of moral obligation; each is bound only by the free, arbitrary [willkührlichen] decision to live in community [Gesellschaft] with others, and if someone does not at all want to limit his free choice [Willkühr], then within the field of the doctrine of right, one can say nothing further against him, other than that he must then remove himself from all human community.[24]

Fichte goes so far as to claim that

> it is originally up to the free and arbitrary choice of every individual to determine whether he wants to live in this particular state or not, although if he wants to live among other human beings at all, then it is not up to his arbitrary choice to determine whether he enters into a state, or whether he wants to remain his own judge.[25]

Fichte's position thus appears to be that a human being's entry into a particular state is essentially an optional matter. However, since it is impossible for human beings to live peacefully together if they are not subject to the authority of a third party entrusted with the task of deciding disputes between them and equipped with the power to enforce its decisions, a human being has no choice but to be part of a state *if* he wishes to live in community with other human beings. Yet this does not mean that a human being has no choice when it comes to the particular state of which he becomes a member, nor that people may

---

24 GA I / 3: 322; FNR: 11f.
25 GA I / 3: 326; FNR: 15.

not, in fact, choose to enter into society with other human beings in such a way that they can all feel secure in relation to each other.

To turn to the powerful objection to contract theories of the state that Hegel offers, the statements cited above provide perfect examples of what he means when he accuses contract theories of the state of making opinion and the arbitrary will into the basis of the state. Moreover, an important aspect of Hegel's account of civil society as the 'state of necessity', however much it otherwise corresponds to Fichte's amoral conception of the state, points to a powerful reason for claiming that contract theories of the state misconstrue the real nature of the state by basing it on an essentially illusory theory of consent. This aspect of Hegel's theory of civil society concerns the previously mentioned condition of mutual dependence found in civil society, which arises in a largely unconscious fashion through individuals striving to satisfy their needs, and which implies that individuals cannot, in fact, live outside the system of needs that forms the economic and social basis of the state. This system of needs, which constitutes a self-reproducing totality, must be thought instead to exist prior to the particular individuals who become caught up in it in their attempts to satisfy their needs, so that the emphasis here falls firmly on the idea of necessity rather than on that of freedom. In this respect, the notion of consent appears out of place, especially if it is taken to involve an empirical act by means of which the state comes into existence.

Significantly, Hegel claims that Fichte comprehends the state merely as an 'external order';[26] for, when taken together with the way in which he refers to civil society as the 'external' state, this claim suggests that Hegel himself thinks there is some kind of link between Fichte's theory of the state and his own theory of civil society. Moreover, Hegel allows that human beings are able to shape the laws and institutions which arise on the basis of the system of needs, by transforming them in accordance with the idea of freedom; and one of the specific ways in which Hegel thinks this has happened in the course of human history shows how the voluntarist aspect of Fichte's conception of the state might be retained even if we discard the radical voluntarism found in his theory of the civil contract. In this way, it becomes possible to regard Fichte as having developed a conception of the state that contains an insight into the type of disposition that often

26 Hegel, *Philosophie des Rechts. Die Vorlesungen von 1819/20 in einer Nachschrift*, 190f.

characterizes the relation of modern, reflective individuals to the state and its laws and institutions; a type of disposition that also finds expression in Hegel's theory of civil society.

Although Hegel ultimately rejects the 'external' conception of the state that we find in Fichte's theory of right, and which he himself thinks is characteristic of modern civil society, he acknowledges the reality of the disposition associated with this conception of the state. In a way that recalls his description of civil society as the 'state of necessity', Hegel describes the disposition in question as one where individuals think of themselves as living in a state only as a matter of necessity,[27] choosing to obey its laws only because they realize that they could not otherwise achieve their own ends.[28] The way in which individuals may think of themselves as living in a state as a matter of necessity implies that they need not, in fact, live in a state, if they could find some other means of realizing their ends, or if they should renounce the ends that make it necessary for them to live in a state; and these possibilities all bring to mind Fichte's distinction between the conditional nature of right and the unconditional nature of morality. Although Hegel's account of the system of needs as the basis of civil society implies that this viewpoint is an essentially illusory one, his remarks concerning the attitude that individuals may have towards state authority mentioned above show that he is nevertheless aware of the different kinds of disposition that may characterize individuals' attitudes towards the laws and institutions of the state, and that among them we must include this essentially erroneous kind of disposition. Another aspect of the necessity found in the 'state of necessity' can be thus understood as a subjective form of necessity: the perception that one needs to live in a state because doing so represents the necessary means of realizing certain ends, whose ultimate source is located in self-interest. Although this subjective form of necessity may go together with a failure to acknowledge the objective form of necessity that has its basis in the system of needs, it is still useful to distinguish these forms of necessity from each other and to regard the subjective form of necessity as in itself significant.

Given the existence of this subjective form of necessity, Fichte's theory of the civil contract might be accorded a metaphorical function that derives from the way in which it serves to illustrate this subjective

---

27 Cf. Hegel, *Vorlesungen über Rechtsphilosophie*, vol. IV, 474.
28 Cf. Hegel, *Vorlesungen über Rechtsphilosophie*, vol. IV, 481.

necessity and the type of reasoning associated with it. His theory of the civil contract may also be accorded a regulative function, of the kind that Kant accords to the social contract, when he claims that it is an idea of reason which enables us to ask what laws could have issued from the united will of a whole nation.[29] This is because the nonmoral grounds that Fichte identifies when he seeks to distinguish right from morality in terms of what motivates individuals to act can be viewed as an attempt on his part to specify the grounds of justification that need to be met for any actual state to count as a legitimate one in the eyes of its citizens, insofar as they are considered to be rational, self-interested agents, but not necessarily moral beings as well. More than anything else, these grounds of justification will concern the state's ability to perform the role of a protective power that guarantees individuals the right to be able to live from their labour. In order to highlight further how the voluntarism found in Fichte's conception of the civil contract can be retained even when the facticity of such a contract is denied, and in a way, moreover, that acknowledges the objective form of necessity found in what Hegel calls the system of needs, I shall now return to Fichte's claim that one does not become a citizen in general but enters into a certain class of citizen at the same time as entering into the state. I argue that this claim can be related to one of Hegel's main attempts to show that civil society has been shaped by human beings seeking to realize their freedom in the course of history, despite having its basis in the objective form of necessity which he associates with the system of needs.

For Hegel, one of the main ways in which the possibility of exercising free choice exists in civil society in the face of the necessity that otherwise characterizes it concerns the type of work that a person does, since in modern civil society people may freely choose to enter a particular trade or occupation, even though a person's choice will be limited by such factors as his natural ability and level of education, so that once again necessity has a significant role to play. By choosing to enter a particular trade or occupation, a person at the same time chooses to

---

29 Cf. Kant, 'Über den Gemeinspruch', 297 / *Political Writings*, 79. Fichte himself makes claims that invite a hypothetical interpretation of the civil contract, as when he states that, 'In fact, since the law is exactly as I myself would have to prescribe it, in accordance with the rule of right, I am subjecting myself to my own immutable will, a will I would necessarily have to possess if I am acting rightfully [*gerecht bin*] and therefore if I am to have any rights at all' (GA I / 3: 398; FNR: 95f.).

enter a certain class (*Stand*).[30] Hegel contrasts this with the way in which the principle of 'subjective particularity' was denied its rights by Plato, who, he claims, assigns to the rulers of the state the task of choosing the class to which each individual belongs.[31] Other examples of the denial of subjective particularity would be when particular trades or occupations are assigned to particular castes or other groups of people within society; while the existence of societies in which subjective particularity is denied its rights in this way, points to the need to transform society in accordance with the idea of the person as an essentially self-determining being. This way of reconciling freedom, in the shape of the choice of one's occupation, and necessity, understood as the existence of the system of needs and one's place within it, is compatible with Fichte's views on the nature of property and the role of the state, because he regards the right to undertake a particular form of labour as itself a form of property, so that one of the main functions of the state will be to ensure that a system is in place which guarantees that each and every person is able to live from his labour. Indeed, a person's absolute and inalienable right to be able to live from his labour constitutes the main object of the property contract. Although, in *The Closed Commercial State*, Fichte places certain limits on the right to enter an occupation of one's own choosing, he does not rule out the possibility of free choice altogether. In fact, Fichte himself suggests that the act of entering a certain occupation may stand in for the voluntarist element contained in his theory of the civil contract when he claims that a person consents to the property contract 'by dedicating himself publicly and openly to a particular occupation'.[32]

Fichte pursues this idea in the first book of *The Closed Commercial State*, which develops in more detail certain points already contained in the second part of the *Foundations of Natural Right*. Fichte here speaks of the members of the two estates that he distinguishes between in terms of the different activities they perform in relation to the end of maintaining life and making it more agreeable, that is, the estate of producers and the estate of artists, as entering into contracts with each other. They do this in the first instance by agreeing to restrict themselves to their respective spheres of activity and then, more positively,

30 Hegel, 'Grundlinien der Philosophie des Rechts' / *Foundations of the Philosophy of Right*, § 206.
31 Hegel, 'Grundlinien der Philosophie des Rechts' / *Foundations of the Philosophy of Right*, § 206 *Anmerkung*.
32 GA I / 4: 9; FNR: 170.

by agreeing to exchange their products, so as to guarantee each other the means to live from their labour and to live as agreeably as possible. Fichte sees the relations between these two estates and the estate of merchants, which has the exclusive right to exchange the natural products and finished articles of the producers and the artists, as also being based on a series of contracts. Fichte's theory of the relations of the estates to each other, insofar as the provision of goods is concerned, shows that despite the contractual terms in which he describes these relations, he has some awareness of the necessity that characterizes the economic life of the state on account of the way in which human beings are dependent on each other for the satisfaction of their needs. Since the state, which oversees the whole process of production and exchange, has to ensure not only that the various estates honour the agreements they have made with each other, but also that there are enough natural products and finished articles available to satisfy the needs of all the members of the state, its planning of the economy will, as previously mentioned, partly consist in making sure that there is always the right number of members belonging to each estate. For this reason, Fichte argues that a person who intends to enter an occupation must make his intention known to the government, which will then either grant or refuse the person in question the right to enter the occupation of his choice, so that there 'can be no occupation in a state without the state's permission'.[33]

This does not mean, however, that the state assigns to each individual their place and role within the state, which is a measure that Hegel thinks Plato advocates. For although the supervisory role that Fichte accords to the state involves the imposition of limits on the extent to which a person will be able to choose the occupation into which he enters, he does not entirely exclude the possibility of free choice, since a person's request to enter a particular occupation or profession may in fact be granted. Moreover, even if this request should be refused, the person in question may still be able to ask to enter another occupation or profession in opposition to other ones. In any case, the state's role in guaranteeing that everyone is able to live from his labour may conceivably require less planning than Fichte himself makes out. The state's performance of this role might be seen instead to amount to such measures as guaranteeing that sufficient jobs are available, that individuals are competent to perform the occupations or trades they

33 GA I / 4: 23; FNR: 187.

wish to enter, and to making sure that everyone has the best possible chance of being able to choose the type of work he does, which will demand such measures as giving people equal access to education and training. There would still be an element of necessity involved, given such factors as differences in ability and the limited availability of certain types of job. Yet, depending on particular circumstances, there would still be some degree of free choice concerning one's specific place within the state, thus allowing the voluntarism found in Fichte's theory of the civil contract to be partially retained, at the same time as according full recognition to the objective necessity identified by Hegel in his theory of civil society.

In the next section, I show that this emphasis on the type of occupation that an individual enters into within the state accords well with Fichte's doctrine of ethical duties given in the third part of *The System of Ethics*, which concerns the systematic application of the concept of morality (*Sittlichkeit*). This doctrine of ethical duties will in turn be shown to open up the possibility of a different understanding of the theory of the state and society developed by Fichte during his professorship at the University of Jena, because it implies that there is an important sense in which right and morality must be thought to stand in an essential relation to each other. The relation in question is a different one to a relation between these concepts that Fichte himself explicitly identifies, and which I shall also mention. These two relations between right and morality do not, however, serve in any way to undermine Fichte's views concerning the fact that individuals may exhibit different dispositions in relation to the laws and institutions of the state, so that his separation of right from morality remains valid.

Fichte's doctrine of ethical duties

In *The System of Ethics*, Fichte is concerned with the form of freedom that is characteristic of acting in accordance with the moral law. This form of freedom is autonomy, which requires subjecting oneself to laws that stem from one's own rational nature. Moral autonomy incorporates, as a condition of its possibility, the formal freedom that constitutes the bare capacity to determine one's own activity in accordance with free choice. This is because acting morally presupposes that one was, in fact, able to act otherwise than one actually did act. As we have seen, Fichte thinks that this formal freedom is made possible in the sensible world by means of the relation of right. The formal freedom which right guarantees does not, however, specify any particular ends that a person ought to make his own, beyond that of respecting, insofar as one's external actions are concerned, the freedom of others. The ends a person sets himself can be thus held to be of an essentially contingent nature. The moral law, by contrast, prescribes rules of action that are unconditionally valid; it therefore commands, as Fichte himself puts it, 'an action that ought to occur purely and simply because it ought to occur'.[34] However, although the moral law prescribes rules that each and every individual ought to follow, it is equally a law that individuals do not necessarily obey, since, given their capacity to exercise free choice, they may, in fact, choose not to submit themselves to the moral law.

As mentioned at the beginning of this chapter, the way in which morality involves a different form of freedom to the form of freedom safeguarded by right has been seen to represent one of the main reasons behind Fichte's separation of right from morality. This separation of right from morality makes its presence felt in Fichte's separate deductions of the particular duties of recognizing the property of others and respecting the inviolability of their bodies undertaken in *The System of Ethics*, in which these duties are held to be conditions of one's becoming an effective tool of the moral law,[35] and of the right to have the inviolability of one's own body respected by others and the right to property undertaken in the *Foundations of Natural Right*.[36] The different justifications that Fichte gives of the demand to respect the right to property and the inviolability of a person's body to those that he gives of the duties to recognize the property of others and to regard their bodies as inviolable accord with his claim in the *Foundations of Natural Right* that the question as to whether the moral law might provide a new sanction for the concept of right is not part of the doctrine of natural right itself, but instead belongs to an account of 'real morality' (*eine reelle Moral*).[37] This appears to confirm that Fichte advocates an absolute separation of right from morality, as does the idea that while right has its ultimate basis in the original right of each human being to enjoy the conditions of free agency in the sensible world, so as to be able to determine oneself as

34 GA I / 5: 66; SE: 57f.
35 GA I / 5: 247ff. and 259ff.; SE: 264ff. and 278ff.
36 GA I / 3: 405ff.; FNR: 103ff.
37 GA I / 3: 359; FNR: 50.

an individual, in the case of morality it is by means of the 'disappearance and annihilation of one's entire individuality that everyone becomes a pure presentation of the moral law in the world of sense'.[38] In line with the idea of an absolute separation of right from morality, Fichte makes a sharp distinction in the following passage between the disposition associated with moral duty and the egoism which is characteristic of right:

> Just as a moral disposition [*moralische Gesinnung*] is the love of duty for duty's sake, so is a political disposition, by contrast, the love of oneself for one's own sake, concern for the security of one's person and property; and the state can without hesitation adopt as its fundamental law: love yourself above all else, and love your fellow citizens for your own sake.[39]

Significantly, in this passage it is by making a distinction between the types of disposition associated with right and morality that Fichte seeks to emphasize their separation, with the disposition that he associates with right corresponding to the kind of disposition that Hegel thinks is characteristic of the members of civil society insofar as they understand society in terms of the 'state of necessity'. The doctrine of ethical duties that Fichte sets out in *The System of Ethics* suggests, however, that right and morality stand in some kind of relation to each other, and that the moral disposition ought ideally to supplant, or at the very least supplement, the egoism that he associates with the juridical and political sphere of right. This becomes evident in Fichte's account of the duties of human beings within a particular profession.

Fichte's account of the ethical duties that arise within a particular profession is based on his claim that morality demands that individuals act as a means of realizing reason.[40] As we shall see, in the present context this appeal to an 'end of reason' can be simply identified with the idea of an ethical, legal and political community that seeks to realize itself to the fullest possible extent, and, in so doing, realizes the freedom of its members in the formal sense and, potentially, also in the sense of moral autonomy. Fichte claims that the realization of the end of reason requires a division of labour, whereby different individuals become responsible for the different tasks that need to be accomplished in order to achieve this end; an arrangement which

38 GA I / 5: 231; SE: 245.
39 GA I / 4: 69; FNR: 237.
40 GA I / 5: 230f.; SE: 245.

involves the establishment of different estates. As we already know, these estates are based on either natural or artificial relations. While the former type of relation characterizes the relations of the members of the family to each other, Fichte uses the term 'profession' to designate the second type of estate, whose relations are based on 'a contingent and free determination of the will'.[41] We encountered in the previous section in connection with Hegel's account of the 'state of necessity' one good reason that Fichte has for describing membership of a profession in this way, namely, that it is to some extent a matter of free choice, or at least ought to be so.[42] The question remains, however, concerning the precise sense in which Fichte thinks that the members of a profession help realize the end of reason through their actions.

We have already seen that the professions themselves subdivide into those that consist in acting immediately upon the community of rational beings and those that consist in acting upon nature for the sake of this community. The first set of professions is made up of that of the scholar, the cleric, the fine artist and the state official, while the second set of professions is made up of people whose occupations involve directing nature or else gathering or tending its products, fashioning the raw materials that nature provides, or facilitating the exchange of objects of need. Although the formal correspondence between this account of the lower professions and the division of labour found in Fichte's *The Closed Commercial State* is obvious, it should not be allowed to obscure a fundamental difference between the relations characteristic of this division of labour when they are viewed from the standpoint of right, on the one hand, and when they are viewed from the standpoint of morality, on the other. For, in the case of right, a person's membership of a particular estate and the relations of the various estates to each other are based on self-interest, whereas, in the case of morality, they are based on a sense of duty. Fichte therefore makes no appeal in *The System of Ethics* to the idea of a contract between the various estates, thus showing that he regards contractual arrangements as belonging to the realm of right alone.

The separation of right from morality is also reflected in the different justifications that Fichte gives of the division of society into various estates. This is because in the case of right this division

41 GA I / 5: 287; SE: 310.
42 Fichte himself acknowledges that the idea that human beings should be able to choose the estates to which they belong is more of a moral demand than a reality (GA I / 5: 244; SE: 260).

aims to ensure the existence of an economic system within which each person is able to live from his labour, so that an external reason exists for entering a profession, that is, a motive that makes entering a profession into merely the means to an end, with the end in question being that of self-preservation, which constitutes the ultimate condition of a finite rational being's ability to act freely and effectively in the sensible world. By contrast, the justification given of such a division in *The System of Ethics* is that it guarantees that one person does not take upon himself a task which another person has already taken on, thereby hindering this second person's activity insofar as it aims to further the end of reason.[43] Moreover, from the moral standpoint there exists the duty to preserve oneself, but only insofar as doing so relates to one's status as an instrument of the moral law. Self-preservation is therefore not to be understood as the final end of action; it is instead only the means to a higher, moral end, which may conceivably demand at some point in the future that one does not preserve one's life but instead sacrifices it for the sake of this higher end.[44]

Although Fichte calls the first set of professions higher ones and the second set lower ones, he claims that any one profession is no more essential than another one insofar as the end of reason is concerned. Indeed, each occupation 'is related to the preservation and free activity of moral beings, and it is thereby sanctified [*geheiligt*] just as much as the highest occupation'.[45] To use the members of the lower professions as an example of how individuals help realize the end of reason through their actions, we might recall how Hegel's account of the 'state of necessity' suggests that a system of right consisting of various laws and institutions arises on the basis of the condition of mutual dependence which he associates with the system of needs; while within this condition of mutual dependence, each individual may choose to enter a trade, profession or other occupation, so that to this extent the ideas of freedom and necessity are reconciled. Although Fichte's

---

43 GA I / 5: 243; SE: 259f. As far as specific duties are concerned, Fichte appears to assume the possibility of a kingdom of ends, in which the moral ends that each member adopts are in perfect harmony with those that the other members adopt; for he asserts that that which the moral law demands of one individual can never conflict with that which it demands of another individual (GA II / 13: 213f.).

44 GA I / 5: 233ff.; SE: 248ff.

45 GA I / 5: 301; SE: 326.

presentation of the civil contract serves to obscure this element of mutual dependency and necessity, it helps explain his claim that the lower professions are just as essential as the other estates, in the sense that, 'Reason's end is furthered in each estate, beginning with that estate that wrests from the soil its fruits, which is a condition for the preservation of our species in the sensible world'.[46] For this claim suggests that the lower professions are as essential as the higher ones to the existence of society because the members of these professions engage in activities that are concerned with the provision of goods and products which are essential to satisfying people's basic needs, as well as those needs whose satisfaction renders life more agreeable.

In this respect, the lower professions play a vital role in guaranteeing all persons, including the members of the higher professions, the possibility of acting freely and purposefully in the world, which depends, in the first instance, on the continued existence of their own bodies. In playing such a role within the amoral 'state of necessity', the lower professions help make possible the actual existence of a moral community, for the realization of the moral law depends on individuals having the freedom not only to form moral ends but also to act in the sensible world in accordance with these ends; and, as with the realization of any end in the sensible world, this will require the continued existence of their own bodies, as well as the absence of such feelings as hunger, which might lead them to act with mechanical necessity. Fichte appears to be making a similar point in the 1812 *Rechtslehre* when he claims that, 'The external ends however, that nature imposes upon us as conditions of the higher end, are our preservation, and our safety. These must therefore be attained, and universally attained, before the moral law can universally appear'.[47]

The way in which the realization of the moral law presupposes the establishment of a condition of right helps explain Fichte's claim that while humanity 'separates itself from citizenship [*Bürgerthume*] in order to elevate itself with absolute freedom to the level of morality [*Moralität*] . . . it can do so only if human beings have first existed within the state'.[48] Fichte in fact appears to make the very strong claim that morality would not be possible at all in the absence of a condition of

46 GA I / 5: 244; SE: 261.
47 GA II / 13: 214.
48 GA I / 4: 17; FNR: 178f.

right. This is suggested by the statement that 'no acting is possible at all before a state has been erected',[49] as well as by the following claim:

> If human beings are to exercise a mutual influence upon one another, then, prior to anything else, their legal [*rechtliches*] relationship has to be assured. This is a condition for any society [*Gesellschaft*]. – The institution through which this occurs is called the *state*.[50]

The last claim is made in relation to the ethical duties pertaining to a profession; and we can therefore interpret it as meaning that the possibility of an ethical condition represented by a society made up of various professions, each with its own set of ethical duties, rests on the prior establishment of a condition of right, in which we also encounter a division of society into various estates, though this time one that is based on self-interest. This does not mean, however, that the establishment of a condition of right will automatically lead to the establishment of an ethical, rather than legal and political, form of community, since this transition ultimately depends on human will. Right is thus seen as a necessary, but not sufficient, condition of morality.

The way in which right forms a condition of moral agency in the sensible world points to another important connection between these two spheres. For it suggests that Fichte's theory of right as developed in the *Foundations of Natural Right* forms part of a more general theory of society, one in which moral autonomy forms the ultimate end of right. One might object to this teleological aspect of Fichte's theory of right, which amounts to reducing right into the means of guaranteeing the formal freedom that constitutes a condition of moral autonomy, as opposed to understanding right to have its own distinctive end. Indeed, this teleological aspect of Fichte's theory of right presents another obstacle to the kind of liberal interpretation of Fichte's political philosophy offered by Frederick Neuhouser, who links his claim that Fichte sees right as having its own distinctive end in the fostering of individuality specifically to the idea of a liberal social order. This is because Fichte's reduction of right into a means in relation to morality suggests that he is attempting to advocate a particular, exclusive conception of the good life – in this case one based on the idea of the division of society into various estates, each with its own particular

49 GA I / 5: 215; SE: 226.
50 GA I / 5: 301; SE: 326.

ethical function within society – whereas this is a move that liberal political theory has traditionally attempted to avoid.

The teleological aspect of Fichte's theory of right suggests another important relation between right and morality, though one that Fichte does not explicitly mention. For it invites the question as to why we cannot equally think of right as being the end and morality the means, in such a way, however, as to avoid reducing morality to *only* a means. I shall now argue that Fichte himself has good reasons for thinking that morality is itself a condition of right and, in this sense, represents a means in relation to the latter, so that right and morality can be seen to stand in a reciprocal relation to each other, with each of them being both an end and a means in relation to the other. In this respect, the teleological aspect of Fichte's theory of right can be interpreted in such a way as to show that the end which right helps realize is not external to right itself, since by making moral autonomy possible, right turns out to be securing the conditions of its own possibility. Conversely, in helping to produce a condition of right, morality would be securing the conditions of its own possibility. In this way, neither right nor morality is reduced to the status of merely a means to an end.

Although it is conceivable that a condition of right could be maintained through people acting from self-interest alone – and Hegel's account of the state of necessity as having its basis in a condition of mutual dependence appears to show that this is indeed possible – the truly effective functioning of a state, in which relations of right exist between individuals, might be thought to require that at least some individuals perform their social or political roles within the state with a sense of commitment and responsibility. These qualities can be considered to be of a specifically moral nature, while a sense of commitment and responsibility, which may require more of an individual than his own self-interest dictates, seems difficult to explain in terms of the methodological assumption of 'universal egoism' upon which Fichte bases his theory of right.[51] The need for at least some individuals to demonstrate certain moral qualities within the state is suggested by Fichte himself when he speaks of virtue (*Tugend*) as being of an essentially social nature, so that one does not fulfil one's duty 'by living the life of a hermit, by separating oneself from others, and simply by

---

51 GA I / 3: 433f.; FNR: 134.

entertaining sublime thoughts and speculations . . . but only by acting in and for society'.[52]

Fichte admittedly fails to develop his own comprehensive theory of virtue. Indeed, his account of this moral concept does not extend beyond a few scattered remarks in *The System of Ethics*, and, when he does mention it, he does not always appear to have a social form of virtue in mind. On one occasion, Fichte speaks of 'the *genius for virtue*' (*Genie zur Tugend*), by which he means an outstanding ability to raise oneself above the laws of nature, in the sense that although external circumstances may provide the stimulus, it is still up to a human being as a free agent to determine himself in response to this stimulus.[53] The freedom that a moral agent enjoys in relation to nature, including himself as a merely natural being, reveals his status as a free and supersensuous being elevated above nature, and virtue is correspondingly held to be 'an actively engendered product of our own freedom . . . an elevation into a completely different order of things'.[54] This tells us that virtue is not something merely given; it is instead something that must be produced by the individual concerned through his own freedom, so as to realize his destiny as a supersensuous being elevated above nature.

Such edifying descriptions of virtue do not, however, suggest a form of virtue that in any way extends beyond the moral agent conceived in abstraction from any kind of social or political context. On the other hand, in his account of the role of a church and its symbol or creed in the moral cultivation (*Bildung*) of human beings, Fichte states that all virtuous people will necessarily aim to achieve among themselves unanimous agreement concerning both their practical convictions and the uniformity of the acting that is to issue from them.[55] This idea can be transferred from the wider body of the church, with its universal symbol or creed, to the narrower body of one of the estates and, more narrowly still, to one of the professions within society, which form essential elements in Fichte's theory of ethical duties. We can then think of the members of these estates and professions as being virtuous insofar as they strive to achieve agreement among themselves concerning their particular roles within the estate and profession to which they belong, and the specific actions that these roles demand,

52 GA I / 5: 213; SE: 223.
53 GA I / 5: 171; SE: 175.
54 GA I / 5: 186; SE: 193.
55 GA I / 5: 213; SE: 224.

actions which ought to be made to harmonize with those of the other members of the same estate and profession. Moreover, Fichte speaks of virtue as having to be cultivated in a human being, and he proceeds to suggest that other human beings will have an important role to play in this process when he refers to the duty of setting a good example. This implies that the wish to emulate others whom one respects will have an essential role to play in the cultivation of virtue (*Bildung zur Tugend*) in an individual.[56] Fichte's conception of virtue thus turns out to contain an intersubjective element after all, and to suggest the existence of a social form of virtue which, insofar as it relates to his theory of ethical duties as they derive from a person's membership of an estate or profession, can be further explicated with reference to Hegel's account of virtue in his philosophy of right.

Hegel associates virtue with the naturally determined character of an individual, and he claims that when it 'represents nothing more than the simple adequacy of the individual to the duties of the circumstances [*Verhältnisse*] to which he belongs, it is *rectitude* [*Rechtschaffenheit*]'.[57] He thus appears to have in mind a specific type of virtue. This type of virtue has a strong social dimension, despite the fact that it relates to an individual's naturally determined character. This becomes evident from the way in which Hegel compares virtue, understood as rectitude, to how the ancients ascribed virtue to a heroic figure such as Hercules. In the latter case, virtue is identified with 'the distinctive natural genius of individuals'.[58] The idea behind this understanding of ancient virtue is that, in the states of antiquity, a fully developed system of ethical duties and norms deriving from an individual's relation to the laws and institutions of the state had yet to evolve. This in turn meant that the performance of ethical actions came to depend on an individual's having the right character, in the sense of possessing the ability to know what was the appropriate thing to do in the particular circumstances and to do it. The wish to emulate the actions of a heroic individual such as Hercules, who is credited with being virtuous in the sense indicated above, then served as the source of ethical norms within a society. It is a different matter in a state with a more

---

56 GA I / 5: 279; SE: 301.
57 Hegel, 'Grundlinien der Philosophie des Rechts' / *Foundations of the Philosophy of Right*, § 150.
58 Hegel, 'Grundlinien der Philosophie des Rechts' / *Foundations of the Philosophy of Right*, § 150 *Anmerkung*.

developed set of laws and institutions, since there will be less need to depend on individual character when it comes to determining what ought to be done. Rather, one must act in accordance with the norms that derive from one's relation to these laws and institutions, so that, according to Hegel, 'it is easy to say *what* someone must do and *what* the duties are which he has to fulfil in order to be virtuous. He must simply do what is prescribed, expressly stated, and known to him within his situation [*in seinen Verhältnisse*]'.[59]

In a modern state there will consequently be less room for the exercise of any distinctive natural ethical genius on the part of certain extraordinary individuals, especially since acting ethically will largely amount to acting as others who perform the same social roles particularly well act, rather than acting in extraordinary ways that serve to distinguish oneself from others. Hegel thinks, in fact, that in the course of human history there has been a move away from the ancient form of virtue towards the more modern one of rectitude. He therefore claims that the age of actual virtues is past, while the age in which we live is the age of rectitude,[60] which consists in acting in a universal manner and in not wanting to distinguish oneself from others.[61]

Yet Hegel describes the virtues themselves as 'the ethical in its particular application'.[62] This notion of applying the ethical in particular situations invites the question as to whether the application of ethical norms amounts to a merely mechanical process in the case of the modern form of virtue that he calls rectitude. Against such a view it can be argued that the successful performance of a social role will sometimes require the exercise of such capacities and qualities as good judgement and a sense of commitment and responsibility when it comes to working out what is the right thing to do in the particular circumstances in which one finds oneself, because the available ethical norms will not provide complete guidance as to how one is to act. This will be especially true in certain exceptional circumstances; and Hegel himself acknowledges that in certain extraordinary circumstances virtue 'in the proper sense' (that is, an individual's natural ability to know what is the right thing to do in the

59 Hegel, 'Grundlinien der Philosophie des Rechts' / *Foundations of the Philosophy of Right*, § 150 *Anmerkung*.
60 Hegel, *Philosophie des Rechts. Die Vorlesungen von 1819/20 in einer Nachschrift*, 125.
61 Hegel, *Vorlesungen über Rechtsphilosophie*, vol. IV, 404.
62 Hegel, 'Grundlinien der Philosophie des Rechts' / *Foundations of the Philosophy of Right*, § 150 *Anmerkung*.

circumstances and to do it) will have a role to play in modern ethical life.[63] In this respect, we can think of the type of virtue required of modern individuals as varying according to different circumstances. The type of virtue required will nevertheless be of a social kind insofar as both its object and its consequences are concerned.

Hegel's analysis of the concept of virtue can be related to Fichte's theory of ethical duties insofar as it concerns the duties deriving from a person's profession in a number of ways. To begin with, the idea that virtue is natural in the sense of being part of an individual's character is not necessarily incompatible with Fichte's conception of virtue as a product of human freedom that elevates a human being above nature. This is because a person's membership of a profession will depend on the possession of certain natural talents and aptitudes, though it will also be up to the individual concerned to develop these talents and aptitudes given to him by nature, so that in this respect there remains an important role for freedom. Secondly, the way in which Fichte associates certain particular duties with the norms that arise in connection with an individual's membership of a wider social whole indicates that he has in mind something very much like the modern form of virtue that Hegel terms 'rectitude'. The fact that virtue will consist in acting in accordance with these norms suggests, moreover, that individuals will need to emulate the actions of those members of the same estate and profession who are commonly considered to be its most exemplary members. This ties in well with Fichte's own suggestion that emulating others whom one respects has an essential role to play in the moral cultivation of an individual. However, unless one wants to reduce ethical action to a merely mechanical process, which is surely something that Fichte would not want to do, at least not during his Jena period, there would also appear to be some room for the 'genius for virtue' that he mentions, in the sense that, in extraordinary circumstances, individuals may need to work out entirely by themselves what is the right thing to do and to do it.

The social form of virtue that can be detected in Fichte's theory of ethical duties and some of his scattered remarks on virtue will be arguably required of at least some people if the state is to function in a truly effective manner, and almost certainly if society is to be given the chance to flourish. The theory of society that emerges when we view

---

63 Hegel, 'Grundlinien der Philosophie des Rechts' / *Foundations of the Philosophy of Right*, § 150 *Anmerkung.*

Fichte's theory of right in the light of his account of the ethical duties connected with a person's profession might therefore be seen as setting out the conditions for a more adequate form of society than the one that we get when his theory of right is viewed in isolation from his theory of ethical duties. Fichte's teleological account of right can, in short, be understood to reveal the further conditions of an effectively functioning state and of a potentially flourishing form of society. In fact, Fichte's own theory of right can be used to illustrate this point, even though his separation of right from morality implies that the idea of virtue is irrelevant when it comes to the legal and political form of community that he associates with the concept of right. This is because Fichte's theory of the constitution of the state opens up some space for the exercise of virtue and even appears to demand its existence in the case of some individuals who perform certain important political functions within the state. My discussion of this issue will, moreover, allow me to establish yet another link between Fichte's social and political philosophy and the radical phase of the French Revolution.

The role of virtue in Fichte's theory of right

In the theory of the constitution of the state that he sets out in § 16 of the *Foundations of Natural Right*, Fichte rejects the idea of a democratic constitution which allows the populace as a whole to exercise executive power, on the grounds that the populace would become judge of their own cause when it came to the administration of justice. This situation would in itself constitute an injustice, and it would also result in insecurity and terror (*das Schrecken*), 'since one would have to fear not only the violent acts of all the others just as he would outside the state, but also, from time to time, the blind fury of an enraged mob that acts unjustly in the name of the law'.[64] By identifying these problems with a direct form of democracy, Fichte thinks he has provided a deduction of the need for representation in a commonwealth. The populace must, in short, alienate the task of exercising executive power, thereby becoming subject to the decisions made by the body they have authorized to exercise this power.

Fichte also rejects the idea of a separation of powers, arguing instead for a constitution in which both the judicial and executive functions of the state are the responsibility of the populace's representatives, who

64 GA I / 3: 439; FNR: 140.

may be one or more persons. Fichte goes even further than this, however, by claiming that the populace's representatives must be responsible for determining the content of law. All particular laws are understood by Fichte to be essentially applications of the one fundamental law, which states that 'these particular human beings [*diese bestimmte Menschen Menge*] are to live alongside one another in accordance with right'.[65] The people's representatives will therefore be responsible for interpreting in more precise terms the content of the civil contract and the common will to which it gives rise. The executive power thus 'includes the entire public power in all its branches'.[66]

Fichte recognizes, however, that this concentration of all power in the hands of a certain group of people or of a single person can be a dangerous thing, so that the persons entrusted with executive power must somehow remain accountable to the populace, for otherwise the result would be despotism. This raises the question as to how such accountability is to be assured; and it is Fichte's answer to this question that not only leaves open some space for the exercise of virtue in his theory of right, but also points to the need for the social type of virtue that can be detected in his theory of ethical duties and in some of his scattered remarks on virtue. Since the issue here is that of the accountability of the people's representatives with respect to the effective functioning of a state in terms of the end of guaranteeing the rights of all, together with the related issue of how to bring about a just legal, social and political order, the significance of the points made below can be thought to extend beyond Fichte's theory of the constitution of the state, many of the details of which one may well want to reject.

To solve the problem as to how the people's representatives are to remain accountable to the populace, Fichte introduces an institution whose task is to oversee the executive power and to judge whether or not public power is being administered properly by the particular persons to whom it has been entrusted. He calls this institution the ephorate (*das Ephorat*). The members of this institution must be elected by the populace, so as to ensure their independence of the government. The ephorate itself lacks any executive power, since its task is simply to examine and decide whether the members of the executive power are acting as reliable interpreters and guarantors of the common will that is generated by means of the civil contract. The ephors

65 GA I / 3: 441; FNR: 142.
66 GA I / 3: 441; FNR: 142f.

cannot, therefore, overrule the judgements made by the government or issue a verdict in any particular case. They can and should, however, suspend all exercise of public power by means of what Fichte calls the state interdict (*das Staatsinterdikt*) if they become convinced that the executive power is not being administered properly, and summon the populace to constitute itself as a whole, that is to say, as the people (*das Volk*). A people's tribunal must then take place. At this tribunal the assembled people must consider the evidence presented to it both by the ephors and the members of the government concerning the claim that the executive power is not being administered properly and decide which party is in the right, with the losing party being judged to be guilty of high treason.

The process by means of which the people constitutes itself as a whole and makes its decision known remains obscure. Fichte restricts himself to stating that although in small states, particularly republican ones, constitutional law could prescribe that the people assemble on a regular basis at specified times so that the magistrates can give them an account of how the state is being administered, in a large state this arrangement might not be feasible, and the populace should therefore be convened only when it is absolutely necessary. He also suggests that rather than the whole populace gathering together in a single place, an investigation and discussion of the issues raised in connection with the state interdict issued by the ephors can be conducted and voted upon in every city and village of the commonwealth. Fichte's theory of the ephorate nevertheless introduces the possibility of a genuine expression of popular sovereignty and an explicitly democratic element that are otherwise lacking in his theory of the constitution of the state, in which he relegates the issue as to whether, and to what extent, the populace must elect its representatives to the realm of politics rather than philosophy, by arguing that the question as to which governmental constitution is best suited for a particular state depends on 'which constitutional form will enable the ephorate to function most strongly'.[67] Indeed, although Fichte argues for the need for representation on the grounds of the inherent injustice and dangers of direct democracy, he ends up introducing what looks very much like a direct form of democracy, when he claims that the people as a whole must decide whether the claims of the ephorate or those of the members of the executive power are justified. Moreover, in

67 GA I / 3: 442; FNR: 144.

order for this arrangement to work, the people need to be in the position to ensure that their will is recognized; and Fichte claims that the solution to this problem consists in meeting the following requirement: 'the power of the people must exceed beyond all measure the power that the executive officials possess'.[68] In other words, the government ought not to have the monopoly of the legitimate use of coercion. Rather, the people must have more coercive means at its disposal than the government has.

As far as the concept of virtue is concerned, Fichte's theory of the ephorate's function in relation to the executive power provides a clear answer to the question that Robespierre posed regarding the topic of political morality to the National Convention on 5 February 1794: the question as to what will repress the body that represents the people if not this body's own virtue?[69] For it is evident that, in Fichte's view, the representative body's own virtue will not be sufficient in this regard, and that an extra safeguard is therefore needed, which is provided by the institution of the ephorate. Yet Fichte can be accused of simply reintroducing the same problem at a different level, since one might ask what guarantee there is that the members of the ephorate will fulfil their function within the state in the appropriate manner. Fichte's discussion of this issue in fact implies his recognition of the importance of the type of virtue of which Robespierre speaks in the same speech on political morality, in which he claims that *la vertu publique* is the fundamental principle of democratic or popular government, while characterizing this type of virtue as love of the *patrie* and its laws, a love that assumes the primacy of the public interest over all particular interests.[70] Robespierre consequently also speaks of substituting morality for egoism.[71] This demand appears difficult to relate to Fichte's theory of right, whose basis is located in a 'universal egoism', so that private interest, rather than the public interest, appears to be the only end of the citizens of the state. I now intend to show, however, that Fichte himself suggests that some individuals at least will need to possess the type of virtue which Robespierre has in mind if a condition of

68 GA I / 3: 453; FNR: 156.
69 Robespierre, 'Sur les principes de morale politique que doivent guider la Convention nationale dans l'administration intérieure de la République', in *Œuvres de Maximilien Robespierre*, vol. x, 356.
70 Robespierre, 'Sur les principes de morale politique', 353.
71 Robespierre, 'Sur les principes de morale politique', 352.

right is to be sustained and even if such a condition is to be introduced in the first place.

The type of virtue in question must be thought of as a social or political form of virtue that is exercised in rather extraordinary circumstances. It can nevertheless be viewed as a heightened form of the kind of virtue demanded by the duties that arise from an individual's membership of a certain profession within society that we find in Fichte's theory of ethical duties, because it concerns a person's specific role within society. As such, it lies somewhere between the type of virtue that Hegel terms rectitude and the type of virtue that the ancients ascribed to a heroic figure like Hercules. It is a type of virtue which is based on the demand to fulfil one's social or political roles conscientiously and with a view to the common interests of all the members of society, rather than in a merely self-serving manner. This will require refusing to be swayed by one's own particular interests or those of others, when one knows them to be incompatible with the common interest. Yet that which is required of any individual will depend on the particular circumstances, so that it is not possible to specify in what exactly the exercise of such virtue consists. Fichte manages, however, to provide us with some examples of what the exercise of this form of virtue might involve, when he identifies certain individuals who will need to possess and exhibit virtue if the people's rights are to be guaranteed, which is, after all, the ultimate aim of right.

The political significance of the concept of virtue in Fichte's theory of right is already apparent from his account of the ephorate, whose members will need to possess and exhibit a genuine concern for the interests of the populace as a whole in the face of the particular interests that may lead the executive power to want to oppress the people. In introducing the need for virtue in relation to the effective functioning of the political constitution of the state, Fichte ends up appealing to the necessity of something which he thinks modern individuals cannot be assumed to possess. In this respect, a measure such as a separation of powers might well be held to be desirable, on the grounds that it would help prevent power from being concentrated in the hands of a few people. In failing to consider such alternatives, Fichte appears to rely heavily on the possession and exercise of virtue by at least some people within the state. The infinite regress to which his account as to how a descent into despotism is to be prevented gives rise, and which he is able to end only by means of an abrupt appeal to the authority of the people, can be used to illustrate this point.

This infinite regress arises because Fichte concedes that the members of the ephorate may themselves lack virtue, when he introduces a worst case scenario, in which a people has become so corrupt that those individuals who are universally recognized as the best among the people, and are thus held to be eminently suited to holding the office of ephor, become corrupt immediately upon taking office and join sides with the executive in order to oppress the people.[72] This possibility leads Fichte to introduce the idea of a right of rebellion, even though rebellion would be unnecessary and a violation of right in cases when the ephorate had not become corrupt and continued to perform properly its function of ensuring that the populace are not being oppressed.

Fichte begins his discussion of the right of rebellion by considering an act of rebellion on the part of one or more private persons, who call the populace together and encourage them to oppose the common will that the executive power claims to represent. Although Fichte thinks that the individuals who instigate such an act of rebellion are to be termed rebels, whereas the people as whole, as the highest power accountable only to God, can never be accused of rebellion, he does allow that these rebels, having incited the populace to constitute itself as the people, may then be judged by the people to have made a legitimate call to rise up against the executive power, with the result that the will of these private persons is confirmed as the true common will. In such cases, the individuals in question are to be regarded as 'the nation's saviors [*Erhalter der Nation*], and its unadorned, natural ephors', on account of 'their heart and virtue [*ihr Herz, und ihre Tugend*]'.[73] In other words, these individuals turn out both to be the true interpreters of the common will and to perform the function which the institution of the ephorate should have performed but failed to do so because of its members' lack of virtue.

This implies that, for Fichte, there is the need in any rightfully constituted state for certain virtuous individuals, whose actions are determined by the idea of the public good, rather than by private interest, and who seek to ensure that this public good prevails. At the same time, in line with Fichte's identification of the kind of disposition whose existence his theory of right must assume, this recognition of the need for virtue does not rule out the possibility that the grounds on which the populace come to decide whether certain individuals are in

---

72 GA I / 3: 456; FNR: 159.
73 GA I / 3: 457; FNR: 161.

fact justified in acting in opposition to the executive power will be based on self-interest alone. Indeed, Fichte himself firmly indicates such a possibility when he states that, 'for so long as the insecurity and the poor administration of the state do not oppress them *all* and do not become universally harmful, every individual will look out only for himself and try to get by as best he can'.[74] He thus suggests that the people will decide in favour of the rebels only when they judge it to be in their own best interests to do so, because the current situation has become intolerable for them as well as for others. Fichte therefore appears to mean by the people in this particular case a group of egoistic individuals who do not care if others are being oppressed as long as the situation has not become unbearable for them personally. Such a scenario makes it difficult to explain why anyone should want to take the considerable risks involved in seeking to assert the rights of the people and to defend the idea of the public good. Yet Fichte's position here is compatible with what he has to say elsewhere, since, as we have seen, acting morally for him requires doing the right thing simply because it is the right thing to do, irrespective of its consequences in relation to oneself.

Fichte gives another explanation as to why the people as a whole may fail to rise up against the executive power when incited to do so, in addition to the idea that they have not all come to find the situation unbearable. This failure concerns the possibility that the people

> have not yet awakened to will their freedom and to know their rights; that they are not yet mature enough to take up the great legal task [*Rechtshandel*] assigned to them; and therefore, that they never should have been incited to rise up in the first place.[75]

Thus, in the event that their act of rebellion should ultimately prove unsuccessful, the individuals who incited the people to constitute itself as a whole and to rise up against the executive power can be considered to have been at fault for not having recognized the people's immaturity. Yet they can still be regarded as 'martyrs of right' (*Märtyrer des Rechts*) according to their own consciences.[76] In other words, when they are viewed from the standpoint of morality, these individuals' actions can be regarded as justified, whereas from the standpoint of right, given these actions' lack of effectiveness in the sensible world,

74 GA I / 3: 457; FNR: 160.
75 GA I / 3: 458; FNR: 161.
76 GA I / 3: 458; FNR: 161.

they are not. In what follows, I show that this understanding of why the people as a whole may fail to rise up against the executive power can be related to Fichte's account of the duties of the state official, which clearly suggests the idea of a type of virtue that has much in common with *la vertu publique* of which Robespierre speaks in his speech on political morality. This will in turn provide another example of the way in which the sphere of right and the sphere of morality may come into contract with each other, with the latter serving to bring about and sustain the former.

Fichte identifies the state official as one of the higher officials of the state who participate in legislation and whose decisions cannot be appealed against. The state official is, in short, a member of the executive power, and, as such, he is considered by Fichte to be nothing more than an administrator of the common will. Since the constitution is the definitive expression of this common will, the state official does not have the right to change it. This invites the question as to what the state official is to do when the positive rule (i.e. that which is stated in the constitution) conflicts with that which reason demands, thus putting him in the position of having to administer measures that he himself considers to be unjust. Fichte argues that in such cases it is the state official's duty to act in accordance with the existing constitution, even though, according to his own conscience, it does not measure up to the purely rational constitution of which he himself has knowledge. Fichte's main reason for making this claim is that society itself and the end towards which it serves as the means, that is, the progressive establishment of a community of rational beings, can exist only if there is a constitution which has been established through the consent of everyone.[77]

It may seem that Fichte in this way reduces the duties of the state official to ones that consist in the simple acceptance of, and obedience to, the existing constitution, irrespective of its actual nature, just as long as it has been consented to. A given constitution might not, for example, unlike the 'Jacobin' constitution of 1793, contain an article asserting the right of existence; whereas Fichte's assertion of the right to be able to live from one's labour as the most basic of all rights indicates that such a constitution must be judged to deviate from the ideal, purely rational one of which the state official, according to

Fichte, ought to be aware.[78] The public official would nevertheless still have to administer this defective constitution, even though it does not guarantee that which is, from the standpoint of reason, the most basic of all rights. The exercise of virtue thus appears to be reduced to the conscientious administration of the constitution of an existing state, irrespective of its actual nature and even when it happens to conflict with the ends of reason. It might be said in Fichte's defence that the way in which he limits the role of the state official to that of an administrator of the existing constitution to which the populace have given their consent may help protect people against any arbitrary acts on the part of the executive power. A closer look at Fichte's account of the role of the state official, however, reveals more scope for the exercise of virtue than Fichte himself at first appears to allow.

To begin with, the fact that for Fichte the members of the executive power are to be entrusted with the task of formulating particular laws ties up with the following role that he assigns to the state official:

> The administrator of the executive power is the natural interpreter of the common will concerning the relationship of individuals to one another within the state; he is the interpreter, not exactly of the will that the individuals actually have, but rather of the will that they must have if they are to exist alongside one another; and this is so, even if not a single person should, in fact, have such a will (as one might well assume to be the case from time to time).[79]

The claim that the common will, which the administrator of the executive power needs to interpret, is one that individuals must themselves have if they are to exist alongside one another, even though these same individuals may not, in fact, have such a will at any given time, can be understood in either a strong or a weak sense. In the weak sense, the claim can be understood to express the idea that the common will would be one that finds expression in any constitution whatsoever which meets the minimum condition of allowing human beings to coexist peacefully, although it may be unjust in other respects. Whereas when it is understood in a strong sense, the claim in question can be seen to express the idea that the common will would be one that could only properly endorse the condition of right presented in Fichte's *Foundations of Natural Right* and then developed with respect to its economic implications in *The Closed Commercial State*. In this case, a

---

78 GA I / 5: 310f.; SE: 337.
79 GA I / 3: 328; FNR: 16.

state's constitution would have to guarantee, above all else, the right of persons to be able to live from their labour, if it is to be classed as a truly legitimate one.

Fichte's account of the duties of the state official suggests that the state official can have knowledge of the common will in the stronger sense while governing in accordance with the common will in the weaker sense with a good conscience. Fichte nevertheless imposes one definite restriction on the kind of constitution which can be held to be a rightful one in the weaker sense of the term, when he claims that the only constitution that is utterly contrary to right is one that aims to preserve everything as it is.[80] Each constitution ought, in other words, to be modifiable, so as to be able to approach the ideal, purely rational constitution. Given this restriction on the kind of constitution which can be considered to be a rightful one even in the weak sense of the term, together with the fact that Fichte views the task of supporting enlightenment as being a matter of conscience (*Gewissenssache*) for someone entrusted with executive power,[81] it could be argued that the state official ought to do all that lies in his power to make the existing constitution conform to the ideal, purely rational one, even though his capacity to do so will be limited by the existing constitution, of which he is the administrator. In his legislative role the state official ought, for example, to formulate and implement enlightened laws that do not, however, directly conflict with the existing constitution. For by living under such laws, the populace may themselves become more enlightened and hence more aware of the inadequacy of the constitution to which they have consented, and which may then be replaced with a better, more rational one. Fichte in fact considers it to be a duty to change a constitution which does not measure up to the standards of a truly rightful, rational one, as soon as the concept of the latter is available and a nation is capable of realizing this concept.[82] Although Fichte does not mention such a duty on the part of the state official in particular, he clearly needs to admit the possibility of such a duty if he is to explain how it is possible for the state official to fulfil his duty of supporting enlightenment.

Fichte also makes the following claim with respect to the existing laws:

80 GA I / 5: 314; SE: 341.
81 GA I / 5: 313; SE: 340.
82 GA I / 3: 459; FNR: 162.

if there should arise general and loud protest against a law that is in itself unjust, and which could be [considered] just only under the presupposition of consent, it is then the governor's absolute duty to renounce this law, no matter how loudly those who profit from the injustice in question might complain about a violation of the contract.[83]

In such a case, the state official would be justified in changing a law not only because he himself knows it to be unjust, but also because the law in question can no longer be held to command universal consent. If this is so, there would appear to be other opportunities for the state official to exercise a social or political form of virtue in a way that remains compatible with Fichte's theory of ethical duties and some of his scattered remarks on virtue.

To begin with, in addition to repealing laws, the state official would also be justified in introducing laws that he knows to be just and which certain sections of the populace have demanded, such as laws that aim to guarantee every person's right to be able to live from his labour, even when other sections of the populace, particularly those people who benefit from the injustices made possible by the existing constitution, view their introduction as a violation of the contract on which the state allegedly rests and as a threat to their own interests. Another possibility is that the state official introduces laws that he knows to be just, or repeals ones he knows to be unjust, and then waits to see if there is a general outcry against the steps he has taken, with the absence of such an outcry against them amounting to an act of tacit consent on the part of the people.[84] In this respect, we can again see how Fichte might have done better to conceive the civil contract in purely hypothetical terms, as Kant does when he claims that the social contract is an idea of reason which enables us to ask what laws could have issued from the united will of a whole nation. The ideal, purely rational constitution, together with the specific laws formulated by the executive power, can be then understood as stating the conditions to which all individuals living together in a single legal and political community could be reasonably expected to submit themselves, irrespective of what they themselves happen to will at any given time. The state official would need to keep this ideal constitution in mind, so as to be able to transform the existing

83 GA I / 5: 311; SE: 338.
84 Although Fichte himself speaks of such tacit consent, he recognizes that in reality an absence of protest might be the result of a lack of knowledge of their rights on the part of the disadvantaged members of society (GA I / 5: 215 and 313; SE: 226 and 340).

constitution in accordance with the ends of reason, despite any objections that might be raised against his actions by people who profit from the injustices of the existing constitution. It would be nevertheless incumbent on the state official to modify the constitution and the system of laws in a way that took account of a nation's level of development, so that the ends of reason are given a real chance of being realized in the sensible world. This is why Fichte himself acknowledges that the state official must be acquainted with the path that humanity in general, and especially his own people, must follow in order to participate in the ideal constitution.[85]

This implies that if the state official should consider conditions to be favourable enough, he might even, as a private person, incite the people to rise up against the executive power of which he is himself a member, while encouraging the people to replace the existing constitution with the ideal one of which he has knowledge. The state official would thus become one of those individuals who, through their 'heart and virtue', together with their more adequate understanding of the common will, turn out to be the nation's saviours. Alternatively, the state official might restrict himself to agitating within the executive power for certain measures to be introduced and for certain steps to be taken in order to realize the ideal constitution and the idea of a purely rational system of laws, claiming that he is a better interpreter of the common will than its other members. Fichte's account of the duties of the state official, together with his views on the right of rebellion, here suggest a direct relation between his social and political philosophy and the radical phase of the French Revolution, especially such features of the latter as the problem of factionalism and the idea of revolutionary government, whose task, according to Robespierre, requires extraordinary activity and measures guided by the public interest, so as to defend the public power against its internal, as well as its external, enemies, and to raise the people to the level of its rights and destiny.[86] Fichte appears to assume, however, that the executive power will not be subject to any internal divisions, probably because he thinks that it will simply reflect the consensus generated by means of the civil contract; while, as we have seen, he favours gradualism over revolutionary action. In this

85 GA I / 5: 311; SE: 338.
86 Robespierre, 'Rapport sur les principes du Gouvernement révolutionnaire', in Œuvres de Maximilien Robespierre, vol. x, 273ff.

respect, philosophical theory and actual history turn out to diverge considerably.

Fichte's account of the duties of the state official nevertheless suggests that the idea of virtue, which forms an essential element in republican rhetoric during the radical phase of the French Revolution, will have an important role to play in political life, despite his recognition of the fact that egoism, rather than virtue, will continue to motivate many members of society. For Fichte, it is especially the people's representatives who will need to demonstrate a political form of virtue, which involves attempting to promote the public interest in the face of opposition from private interests, by seeking to ensure that a condition of right prevails and that progress towards the ideal constitution and a purely rational system of laws can be made. It is arguably the case that the social equivalent of this type of virtue would be required, though to a lesser extent perhaps, of many other members of society, upon whose actions the effective functioning of society and the state depends.

One of the main ways in which morality is to be understood as a condition of right therefore concerns the idea that individuals will need to act from a sense of duty as well as from self-interest when it comes to performing their roles within society and the state, so as to make both right and morality effective in the sensible world. This way of acting is itself made possible by a condition of right, because right guarantees individuals the formal freedom required for them to be able to act in a morally autonomous manner. In this respect, right and morality must be thought to stand in a reciprocal relation to each other, thus suggesting a positive relation of right to morality that one might not have expected given the way in which Fichte separates them in the *Foundations of Natural Right*. This gives rise to the problem as to how moral actions can take place when one of their main conditions, which is the establishment of a constitution that accords with the principles of right, has yet to be established; and it is here that Fichte needs to introduce the idea of certain exceptional, virtuous individuals, such as the enlightened state official, who are capable of acting in a morally autonomous manner, even when the conditions of doing so are not yet fully present. The ahistorical character of Fichte's theory of right and his predominantly conceptual account of the relation of right to morality, however, prevent him from considering this problem in more detail. Had Fichte done so, the concept of virtue would possibly have come to assume a more prominent place in the theory of the state and society that he developed during his professorship at the University of Jena.

The conception of the relation of right to morality outlined above might appear to run counter to Fichte's claim that acting in accordance with duty means acting from a sense of duty alone and not in any way from inclination. It is not immediately obvious that this view of duty can be reconciled with his account of the ethical duties deriving from one's profession, because the people whose duty is to sustain a condition of right will be typically also seeking to guarantee for themselves the possibility of acting effectively in the sensible world, which includes their own self-preservation as its most fundamental condition. Perhaps, then, it is better to say that individuals have both an incentive and a duty to sustain a condition of right. This explanation has the advantage both of allowing that right and morality stand in an essential relation to each other and of being compatible with some of the claims that Fichte makes concerning the relation of nonmoral incentives to the moral law, which indicate that he has in mind a form of willing in which nonmoral incentives are subordinated to moral ones, rather than an acting from moral incentives alone. For example, when discussing the drive for happiness, which he describes as being based on 'the natural drive', Fichte claims that the moral law demands that I entirely subordinate (*unterordne*) the natural drive to a 'higher impulse'.[87] This could be interpreted as meaning that the drive for happiness can be allowed to motivate actions, but only insofar as this drive is in harmony with the moral law. In this respect, the inclination to promote the existence of a condition of right, which can be held to stem from a concern with one's own welfare, and is therefore linked to the natural drive for happiness, and the moral duty to do the same thing, need not be viewed as mutually exclusive. This compatibility between self-interest and virtue represents a fairly moderate position, which combines a concern for private rights, particularly the right to be able to live from one's labour, with a concern for the common good. As I argue in the next chapter, this moderate position is preferable to the idea of acting from a sense of duty alone, as becomes evident when we turn to Fichte's attempt in the *Addresses to the German Nation* to explain the possibility of a form of virtue that does appear to consist in acting from a sense of duty alone.

It also needs to be stressed, however, that, in line with Fichte's separation of right from morality, the reciprocal relation of right to morality outlined above must be regarded as an ultimately contingent

87 GA I / 5: 277; SE: 299.

one. This is because it is conceivable that a given state, in which relations of right existed between human beings, could sustain itself even though it is based entirely on self-interest, that is, on the type of reasoning that we encounter in Fichte's attempt in the *Foundations of Natural Right* to explain the separation of right from morality in terms of what motivates persons to act. This type of condition would be one in which legal, social and political relations are determined solely by the ends of securing one's own self-preservation and pursuing one's own personal aims. The desirability of living in a state in which moral qualities such as a sense of commitment and responsibility with respect to one's social roles, together with a concern for the common good, are entirely lacking may be denied. Yet this is not to say that such a state could not maintain itself on the basis of the purely self-interested actions of its members.

Fichte's separation of right from morality, when taken in conjunction with his theory of the ethical duties deriving from a person's profession, thus presents us with a conception of society and the state consisting of two opposing poles, each with their corresponding dispositions. The first pole is that of a state based on 'universal egoism' alone, while the second pole involves the idea of the establishment of a fully ethical community, in which the moral dispositions of its members means that right becomes no longer necessary, so that the state 'falls away as a *legislative and coercive power*'.[88] I have suggested that when the *Foundations of Natural Right* and *The System of Ethics* are read in the light of each other, Fichte's ideal state might be thought to lie somewhere between these two poles, since it involves a conception of society in which ethical virtue plays an important role in making a condition of right function effectively and in giving society the possibility to flourish, while the condition of right in turn enables individuals to act autonomously in the world, by guaranteeing such individual rights as the right to be able to live from one's labour. This conception of society and the state is, moreover, one in which individuals are held to be of equal value insofar as they each play a role in sustaining and promoting the social and political whole of which they are members. They are therefore able to think of themselves as being engaged in a common project. This conception of society and the state appears to overcome a particular problem with Fichte's theory of right.

88 GA I / 5: 227; SE: 241.

The problem in question is that of the alienation of one human being from another human being with respect to their productive activity. This problem stems from the way in which right establishes fixed boundaries between one person's property and another person's property, that is, between one person's activity within society and the products of this activity and another person's activity within society and its products.[89] In the light of what has been said above, we can imagine two possible scenarios: one in which people perform the actions demanded by the profession to which they belong purely in accordance with the end of being able to secure the means to live, with only contractual relations existing between individuals, and one in which people perform these same actions also in accordance with a sense of duty towards the other members of the profession to which they belong and towards society as a whole. While the first scenario represents the kind of alienation described above, the second scenario represents the possible overcoming of this alienation. Admittedly, we here face the problem that Fichte's world of farmers, artisans, merchants, high-ranking state officials, clerics and philosophers presents us with a traditional view of society that understands the relation in which the various classes of people stand to each other and to society as a whole in organic terms, with each member helping to sustain the whole of which the he is a part. Such an understanding of society is evident from the following passage from *The System of Ethics*: 'The higher classes constitute the mind [*der Geist*] of the single large whole of humanity; the lower classes constitute its limbs; the former are the thinking and designing part, the latter the executive part'.[90] Although one may well

89 Cf. Verweyen, *Recht und Sittlichkeit in J. G. Fichtes Gesellschaftslehre*, 123.
90 GA I / 5: 316; SE: 344. Fichte in fact sees right as paving the way for morality also in the sense that by uniting individuals, though only by means of the bonds of self-interest, the state constitutes a form of community that serves as a provisional step towards the fuller form of community that morality aims to bring about. As Fichte himself expresses this idea: 'Thus in the state, nature re-unites what she had previously separated when she produced several individuals ... Humanity was divided into several independent members; the natural institution of the state already cancels this independence provisionally and molds individual groups into a whole, until morality [*Sittlichkeit*] re-creates the entire species as one' (GA I / 4: 14; FNR: 176). He then goes on to compare the state to an organized product of nature, by which he means one that must be understood in teleological rather than mechanical terms, in the sense of exhibiting an internal purposiveness, with its parts serving to produce the whole, which is itself the end for which its various members are united. Whether Fichte is justified in describing the state in organic terms in this section of the *Foundations of Natural Right* is another matter, however, since such a description appears to conflict with the individualistic premises of

doubt the extent to which this model of society can be realized given the historical changes that led to the dissolution of an organic model of society based on a division of people into particular estates, such as the increased mechanization of labour, this does not by itself mean that the conceptual links between right and morality that we find developed in Fichte's social and political philosophy from his Jena period are not valid ones.

We should not, however, view such conceptual links between right and morality, which are of a contingent nature insofar as their application to the conditions of the sensible world is concerned, as inviting the complete moralization of right. By identifying certain fundamental differences between right and morality, while also indicating some important links between them, Fichte succeeds in presenting us with a range of scenarios, beginning with the amoral 'state of necessity' and ending with a utopian vision of the abolition of the state. Between these two poles we have a conception of society and the state in which right and morality are brought into relative harmony with each other, thereby making possible a more flourishing form of human society, whose possibility a purely amoral conception of the state is arguably unable to explain. This range of scenarios depends on the separation of right from morality, as well as on the idea that they can be nevertheless understood to stand in a reciprocal relation to each other. Fichte's separation of right from morality thus remains valid insofar as it helps make us aware of the possibility of these different scenarios and the ways in which they are linked to a certain type of disposition, so that Fichte manages to shift attention to the subjective dimension of an individual's relation to the social and political world to which he belongs. The insights contained in this aspect of Fichte's account of the relation of right to morality would be obscured if one were to seek to reduce right and morality to a common foundation, and in such a way, moreover, as to elide the differences between them that Fichte identifies.

In his *Addresses to the German Nation*, Fichte came, by contrast, to develop an account as to how a fully ethical community might be produced, so as to overcome the amoral conception of the state developed in his *Foundations of Natural Right*. In the *Addresses to the German Nation*, Fichte also attempts to realize his ideas concerning the role of

his contract theory of the state. Cf. Verweyen, *Recht und Sittlichkeit in J. G. Fichtes Gesellschaftslehre*, 112f. We can, perhaps, be said to encounter here a certain tension between the more modern and the more traditional aspects of Fichte's social and political philosophy.

the scholar in society, which has already been alluded to in connection with his theory of ethical duties. In this respect, the *Addresses to the German Nation* does not represent a complete break with some of the central concerns that Fichte sought to deal with during his Jena period, but, rather, an attempt, in different historical circumstances, to develop some of his earlier ideas. To this extent, the interpretation and discussion of Fichte's Jena theory of the state and society given in this chapter and the previous ones opens the way for a better understanding of the *Addresses to the German Nation* with regard to the two following interconnected issues: the moral vocation of the scholar, which itself serves as an example of what it means in Fichte's view to fulfil the social duties connected with membership of a certain profession, and the problem as to how a fully ethical community might be brought into existence.

By showing how Fichte attempts to deal with these issues in the *Addresses to the German Nation*, I demonstrate that the role he accords to the scholar in society and the means of producing a distinctly moral form of community that he identifies both turn out to be highly problematic, and that the position Fichte developed during his Jena period, with its separation of right from morality, is accordingly to be preferred. From an historical perspective, the problematic nature of any appeal to the idea of a fully ethical community should not surprise us, perhaps, since the moralization of politics, in which the language of virtue played an essential part, can be identified as one of the main factors leading to the French Revolution's descent into state-sponsored terrorism.[91] Fichte's attempt to explain the complete moralization of society and, by implication, of the sphere of politics, will be likewise shown to contain its own tensions and to imply certain undesirable

---

91 Cf. Higonnet, *Goodness beyond Virtue*, 127ff. and 240ff. As far as the relation of the language of virtue to the period of the French Revolution known as the Terror is concerned, some Jacobins were happy to acknowledge the necessity of a relation between virtue and terror under certain circumstances, as is evident from Robespierre's claim that, 'If the mainspring of popular government in time of peace is virtue, the mainspring of popular government in revolution is at once virtue and terror: virtue, without which terror is fatal; terror, without which virtue is powerless'. Robespierre, 'Sur les principes de morale politique', 357. By mentioning here the way in which the language of virtue possibly played a significant role in the French Revolution's descent into state-sponsored terrorism, I do not mean to suggest that Fichte's own use of the language of virtue in the *Addresses to the German Nation* might have aimed at, let alone led to, the emergence of state-sponsored terrorism. We shall see, however, that something Fichte has to say concerning love of fatherland contains intimations of extreme violence, since it implies a valorization of war.

consequences. Although these tensions and consequences are ones that play themselves out at the level of philosophical theory, the historical circumstances in which the *Addresses to the German Nation* were delivered, and the conception of the scholar's moral vocation that Fichte believed himself to be realizing when delivering them, suggest that it was his intention that they should also play themselves out at the level of actual politics.

5

THE ROLE OF VIRTUE IN THE
ADDRESSES TO THE GERMAN NATION

Given its status as a foundational text in nationalist political thought, the main emphasis in discussions of Fichte's *Addresses to the German Nation* has not surprisingly tended to be on the issue of the kind of nationalism that is to be found in this text, particularly the question as to whether it contains an ethnic nationalism, based on descent, or a cultural nationalism, which defines nationality in terms of linguistic and cultural differences, or a mixture of both these forms of nationalism.[1] Although the *Addresses to the German Nation* clearly does constitute an attempt on Fichte's part to shape a German national identity, in what follows I focus on the question of the relation of this attempt to shape a German national identity to Fichte's ideas concerning the moral vocation (*Bestimmung*) of the scholar (*der Gelehrte*) in society, and on the means that Fichte employs to achieve the end of shaping a German national identity. By so doing, I draw attention to at least two elements of continuity that must be thought to exist between the period of Fichte's professorship at the University of Jena and his *Addresses to the German Nation*, which were delivered and then published in the period 1807–08, in the wake of Napoleon's defeat and subjugation of Prussia, while Fichte was in Berlin without an academic position, having moved there in 1799 after losing his professorship at Jena in the wake of the Atheism Controversy. These two elements

---

1 For a discussion of these issues, which argues that the last mixed form of nationalism is to be found in the *Addresses to the German Nation*, see Abizadeh, 'Was Fichte an Ethnic Nationalist? On Cultural Nationalism and its Double'. For an older account of Fichte's nationalism, which stresses the differences between it and his earlier views, whereas I point to the existence of some significant elements of continuity, see Kohn, 'The Paradox of Fichte's Nationalism'.

of continuity are as follows: the important role that Fichte assigns to the scholar in society, which we have already touched upon in relation to his theory of ethical duties; and the need for a social or political form of virtue of the kind discussed in the previous chapter; a need which here takes on a particular urgency, because of the humiliating and precarious situation of the German nation in the face of French hegemony. In the *Addresses to the German Nation,* Fichte no longer defines a state's natural frontiers in terms of its need to become self-sufficient, as in *The Closed Commercial State.* He instead defines them in linguistic terms, claiming that

> the first, original and truly natural frontiers of states are undoubtedly their inner frontiers. Those who speak the same language are already, before all human art, joined together by mere nature with a multitude of invisible ties ... they belong together and are naturally one, an indivisible whole.[2]

We shall later see how exactly Fichte defines the German nation in terms of a shared language; while Fichte's identification of state and nation, together with his definition of a state's natural frontiers in terms of a shared language, will be shown to prepare the way for a complete moralization of politics,[3] which contrasts with his earlier separation of the legal and political sphere of right from the sphere of ethics.

As regards the issue of the vocation of the scholar, among philosophers Fichte developed what is arguably one of the most self-conscious accounts of the role of the intellectual in society. Already in 1794, shortly after having taken up his first academic appointment as a professor at the University of Jena, he gave a series of lectures that were later published under the title *Some Lectures concerning the Scholar's Vocation (Einige Vorlesungen über die Bestimmung des Gelehrten).* In these lectures, Fichte sets out his own understanding of the significance

---

2 GA I / 10: 267; AGN: 166.
3 I do not mean by the 'moralization of politics' the type of 'we' versus 'they' mentality and the tendency to express this opposition in such moral terms as those between 'good' and 'evil' that has been said to characterize the attitude of traditional European political parties, with their emphasis on the idea of a post-political liberal democratic consensus, to the rise of right-wing populism. Cf. Mouffe, *On the Political,* 72ff. For this tendency to formulate political antagonisms in moral terms does not mean that politics has itself become more moral, whereas, as we shall see, Fichte's moralization of politics is about making politics more moral, in the sense of producing virtuous citizens who act always in the interests of the social and political whole to which they belong.

and social function of his scholarly activity as well as that of the scholar in general. I compare Fichte's conception of the scholar's vocation as developed in these lectures to the role that he assumes for himself in the *Addresses to the German Nation*. I suggest that the *Addresses to the German Nation* represents an attempt on Fichte's part to intervene in history in a way that accords with, and thus realizes, the conception of the scholar's vocation that he had already developed in his Jena lectures on this topic. In this way, the *Addresses to the German Nation* turns out to provide an example of how a member of society belonging to a particular estate and profession, namely, the scholar, exhibits the social form of virtue that Fichte himself identifies in his theory of ethical duties in *The System of Ethics*. This attempted intervention in the course of human history will be shown, however, to raise questions concerning Fichte's account of the role that the scholar's knowledge of history plays in relation to the task of fulfilling his moral vocation. Fichte will, in fact, be shown to use history in a way that might be considered to be immoral, despite his insistence on the moral nature of the scholar's vocation. This point will be illustrated by comparing Fichte's use of history in the *Addresses to the German Nation* to Nietzsche's claim that history should be made to serve the needs of life and action, together with his account of how a 'monumental' form of history can be made to serve this end.

While Fichte's use of history in the *Addresses to the German Nation* can be seen to constitute an instrumentalization of history, I go on to look at the immediate end which Fichte hopes to realize by employing history simply as the means to an end, which is the introduction of a German national education (*deutsche National-Erziehung*). This system of education aims to produce citizens who exhibit the social form of virtue which can be detected in Fichte's Jena theory of ethical duties, and its ultimate aim can therefore be characterized as that of producing a genuine ethical community. Although Fichte is thus able to offer an explanation of the possibility of the kind of moral community that is difficult to explain in terms of his theory of right, which has accordingly been criticized for its failure to develop the implications of the notions of intersubjectivity and mutual recognition that feature in his deduction of the concept of right, I argue that the way in which Fichte develops the idea of such a community suggests that a genuine ethical community is not necessarily something to be welcomed, insofar as its realization in the sensible world is concerned.

Fichte on the vocation of the scholar

Fichte begins the first of the lectures he gave in Jena on the topic of the vocation of the scholar by stressing the social nature of this vocation. He does this by pointing to the fact that when one speaks of the scholar, one does so in contradistinction to other human beings engaged in different activities within society. The scholar's vocation is consequently said to be one that is conceivable only within society.[4] The scholar is not simply a member (*Mitglied*) of society, however; he is also the member of a particular estate (*ein Glied eines besonderen Standes*) within society, the estate of scholars.[5] For the scholar dedicates himself to performing a particular function within society, in contradistinction to other functions whose ultimate end is also to bring about the ennoblement of humankind by means of the advance of culture with respect to all human beings. Fichte accords the scholar pride of place in this process, describing the vocation of the estate of scholars as 'the *supreme supervision of the actual progress of the human race in general and the unceasing promotion of this progress*'.[6] Fichte also gives expression to the sense of common identity and purpose that comes from being a member of the estate of scholars, while identifying truth as the main object of the scholar's activity, at the beginning of the fourth lecture, which deals specifically with the scholar's vocation in society, when he addresses his students at the University of Jena as follows:

> I am thus supposed to speak as a scholar before prospective scholars on the subject of the scholar's vocation. I am supposed to examine this subject thoroughly and, if possible, exhaustively – omitting nothing from my presentation of the truth [*Wahrheit*].[7]

Since Fichte identifies the concept of truth as the primary object of the scholar's activity, so that the scholar's role in advancing human culture is very much linked to this concept, he accordingly describes himself later in the same lecture in the following way:

> I am a priest of truth [*ein Priester der Wahrheit*]. I am in its pay, and thus I have committed myself to do, to risk, and to suffer anything for its sake.

4 GA I / 3: 27; EPW: 146.
5 GA I / 3: 42; EPW: 161.
6 GA I / 3: 54; EPW: 172.
7 GA I / 3: 50; EPW: 169. Translation modified.

If I should be pursued and hated for the truth's sake, if I should die in
its service, what more would I have done than what I simply had to do?[8]

While the passionate terms in which Fichte describes his own vocation
as a scholar are suggestive of the idea of martyrdom and the fate of
a religious teacher such as Jesus, he also implies that it is the duty of
the scholar to adopt a dispassionate, objective approach to the discovery of truth, when he states that the object of his lectures needs to be
investigated coldly, as if it had no relation to himself and his audience,
like a concept from a completely alien world.[9] How, then, does the
scholar serve the cause of truth and human progress by means of an
objective mode of inquiry?

To begin with, the scholar must develop his own predisposition
(*Anlage*) to achieve complete knowledge of the whole human being,
that is to say, knowledge of what human beings essentially are. The
scholar must also strive to produce a science (*Wissenschaft*) of the
means to develop human predispositions and satisfy human needs.
While the first type of knowledge is based on principles given by pure
reason, the second form of knowledge, which relates to the more prag-
matic task of discovering the means of developing human capacities
and satisfying human needs, is partly based on experience, making it
into a historico-philosophical form of knowledge. The historical element derives from the fact that, in order to apply his knowledge of
what human beings essentially are, which requires knowing the path
they must travel so as to develop and realize their capacities, the scholar
must know at what level of culture the society of which he is himself a
member currently stands. For only in this way is he able to put himself
in the position of knowing what is the next level of culture to which this
society can progress and how it should do so. Whereas with regard to
the stages of human culture themselves, Fichte makes the implausible
claim that it is possible to estimate the movement of the human race
and identify the individual stages that it must traverse on the basis of
rational grounds alone, that is, under the presupposition of an experience in general but independently of any particular experiences. In
addition to knowledge that derives from purely rational principles, the
scholar is consequently required to possess a form of knowledge that is
'merely historical' (*blos historisch*). This, in turn, demands both an investigation of the events of the past, though from a viewpoint that has

8 GA I / 3: 58; EPW: 176.
9 GA I / 3: 51; EPW: 169.

been clarified by means of philosophy, and observation of the scholar's contemporaries.[10]

The scholar's possession of all the forms of knowledge mentioned above is thus understood to enable him to advance human culture by showing his society how it can progress from the stage at which it currently stands to the next stage in humanity's historical task of perfecting itself. Given the scholar's function in society, it can also be said that it is the scholar's duty to acquire all these forms of knowledge. Fichte himself claims that the scholar has the particular duty to develop within himself to the highest possible degree the two main social talents of receptivity (*Empfänglichkeit*) and the art of communication (*Mittheilungsfertigkeit*).[11] In the case of the scholar, the former talent requires his becoming acquainted with all the previous knowledge in his field, and it will include acquiring sufficient empirical knowledge of the kind mentioned above; while the latter talent requires being able to communicate his knowledge and discoveries, which is something the scholar must do if he is to be of benefit to society by helping to promote the advance of human culture. At the end of his fourth lecture on the vocation of the scholar, Fichte suggests that he is himself seeking to fulfil this last duty in these lectures, when he makes clear the practical intent that lies behind them, and, specifically, his wish to develop a certain kind of disposition in the members of his audience:

> I frankly admit that I would like to use this position in which providence has placed me in order to disseminate a more manly way of thinking, a stronger sense of elevation and dignity, and a more intense desire to fulfil one's vocation despite every danger. I would like to broadcast this in every direction, as far as the German language extends [*soweit die deutsche Sprache reicht*] and even further if I could.[12]

In this passage, Fichte clearly ties the possibility of his lectures having any practical effect to the German language, the language in which he addresses his audience. He does the same thing in the later *Addresses to the German Nation*, when he states that these addresses are aimed not only at his immediate audience but also, in the hope that the members of the latter will spread the message contained in them to all who might be capable of understanding this message 'as far as the German

---

10 GA I / 3: 53; EPW: 171f.
11 GA I / 3: 55; EPW: 173.
12 GA I / 3: 59; EPW: 176f.

tongue extends [*so weit die deutsche Zunge reicht*]'.[13] Fichte's conscious
acceptance of the fact that the practical intent that informs his
scholarly activity is, with respect to the possibility of its having any
effect in the wider world, dependent on the medium through which
its results are communicated to the public, already suggests some
continuity between his Jena lectures on the scholar's vocation and
the later *Addresses to the German Nation*. I show below that these
addresses in other ways constitute an attempt on Fichte's part to
realize his conception of the scholar's vocation, as developed in his
earlier lectures on this topic. This will in turn raise questions concerning the precise nature of the notion of 'truth' with which Fichte
operates in the *Addresses to the German Nation*, insofar as it relates to
the 'merely' historical form of knowledge which he thinks the scholar
ought to possess in order to be able to fulfil his social duty of advancing human culture.

Fichte's (mis)use of history

As Fichte makes clear at the beginning of his First Address, the *Addresses
to the German Nation* represents a continuation of the series of lectures
that he gave in the winter of 1804–05 at the same venue, the Berlin
Academy of Sciences, and to which he gave the title *The Characteristics
of the Present Age* (*Die Grundzüge des gegenwärtigen Zeitalters*). In these
lectures, Fichte develops a speculative theory of history characterized
by a 'world plan' (*Weltplan*) from which it is possible to deduce all the
main epochs of human life on earth, with each epoch being governed
by its own distinctive principle.[14] The epochs in question are: (1) the
state of innocence of the human race, in which reason is at work but
only in the form of instinct; (2) the state of progressive sin, in which
reason has been transformed into an external ruling authority, as, for
example, in the form of the doctrines and institutions of the Christian
Church; (3) the state of completed sinfulness, in which human beings
have liberated themselves from any external authority, and which, as a
single epoch, can be identified with the Enlightenment and its consequences; (4) the state of progressive justification, in which truth
comes to be regarded as the highest of all things; and, finally, (5) the
state of completed justification and sanctification, in which humanity,

13 GA I / 10: 285; AGN: 183.
14 GA I / 8: 197; CPA: 4.

by its own efforts, forms itself into an adequate and fitting image of reason (*sich selber zum getroffenen Abdrucke der Vernunft aufbauet*).[15]

At the time he gave these lectures, Fichte held the view that his own age belonged to the third epoch, the state of completed sinfulness. In the lectures themselves, he accordingly attempts to convince his audience that this is, in fact, the case, by showing how the scientific, moral, political and religious phenomena of the present age all point in this direction. Fichte characterizes the age in question in the following manner: it will only accept as binding something which it can comprehend.[16] Fichte sees this demand for insight, which he thinks is coupled with an empiricism that is not in the position to gain genuine knowledge of truth, and the present age's consequent rejection of authority, as resulting in a condition of moral degeneration, in which the desires for self-preservation and personal well-being alone are what motivate human actions.[17] Thus, in terms of what motivates human actions, it is difficult not to think of the present age as one that, as regards its legal and political arrangements and the dispositions of its members, closely corresponds to the theory of right which Fichte developed during his Jena period.

Since the present age belongs to only the third period of the whole of human history, two further epochs must be thought to lie in the future. This in itself shows how Fichte's idea of a world plan constitutes a form of knowledge that is independent of experience, since how can an age which has yet to come be characterized on the basis of experience alone? Indeed, in the lectures on *The Characteristics of the Present Age*, Fichte claims that the philosopher must be able to describe time as a whole and all its possible epochs in *a priori* terms.[18] For only in this way can a truly philosophical standpoint be attained, a standpoint which is able to reduce the manifold phenomena that experience provides, including, we may assume, particular historical events, to the unity of a single common principle, that is, the idea of a world plan. This reduction of empirical phenomena to a common principle in turn depends on the possibility of being able to 'deduce and completely explain' these empirical phenomena in terms of this principle.[19] Whatever one makes of such bold claims, it is clear that Fichte's

15 GA I / 8: 201; CPA: 9f.
16 GA I / 8: 208f.; CPA: 20.
17 GA I / 8: 212f.: CPA: 25.
18 GA I / 8: 196; CPA: 3.
19 GA I / 8: 196; CPA: 2.

idea of a world plan consisting of five epochs represents a more fully worked out theory of the movement of the human race and the identification of the individual stages in the progress of human culture already hinted at in his Jena lectures concerning the vocation of the scholar. This idea of a world plan, which assumes the possibility of an *a priori* knowledge of history, is then presupposed in the *Addresses to the German Nation*. Yet there is an important difference between these addresses and *The Characteristics of the Present Age*, a difference that gives the *Addresses to the German Nation* a practical intent that is far less evident in the more contemplative earlier series of lectures. This practical intent again suggests a link between these addresses and Fichte's Jena lectures on the vocation of the scholar, in which the scholar is accorded a practical role to play in society.

This difference concerns the fact that by the time Fichte came to deliver the *Addresses to the German Nation*, he had begun to see the transition from the current epoch, which 'has mere sensuous self-interest as the impulse of all its vital stirrings and motions',[20] to the next epoch, in which truth comes to be regarded as the highest of all things, as already under way. In the light of this difference between *The Characteristics of the Present Age* and the *Addresses to the German Nation*, we can think of Fichte as seeking to demonstrate to his audience in the latter that this transition is, in fact, already happening and as helping to bring about the transition in question by means of his own scholarly activity. This may seem strange given that Fichte's idea of a world plan implies that there is some kind of necessity at work in history, with all of the five epochs he identifies having to manifest themselves at some point in time. Such an idea is suggested by Fichte himself when he claims that the life of the human race 'does not depend upon blind chance', but instead 'proceeds and moves onward according to a settled plan which *must* necessarily be fulfilled, and therefore *shall* certainly be fulfilled'.[21] Yet there are some grounds for thinking that Fichte wants to reconcile the idea of necessity with the idea that human freedom has a role to play in this process, though it may simply amount to bringing about sooner rather than later changes that would eventually have to take place in any case. For he claims that the world plan involves the human race forming and cultivating itself into a

20 GA I / 10: 104; AGN: 9.
21 GA I / 8: 206; CPA: 16.

pure and express image of reason 'with freedom'.[22] Moreover, I show below that the *Addresses to the German Nation* suggests one way in which human freedom might have a role to play in this process, namely, through the scholar taking upon himself the task of encouraging human beings to complete the historical process of which he himself has knowledge. This will lead to a discussion of Fichte's use of history in the *Addresses to the German Nation*, whereas I do not intend to consider in any detail the possible merits or demerits of his speculative philosophy of history.[23]

Fichte sees the transition from the epoch which he describes as the state of completed sinfulness to the next one, in which truth comes to be regarded as the highest of all things, as already under way because historical events have led, in the case of the German nation, to the destruction of the principle of self-interest through its complete development. What this means, as Fichte himself explains in the First Address, is that given the German nation's complete subjection to an alien power, that is, the conquering French, its members have become subject to the ends of this alien power and therefore no longer have a will of their own, so that selfishness 'has lost its self and the capacity to posit its ends independently'.[24] Yet it was egoism that weakened the German nation in the first place, making it possible for another nation to subjugate it; and it is in this way that the principle of self-interest can be said to have destroyed itself through its own complete development.

In the midst of this historical situation, Fichte seeks to show how the transition to the next epoch, in which truth comes to be seen as the highest of all things, can be fully effected by means of a German national education, which aims 'to form the Germans into a totality that in all its individual parts is driven and animated by the same single interest'.[25] The *Addresses to the German Nation* therefore does not represent, as one might have expected, a direct attempt to rouse the German nation to oppose violently the French conqueror; it instead represents

22 GA I / 8: 206; CPA: 16.
23 For a defence of Fichte's philosophy of history, in the face of the particular objection that such a speculative theory of history is unable to comprehend history as a living reality that cannot be expressed by means of intellectual constructions, based on the claim that it is, in fact, rich in possibilities when it comes to understanding the problem of the relationship of history to thought, see Hammacher, 'Comment Fichte accède à l'histoire'.
24 GA I / 10: 109; AGN: 13.
25 GA I / 10: 114; AGN: 19.

an attempt to point the way to the moral renewal of the German nation by means of a system of national education, with the development of a new national self ushering in the possibility of a new age, in which the blind pursuit of self-interest will be replaced by the conscious willing of a collective interest. This will in turn, Fichte believes, eventually enable the German nation to regain its independence. In other words, the struggle has become one of moral principles as opposed to physical force. As Fichte himself expresses it: 'The armed struggle is ended; now there begins, if we so will it, the new battle of principles, of morals [*Sitten*] and of character'.[26]

In this way, Fichte can be seen to understand himself, in line with his conception of the scholar's vocation already outlined during his Jena period, as charged with the task of furthering human progress by means of his privileged knowledge of the course that human history must take, together with the knowledge he has gained through his contemplation of the contemporary world in the light of the first type of knowledge, and, finally, his ability to communicate what he knows.[27] When both of these forms of knowledge are taken together, we have a historico-philosophical form of knowledge that enables the scholar, who happens to be Fichte himself, to fulfil his duty of advancing human culture, by showing his audience how society can progress from the stage at which it currently stands to the next, higher stage in world history. Given the way in which this task relates to the moral aspect of the scholar's vocation, Fichte's delivery of the *Addresses to the German Nation* must be seen as a moral act rather than a political one.

Having taking upon himself such a task in accordance with his ideas concerning the vocation of the scholar, Fichte needs to show why the German nation is uniquely suited to implement the new system of education that will lead to the moral renewal not only of the German nation itself but also, it is to be hoped, through its example, of the rest of humankind, in this way facilitating the full transition from the third epoch of human history to the fourth one.

26 GA I / 10: 275; AGN: 174.
27 In the *Addresses to the German Nation*, Fichte accordingly describes the vocation of the scholar as the task of taking the human race forward 'according to a clear concept and with deliberate art', which means that the scholar 'must always be in advance of the present, must comprehend the future and be able to implant it in the present for its later development. This requires a clear overview of the state of the world until now, a free capacity for pure thought independent of appearance, and, so that he can express himself [*sich mittheilen könne*], the mastery of language down to its living and creative root' (GA I / 10: 238f.; AGN: 139).

This leads Fichte to identify the various characteristics of the German nation that make it fundamentally different from other nations and eminently suited to perform the historical task of bringing about a new epoch in world history. It is here that Fichte makes various appeals to historical fact, despite his denigration of history as a discipline because of its status as 'mere empiricism' (*bloße Empirie*), that is to say, its status as nothing more than a collection of facts and a set of claims based upon these facts.[28] Fichte's use of the 'merely' historical will, however, be shown to raise questions concerning the notion of 'truth' as it pertains to the scholar's role in public life. To show how it does so, I first need to outline Fichte's attempt to demonstrate the uniqueness of the German nation and its consequent fitness for the historical task he wishes to assign to it.

In the Fourth Address Fichte explains the essential differences between the German nation and other nations in terms of language. While the Germans are said to have retained and developed an 'original' language, which can be traced back to the earliest days of the race, other nations have at some point adopted a foreign language, which they subsequently came to modify. Fichte here has in mind the way in which the Romance languages derive from Latin. This essential linguistic difference is then held to have had certain fundamental cultural differences as its consequences. The way in which Fichte rests his case on a theory of language that is so closely tied to the history of Western Europe clearly restricts the possible validity of his argument to the differences between the German nation and nations that speak what he calls a 'neo-Latin' language.

This theory of language denies that the sound which expresses a concept is purely a matter of convention, in which case the link between a certain concept and a certain sound would be an arbitrary one. The relation between concept and sound is instead determined by a necessary law, with objects being represented in language by a particular sound in a way that is analogous to how objects are necessarily represented as having a particular appearance in an individual's sense organs. Originally, language is, in fact, simply 'the designation of objects of immediate sensuous perception'.[29] Given the necessary law which determines the relation of the sound to the object that it represents, and for which it provides the concept by means of which

28 GA I / 8: 301; CPA: 150.
29 GA I / 10: 147; AGN: 51.

this object is designated, Fichte claims that there is essentially only one language. This original language, however, became particularized through becoming subject to such influences as that of climate, though even here language can be said to develop in accordance with a law, namely, that the original language must develop in a certain way given the local conditions to which it is subject.

Although Fichte explains the origins of language in terms of the designation of objects perceived through the senses, he also speaks of a people raising itself from the stage of sensuous perception to grasp a supersensuous world. This leads to the identification of a supersensuous organ, which is the self as the soul or mind as distinct from the physical body, and to a corresponding increase in the stock of language on account of the introduction of words that designate concepts that do not derive from sense experience. Fichte claims, however, that the objects of this supersensuous organ

> could be designated in language only by it being said that their particular relation to their organ is like the relation of this or that particular sensuous object to its sense organ; that in this relation a particular supersensuous thing is equated with a particular sensuous thing, and thanks to this equation its place in the supersensuous organ can be indicated through language.[30]

In other words, human beings can use language to express these supersensuous objects only by means of such devices as analogy and metaphor, so that language based on sense perception must be employed to stimulate the person, who wishes to arrive at the supersensuous object itself, to 'set in motion' the spiritual organ by means of which he is able to grasp such an object.

Since the symbolic mode of designating supersensuous objects is ultimately tied to the language based on sense perception spoken by a particular people, Fichte goes on to argue that it must correspond to the stage of development reached by the faculty of sensuous cognition attained by such a people. Spiritual development thus proceeds in tandem with the development of knowledge based on sense experience. Fichte gives as an example of what he means by this process the symbolic representation of something that arises through clear knowledge as opposed to obscure feeling. This supersensuous object is both in the Greek and in the German languages designated by the word

---

30 GA I / 10: 147; AGN: 51.

'idea' (*Idee*), and it corresponds, or so Fichte claims, to that which the Germans designate by means of the word 'vision' (*Gesicht*) as used by Luther in his translation of the Bible.[31] In sensory terms, the words 'idea' and 'vision' mean something that can be perceived only by means of the physical eye but not through any other sense. This allows these words to be given the supersensuous signification of something that can be grasped only by the mind's eye and not at all by the body. Such an analogy, however, could only have been developed by a people that had already reached the stage of knowing that things may reveal themselves to all or several senses, or, as in the present case, to one sense alone, the sense of sight, and was also aware that this image was the most suitable means of designating the concept in question.

Since the symbolic representation of supersensuous objects is based on the level of sensuous knowledge achieved by a given people, there exists a certain necessity with respect to the relation between the former and the latter. In short, the symbol employed to express the supersensuous object will be of such a kind that it is easily rendered intelligible by means of its relation to the sensory knowledge embedded in the original language. The relation of the symbol to what it expresses is therefore again not an arbitrary one. The way in which a language concerning supersensuous objects is rooted in language that derives from immediate sensuous experience makes it intelligible to anyone who speaks a language which, like German, according to Fichte, is characterized by a symbolic representation of supersensuous objects that corresponds to the level of development attained by a nation with respect to its sensuous knowledge.

When a nation's symbolic representation of supersensuous objects proceeds in tandem with the development of its knowledge based on sense experience and the language which embodies this knowledge, its language as a whole can be said to develop by means of a natural progression. This leads Fichte to describe such a language as one that

> from the moment its first sound broke forth in the same people, has developed uninterruptedly out of the actual common life of that people; a language that admitted no element that did not express an intuition actually experienced by this people, an intuition that coheres with all the others in an interlocking system.[32]

31 GA I / 10: 148; AGN: 51f.
32 GA I / 10: 150; AGN: 53.

This natural progression is broken, however, when a nation adopts a foreign language and the symbolic representations of supersensuous objects contained in the adopted language do not correspond to the stage of knowledge based on sense experience that this nation has thus far attained. In such cases, the nation in question will lack the intuitions needed to render the symbolic representations of supersensuous objects intelligible, though its members may have the symbols and their spiritual meaning explained to them, in which case they would receive 'only the flat and lifeless history of an alien culture'.[33] On these grounds, Fichte claims that, as far as the supersensuous part of language is concerned, such a nation will come to speak a language that may 'give the appearance of vitality' but is, in fact, essentially 'dead and cut off from its living root by the admittance of the new sphere of intuitions and the abruption of the old'.[34]

The fundamental difference between the German nation and other nations is thus held to rest on the fact that 'the Germans still speak a living language and have done so ever since it first streamed forth from nature, whereas the other Teutonic tribes speak a language that stirs only the surface yet is dead at the root'.[35] In the case of these tribes, the natural, organic development of the languages they spoke was broken by their adoption of a foreign language containing symbolic representations of supersensuous objects which did not correspond to the stage of sensuous knowledge that they had attained and which was embodied in their original languages. We shall shortly see why Fichte speaks specifically of other Teutonic tribes, but I first need to mention that he views this difference between the development of the languages spoken by these tribes and the language spoken by the Germans as having had certain consequences with respect to culture, resulting in a further set of differences between the German nation and other nations. Fichte lists these consequences at the end of the Fourth Address and then discusses them in more detail in the Fifth Address. They include the continuing unity of life and spiritual culture in the case of the Germans, and their separation in the case of the other nations; the seriousness and diligence of the Germans, as opposed to the playfulness and carefree nature of the other nations; and, as a result of these last two differences, the capacity of the great

33 GA I / 10: 150f.; AGN: 54.
34 GA I / 10: 151; AGN: 55.
35 GA I / 10: 154; AGN: 58.

mass of the German nation to be educated, together with a willingness on the part of educators to undertake the task of educating the people, whereas the cultivated classes of the other nations have divorced themselves from the people, viewing them as 'nothing more than the blind instrument of their plans'.[36]

Since the consequences mentioned above are held to follow from the division between the German nation and other nations that Fichte establishes on the basis of his theory of language, one way of casting doubt on the essential characteristics that Fichte attributes to the German nation in opposition to other nations would be to criticize his theory of the origins and development of language. There is no evidence that Fichte accords this theory the status of a merely hypothetical account of how languages might have arisen and developed, rather than that of a theory about how languages actually did arise and develop. Indeed, the essential role that Fichte's theory of language plays in the *Addresses to the German Nation* strongly suggests that Fichte thinks of this theory as having an objective status, whereas a merely hypothetical account of the origins and development of language would lack the argumentative force demanded by his overall strategy of getting his audience to accept the need for a German national education and to believe in the unique destiny of the German nation with respect to the task of developing and implementing such a system of education.

Interestingly, though, to accord to Fichte's theory of language anything more than a hypothetical status would appear to violate his own strictures concerning the limits of historical explanation, which is, after all, a form of explanation that his theory of language itself involves, since it explains language in terms of its origins and certain developments that it underwent, developments that are held to have been different in the case of different nations and to relate to certain experiences which, historically, these nations underwent. For in *The Characteristics of the Present Age*, Fichte denies history the right to explain the origin of human language on the grounds that language, as one of the conditions of experience in general, is a condition of the possibility of history itself, so that the latter must itself presuppose the existence of language and is not, therefore, in the position to explain it.[37] This is a valid point, perhaps, but it raises the question as to what enables philosophy to explain the origins of human language in a way that

36 GA I / 10: 156; AGN: 59.   37 GA I / 8: 298; CPA: 146.

history cannot do, when it also presupposes the existence of language? As far as I can see, Fichte does not even attempt to answer this question.

Fichte also does not seem particularly concerned about substantiating his claims regarding the differences between the German language and those spoken by the other Teutonic races, by providing at least some historical evidence beyond the fact that the speakers of the 'neo-Latin' languages came to adopt a foreign language. In the case of the German language, a finer knowledge of the way in which this language developed might have led Fichte to realize that it is not, in fact, as 'original' as he claims it to be. For, despite appearances, it can itself be seen to contain many borrowings from foreign languages in the form of 'loan coinages', which, although they are made up of words that are German in origin, would probably never have been coined or have acquired their modern meaning if it were not for the foreign model on which they are based.[38] This pervasive, but subtle, influence of foreign languages on the German language, of which Fichte, not surprisingly perhaps, does not appear to have been aware, means that we might think of the Germans as speaking a language which contains elements that, according to Fichte's own account of language, should be unintelligible to them without the kind of historical explanation which he thinks only a 'dead' language is in need of. I suggest below, however, that the kind of detailed historical knowledge needed to identify such 'foreign' words within the German language is, in any case, not something that Fichte thinks the scholar has a duty to acquire, since it would be superfluous to the scholar's main purpose.

We might also ask whether the consequences that Fichte derives from his theory concerning the origins and development of language do actually follow from the premises found in this theory. I do not intend to pursue this point, however. I show instead that Fichte is to be seen as consciously adopting a strategy that does not, in fact, rely on adequate argumentation for, and justification of, the claims he makes, though it also invites the suspicion that he attempts to mask this lack of genuine argument and justification. This becomes evident if we look more closely at Fichte's use of historical fact in the *Addresses to the German Nation*. We have seen that in his Jena period Fichte held the view that acquiring historical knowledge constitutes one of the main duties of the scholar, because such

---

38 For an illuminating discussion of this issue, see Martyn, 'Borrowed Fatherland: Nationalism and Language Purism in Fichte's *Addresses to the German Nation*'.

knowledge enables the scholar to perform the task of helping to advance human culture. Fichte's use of historical knowledge in the *Addresses to the German Nation* provides an example of how he himself came to undertake such a task.

Fichte appeals to historical fact when he claims at the beginning of the Fourth Address that the German nation and the nations that came to speak neo-Latin languages were originally from the same stem and are, as such, all of Teutonic descent. Yet, whereas the Germans remained in their original homeland, the other races migrated to other territories, where they came in one way or another to adopt a foreign language. Fichte views this change of territory as not being especially significant in itself, since, or so he claims, natural habitat does not form national character; rather the latter prevails over and alters this habitat after its own image. In short, language, above all else, determines national character, so that it is the change in language brought about by a change of territory, and not this change of territory itself, that is of fundamental importance. If, for the sake of argument, we accept Fichte's theory of language, it is true that the idea of a change of territory is not essential to his argument, because even if the nations that came to speak a neo-Latin language were not of Teutonic origin, the claim that they came at some point to adopt a foreign language, with all the consequences that, according to Fichte, flow from this event, might still be thought to hold. It is nevertheless disconcerting to read Fichte claim in connection with this change of territory that it is an event which 'lies clearly and incontestably before the eyes of all',[39] without attempting to offer any further justification of this claim.

Significantly, at certain points in the *Addresses to the German Nation* Fichte seeks to highlight the logical rigour of the method he employs to identify the consequences that allegedly follow from his distinction between the original language spoken by the German nation and the 'dead' languages spoken by other nations. In the Fifth Address, for example, Fichte speaks of deducing these consequences, 'taking care only that this deduction is correct', whereas the question as to 'whether the variety of phenomena which ought to exist according to this deduction occurs in actual experience or not' is left to his audience and to any other observer to decide.[40] Fichte's use of the words 'ought to exist' implies that the correctness of the deduction itself is not to be doubted, so that the different characteristics exhibited by the Germans, on the one hand, and by the nations that speak a neo-Latin

---

39 GA I / 10: 143; AGN: 48.   40 GA I / 10: 157; AGN: 60.

language, on the other, 'ought' to exist or to have existed, that is, to have manifested themselves in the course of human history, even if they have not in fact done so.

In the Sixth Address, Fichte nevertheless seeks to show that the Germans have actually manifested themselves in the ways implied by his 'deduction' of the consequences that follow from the distinction between the 'original' language spoken by the Germans and the 'dead' languages spoken by the other nations. He does this by citing such episodes from German history as the spiritual renewal brought about by Luther and the Reformation which he initiated. This is then described as 'proof of German seriousness and German soul [*ein Beleg von Deutschem Ernst und Gemüth*]', while, in the positive response of the German people to the Reformation, one sees 'proof of the particularity of the German people [*einen Beleg von der Eigenthümlichkeit des Deutschen Volkes*]'.[41] Fichte also cites the achievements of the German free imperial cities as examples of the uniqueness of the German nation. Yet, given the lack of historical evidence that he provides in support of the version of German history that he serves up to his audience, which consists mainly of value judgements concerning the significance and greatness of the historical events he mentions, Fichte's use of history assumes a highly tendentious appearance, with historical fact being made to conform to a set of claims concerning the originality and uniqueness of the German nation, whose truth has allegedly been already established. As we have seen, this set of claims is based on a theory of language that itself rests on extremely shaky foundations insofar as the historical evidence for it is concerned.

There is, however, a rather simple explanation of Fichte's use of historical fact in the *Addresses to the German Nation* that relates back to his early lectures on the vocation of the scholar, and which concerns the 'truth' with which these addresses are primarily concerned. When Fichte speaks of truth in the *Addresses to the German Nation*, he can be seen to have in mind the higher truth which forms the background to these addresses. This is the truth concerning the historical task of the German nation to usher in the new age that is to follow the age in which self-interest is the guiding principle, namely, the age in which truth comes to be regarded as the highest of all things. As we have seen, in this respect the *Addresses to the German Nation* constitutes an attempt to realize the conception of the scholar's vocation outlined in Fichte's

---

41 GA I / 10: 173f.; AGN: 76.

earlier Jena lectures on this subject. We may therefore think of the task which Fichte sets the scholar as leading him to sanction the reduction of historical detail to the status of a means to an end, with the end in question being that of getting the Germans to initiate the system of education which will lead to the moral renewal of the German nation, and which, in Fichte's view, represents the only real chance of both freeing this nation from foreign domination and introducing a new age in which truth comes to be regarded as the highest of all things. Consequently, when Fichte refers to actual historical events, he concentrates on the spiritual renewal brought about by the Reformation, the glories of the free imperial cities, including the North German Hanseatic cities, and the successful resistance offered by some German tribes to the invading Romans, thereby confronting his predominantly Protestant North German audience, rather than the German nation as a whole defined in terms of its possession of a common language, with the type of historical event with which they could identify themselves, since it was already likely to form part of their own conception of German greatness.[42] The ultimate end of this strategy is, then, to be understood as that of making Fichte's audience accept the proposals that he makes concerning the introduction of a German national education, which form the content of some of the other addresses.

This reduction of historical fact to the status of a means to an end does not require any attempt on Fichte's part to be as objective as he possibly can be with respect to the historical claims he makes, though Fichte tends to mask this lack of objectivity by the use of such terms as 'deduction' and 'proof', which imply logical rigour. This instrumentalization of history is nevertheless compatible with Fichte's earlier theory of the duties of the scholar. For although the acquisition of historical knowledge is considered to be one of the scholar's main duties, it is a duty only insofar as the possession of such knowledge is necessary in relation to the task of advancing human culture, which represents the highest duty and vocation of the scholar. On the other hand, Fichte's use of history raises questions concerning an intellectual's responsibility when it comes to his employment of what he

42 This tendency is especially evident in the concluding Fourteenth Address when Fichte appeals to the German nation as a whole in the name of its 'forefathers' (*Vorfahren*), whom he identifies as those German tribes that resisted the Roman invaders and those Germans who engaged in the struggle for religious freedom, by which Fichte obviously means the Reformation (GA I / 10: 295f.; AGN: 193f.).

alleges to be historical fact, especially when one might doubt the
validity of the kind of higher philosophical truth that Fichte has in
mind. After all, the attempt to be as objective as one possibly can be
with respect to the evidence presented to us by history could itself be
viewed as a duty imposed on the scholar by the notion of 'truth'. In
implicitly denying that such a duty exists, Fichte anticipates Nietzsche's
views on the use of history as found in his essay *On the Uses and
Disadvantages of History for Life* (*Vom Nutzen und Nachtheil der Historie
für das Leben*). Indeed, Fichte's approach in the *Addresses to the German
Nation* will be shown to illustrate some of Nietzsche's main ideas concerning the use of history 'for the sake of life and action [*zum Leben und
zur That*]',[43] while Fichte may be seen as attempting to put these ideas
into practice by means of his own scholarly activity.

Nietzsche's claim that we need history for the sake of life and action
represents a reaction against the historicism, with its pretensions to
pure objectivity, that had become prevalent in Germany by the time
he wrote his essay *On the Uses and Disadvantages of History for Life*,
which was published in 1874 and came to form part of the collection
of articles entitled *Untimely Meditations* (*Unzeitgemässe Betrachtungen*).
Significantly, Fichte is also keen to stress in the *Addresses to the German
Nation* that intellectual activity should be related to life and action. He
claims, for example, that the national education he envisages for all
Germans must produce knowledge that 'shall of necessity intervene
directly in life'.[44] Knowledge would here be doing something that
Fichte must think it already does in his own philosophy, since the latter
uses the German language which, as an original language, employs a
supersensuous language that has developed naturally on the basis of
the sensuous knowledge embedded in everyday language, and which,
therefore, 'has the power to intervene directly in life and to stimulate
it'.[45] The spiritual culture of a people that speaks such a language is in
this way able to influence life.[46] The relation between spiritual culture
and life is, in fact, so close that the former does not so much influence
the latter as it 'is itself the life of him who thinks thus'.[47]

In the case of the Germans, then, knowledge and life do not stand
opposed to each other but are instead unified within a single,

43 Nietzsche, 'Unzeitgemässe Betrachtungen', 241 / *Untimely Meditations*, 59.
44 GA I / 10: 134; AGN: 38.
45 GA I / 10: 149; AGN: 53.
46 GA I / 10: 157f.; AGN: 61.
47 GA I / 10: 161; AGN: 64.

indivisible experience of which they form constitutive elements. Fichte's *Addresses to the German Nation* provides an example of what this might mean. This is because knowledge, more specifically, historical knowledge insofar as it has come to form an integral part of the shared experience of the German nation, or at least of its Protestant members, has become intimately bound up in Fichte's mind, and, he hopes, in his audience's minds, with the destiny of the German nation as a whole. Is there any way of specifying more closely the kind of use of history that is here at work? Clearly, it is not a form of history that pays close attention to historical fact and seeks to base itself on firm historical evidence. It does not, therefore, appear to have much in common with the kind of historicism that is the target of Nietzsche's criticism in *On the Uses and Disadvantages of History for Life*. On the other hand, Nietzsche's thoughts on how history can be made to serve the needs of life and action provide a possible answer to this question.

Nietzsche identifies three kinds of history that can serve the needs of life and action: the monumental, the antiquarian and the critical forms of history. The critical form of history consists in an analysis and scrupulous examination of the past that gives rise to the awareness that every past is worthy of being condemned. This form of history is useful to life and action because it in this way enables one to throw off the burdens of the past.[48] The use of such a critical approach to the past would obviously prove to be counterproductive in relation to Fichte's attempt to inspire his audience by means of an appeal to what they would themselves regard as great moments in the history of the German nation, so that we cannot think of him as employing a critical form of history in the *Addresses to the German Nation*. By contrast, the antiquarian form of history is concerned with a preservation and veneration of the past that serves to make people content with present conditions, however wretched they may in fact be.[49] Yet making people content with their present circumstances by means of an appeal to the past can hardly be said to be what Fichte has in mind. Indeed, in the First Address he expressly condemns any attempt to make the Germans content with their present humiliating situation. Consequently, although Fichte does not explicitly make this point, we may assume that any appeal to a glorious past as a source of comfort, as opposed to a spur to action, is to be condemned. This leaves us with the monumental form of history.

48 Nietzsche, 'Unzeitgemässe Betrachtungen', 265f. / *Untimely Meditations*, 75ff.
49 Nietzsche, 'Unzeitgemässe Betrachtungen', 261ff. / *Untimely Meditations*, 72ff.

Monumental history involves an appeal to the kinds of models from the past which are lacking among one's contemporaries, with the aim of inspiring oneself and others and dispelling a mood of resignation, replacing it with the type of attitude that is needed to achieve some goal, such as that of the happiness of a nation or of mankind as whole.[50] To this extent, the monumental form of history closely corresponds to Fichte's use of history in the *Addresses to the German Nation*, in which he employs examples from German history to make his audience believe in the unique destiny of the German nation. As we have seen, this destiny consists in introducing and implementing a system of education which will in time lead to the moral renewal of the German nation itself and, potentially, of the rest of humankind. Yet, as Nietzsche points out, in order for it to be effective, the monumental form of history 'will have no use for ... absolute veracity [*Wahrhaftigkeit*]: it will always have to deal in approximations and generalities',[51] with the result that 'the past itself suffers *harm*: whole segments of it are forgotten ... and only individual embellished facts rise out of it like islands'.[52] This seems to me to be a fair description of Fichte's use of history in the *Addresses to the German Nation*, though this is not to say that Nietzsche had Fichte in mind. Rather, Nietzsche identifies a general tendency regarding the use of history which can be employed to describe Fichte's approach. In the following passage, Fichte himself acknowledges that the philosopher's and, consequently, his own use of history is highly selective and dependent on the end which it is made to serve:

> the use which he makes of history is not to prove anything by it, for his principles are already proved independently of history; but only to illustrate and make good in the actual world of history, that which is already understood without its aid. Throughout the whole course of events, therefore, he selects only the instances in which humanity really advances towards the true end of its being, and appeals only to these instances, – laying aside and rejecting everything else; and as he does not intend to prove historically that humanity has to pursue this course, having already proved it philosophically, he only points out, for the purposes of illustration, the occasions on which this has been visible in history.[53]

50 Nietzsche 'Unzeitgemässe Betrachtungen', 254ff. / *Untimely Meditations*, 68f.
51 Nietzsche, 'Unzeitgemässe Betrachtungen', 257 / *Untimely Meditations*, 70
52 Nietzsche, 'Unzeitgemässe Betrachtungen', 258 / *Untimely Meditations*, 71
53 GA I / 8: 304; CPA: 154f.

While the idea that history should be made to serve the needs of life and action, together with the idea that this may require the suppression of any attempt to provide an objective account and evaluation of the available historical evidence, are compatible with the kind of immoralism that is typically attributed to Nietzsche, these ideas appear to constitute a rather incongruous element in Fichte's case, given his understanding of the scholar's vocation as a primarily moral one and the role that he assigns to truth in relation to this vocation. Fichte's use of history in the *Addresses to the German Nation* is certainly highly selective and he is clearly not concerned with establishing the accuracy of his characterization of the historical events to which he refers. Although this approach can be viewed as a matter of omission rather than a deliberate distortion of the 'merely' historical,[54] it does, I think, point to a misuse of history on Fichte's part, in the sense that historical fact is reduced simply to the status of a means to an end, as opposed to its being accorded any value in itself, in which case a more scrupulous attention to historical detail and evidence would be demanded.[55] We can consequently think of the scholar's duty to study history, which Fichte alludes to in his Jena lectures on the vocation of the scholar, as extending only to gaining a type of knowledge of history that can be utilized in pursuit of the higher end of advancing human culture and morality. In this respect, the following claim made by Nietzsche concerning the study of history would appear to be one that Fichte might himself have made:

> The study of history is something salutary and fruitful for the future only as the attendant of a mighty new current of life, of an evolving culture for example, that is to say only when it is dominated and directed by a higher force and does not itself dominate and direct.[56]

54 Nietzsche recognizes the potential for deception in the case of the monumental form of history and identifies some of its possible consequences when he claims that, 'Monumental history deceives by analogies: with seductive similarities it inspires the courageous to foolhardiness and the inspired to fanaticism'. Nietzsche, 'Unzeitgemässe Betrachtungen', 258 / *Untimely Meditations*, 71.

55 Fichte himself insists that the philosopher would deserve blame if he asserted a fact that had never taken place, but he then distinguishes between the fact that something occurred and the manner in which it occurred, which may imply many other facts that can be left to the 'empirical' historian (*dem empirischen Historiker*) (GA I / 8: 305; CPA: 156). Yet what precisely does he mean by this distinction? Does it allow, for example, that while the philosopher has a duty to be right about the general facts he mentions, he does not have a duty to be scrupulous regarding the facts concerning the manner in which they occurred, whatever this may mean exactly?

56 Nietzsche, 'Unzeitgemässe Betrachtungen', 253 / *Untimely Meditations*, 67.

Fichte's instrumentalization of history begins to look all the more dangerous when we consider the way in which his interpretation of certain historical events and their consequences is accompanied by the use of such terms as 'deduction', which appear designed to give what he says the appearance of logical rigour and of truth, in the sense of something that no rational being could possibly deny because it follows of necessity. For it seems relatively easy to think of ways in which such a use of history, when combined with such lofty sounding terms as 'truth', might be used to convince people of the need to pursue some sinister end that could also be associated with the notion of the moral regeneration of a whole nation. In this respect, one might well prefer the more modest aims of an approach which is 'merely' historical, in the sense that it concentrates on providing and evaluating historical evidence when making certain claims regarding the past.

Perhaps, though, Fichte was himself well aware of the immoralism that is latent in his conception of the scholar's vocation. In the theory of ethical duties that he sets out in *The System of Ethics*, in which we encounter the idea of an estate of scholars with its own distinctive function within society, Fichte identifies the proper virtue of the scholar as 'a strict love of truth'.[57] Yet, in the very same work, he makes the following claim concerning what he takes to be one of the scholar's fundamental rights: 'One must be allowed to put forward anything of which one believes oneself to be convinced, no matter how dangerous or terrible it might seem'.[58] We can regard Fichte's own use of history, in which historical fact serves merely as the means to an end which Fichte considers to be a higher one, as providing an example of how a scholar might avail himself of this alleged right with all its hidden dangers.

There is a certain irony here concerning the relation of the means to the end. For, as we have seen, in the *Addresses to the German Nation* Fichte is seeking to intervene in the course of history so as to help bring about the transition to the next epoch of human history, which is the epoch in which truth comes to be regarded as the highest of all things. Yet, when it comes to the means he employs to bring about this transition, Fichte appears not to regard truth as the highest of all things insofar as it concerns historical fact and historical evidence. He would himself, of course, regard truth as having a different meaning

57 GA I / 5: 303; SE: 328.
58 GA I / 5: 225; SE: 239.

and value in each case: in one case, there is a higher, philosophical truth, while, in the other one, there is a lower, merely empirical truth. Nevertheless, is it not possible to view such appeals to a higher truth as suspect and open to abuse? With regard to Fichte's own use, or misuse, of history, a fuller consideration of this problem requires a closer look at the end towards which history is being put to use in the *Addresses to the German Nation*. As we already know, this is the end of convincing Fichte's audience to accept the need for a German national education, a system of education that, as we shall see below, is designed to produce virtuous citizens and thus to bring about a truly ethical form of community. I show, however, that the creation of such a community comes at a price.

Producing virtue

Fichte speaks of a German national education because the new system of education he proposes is one that all German people will enter as opposed to only the members of a certain class.[59] As previously mentioned, the aim of this system of education is to form the German nation into a totality, with all its members being driven and animated by the same single interest, namely, that of the German nation as a whole. The aim of a German national education is, in short, to produce virtuous human beings who think and act in accordance with the interests of the nation as a whole, rather than in accordance with their own personal interests alone. Although the theory of ethical duties that Fichte developed during his Jena period also features a demand for virtue, I suggested in the last chapter that Fichte leaves room for a conception of virtue which involves subordinating personal interests to the demands of morality, particularly the welfare of the social whole to which one belongs, but does not amount to eradicating personal interest altogether. Fichte can be seen instead to develop a theory of society which considers acting on behalf of the social whole to be compatible with acting in accordance with the end of self-preservation viewed as the ultimate condition of a finite rational being's capacity to act freely and effectively in the world; an end that Fichte thinks can be properly secured in a way that accords with the idea of

---

59 GA I / 10: 114; AGN: 19. Rather than classes in the modern sense, Fichte refers to *Stände*, which is, of course, in line with his earlier theory of the division of society into various estates.

self-determination by guaranteeing all persons the right to be able to live from their labour. This raises the question as to what extent the German national education that Fichte has in mind, insofar as it aims at producing virtuous citizens, is compatible with this earlier position. I show below that it is not compatible with it because its aim turns out to be the production of human beings who cannot will otherwise than in accordance with the demands of morality, leading to the suppression of human freedom rather than its realization.

In the *Addresses to the German Nation,* Fichte's account of what a German national education actually involves is rather short on specific details.[60] This is, perhaps, a reflection of the fact that Fichte sees the type of education proposed and already being put into practice by the Swiss pedagogical reformer Johann Heinrich Pestalozzi as providing the basis for this German national education. Fichte in fact spends much of the Ninth Address discussing Pestalozzi's proposals. It is clear from what Fichte says in the Second Address, however, that the starting-point of this system of education consists in certain mental activities and tasks whose aim is to foster in the pupil the ability to form images of states of affairs that do not exist in reality but which ought to exist. Fichte himself speaks of 'an image of the human social order, as it absolutely [*schlechthin*] ought to be according to the law of reason',[61] and we may therefore assume that it is especially the image of such a social order which the pupil should be led to form in his or her mind. Since the images the pupil learns to form are products of his or her self-activity, rather than a copy of something that already exists, he or she will come to take pleasure in his or her own imaginative powers and in this way gain a love of learning. The pupil will also come to recognize that these images develop according to certain necessary laws, namely, the laws that govern thinking in general, so that in the process of forming such images, the pupil is able to gain knowledge of these laws. Thus, on the one hand, the learning process that is characteristic of the German national education which Fichte proposes involves a process of self-determination, in the sense that what the pupil learns is a result of his or her own self-activity; while, on the

---

60 A number of specific proposals not mentioned in the *Addresses to the German Nation* are outlined in some of Fichte's other writings from the same period. See Schottky, 'Fichtes Nationalstaatsgedanke auf der Grundlage unveröffentlicher Manuskripte von 1807', 121ff.

61 GA I / 10: 127f.; AGN: 31. Translation slightly modified.

other hand, this process turns out to be subject to certain laws. The question of the relation between freedom and necessity in Fichte's system of education is something to which I intend to return in relation to the idea of conscience.

I first need to mention, however, that for Fichte this purely theoretical form of activity has consequences for the pupil's moral development. For by coming to recognize and comprehend the laws governing all mental activity, irrespective of its particular object, that is, the laws which pertain to any possible experience whatsoever, the pupil achieves a supersensuous knowledge which transports him or her into a new order of things, in which he or she is impelled by a love that does not aim at sensuous enjoyment but only at mental activity in general. Fichte claims that this love, which lacks any sensuous motive, is, in terms of its form, the same as the moral will, which never allows sensuous enjoyment to become the motive of action. The love of learning and the desire to engage in mental activity for its own sake produced in the pupil is thus held to constitute an important preliminary stage in the formation of a pure will. This merely formal agreement between the kind of purely theoretical knowledge mentioned above and a pure moral will, however, does not explain how it is that the pupil comes to project the image of a social order, which he or she may then seek to realize in and through his or her own activity, once he or she has become independent on leaving the German national education that Fichte proposes.

Fichte's solution to this problem is for all the pupils to live in isolation from the wider society so as to avoid its influences, and to 'live in fellowship [*in Gemeinschaft leben*] with one another and thus form an independent and self-sustaining commonwealth [*Gemein-Wesen*]', with its own rationally determined constitution.[62] The pupils will, in other words, in the first instance gain the image of the social order which they are to project in their minds by living in the community of which they are themselves active members. Fichte does not say much about the actual constitution of this community, though he makes clear that it should be arranged in such a way as to ensure that the pupil genuinely wills to act in accordance with the interests of the community as a whole, rather than simply acting in conformity with the rules governing this community. In other words, the pupil's actions should be morally motivated, determined by a sense of duty as

---

62 GA I / 10: 128; AGN: 32.

opposed to a concern merely to avoid certain sanctions. We can here detect an analogy between Fichte's earlier distinction between the ethical duties connected with the moral demand to act on behalf of society as a whole and a person's acting in ways that conform to the principles of right but do not necessarily involve any moral form of motivation. Yet, whereas Fichte distinguishes between the type of disposition required by morality and the one required by right in the social and political philosophy of his Jena period, he attempts in the *Addresses to the German Nation* to overcome this distinction by means of the system of education that he proposes, so as to show how virtuous, rather than merely law-abiding citizens, can be created. The ethical disposition to act on behalf of the community as a whole is to be fostered by such activities as physical labour and 'the mechanical but here idealised labours of agriculture and of various handicrafts', together with such measures as stipulating that anyone who excels at one of these activities will be expected to help instruct the other members of the community in them.[63]

Fichte in fact seems to have in mind a miniature closed commercial state, as indeed is already suggested by his description of the community in which the pupils are to live as an independent and self-sustaining commonwealth. He maintains that the school they attend should have the appearance of supporting itself even if, unknown to the pupils themselves, some essential items need to be brought in from the wider society. Fichte accordingly stipulates that the 'basic law of this little agrarian state is this: that no article may be used for food, clothing, and so on, nor, as far as this is possible, any tool, that is not produced and manufactured within it'; while the effort needed to make sure that this miniature state remains independent and self-sufficient will foster in the pupils the idea that each 'must know that he is entirely indebted to the whole and prospers or starves ... when the whole prospers or starves'.[64] It is by being brought up and educated in such a community that a picture of the relevant social order is produced in the pupil's mind, and the relations that the pupil will enter into on becoming a member of the larger state and of a family 'are thereby presented to him in living intuition, and take ineradicable root in his soul [*Gemüth*]'.[65]

63 GA I / 10: 129; AGN: 33.
64 GA I / 10: 237f.; AGN: 138.
65 GA I / 10: 238; AGN: 138.

Since life in a small-scale miniature agrarian state is to prepare the pupil for his or her eventual entry into the larger state, we may assume that Fichte's views concerning the economic life of the latter remain largely unchanged from the time he wrote *The Closed Commercial State*. Indeed, in the Thirteenth Address, Fichte refers to how he had himself counselled the Germans 'to make themselves independent of world trade and to establish a closed commercial state', and he claims, moreover, that 'besides the unity of the Germans among themselves, their internal self-sufficiency and commercial independence are the second means to their salvation and thereby the salvation of Europe'.[66] What has changed, however, is that the economic proposals announced in this earlier work are no longer viewed primarily in terms of the end of securing the conditions of a self-interested finite rational being's agency in the world. Rather, they are now understood in terms of the ethical purpose of getting people to act for the sake of the community as a whole, which means acting to secure the community's independence and self-sufficiency, with this end now being treated as an end in itself. Although the notion of acting for the sake of the community as a whole is already to be found in Fichte's theory of ethical duties from his Jena period, Fichte appears to want to downplay, if not altogether exclude, the idea that self-interest might constitute another, complementary source of motivation, whose ends are to be acknowledged as valid in themselves. This shift in emphasis finds its most radical expression in the Eighth Address in the *Addresses to the German Nation* in Fichte's account of love of fatherland (*Vaterlandsliebe*), which, Fichte claims, can be more accurately expressed as the love of the individual for his nation.[67]

Fichte asserts that 'people and fatherland far exceed the state, in the ordinary signification of the word', and by the state in the ordinary sense of the term he means the kind of social order whose 'concept demands certain justice [*Recht*], internal peace, that each through his own industry earns his crust and prolongs his sensuous existence for as long as it is God's will to grant it to him'.[68] This description of the state corresponds, broadly speaking, to the amoral conception of the state found in Fichte's *Foundations of Natural Right*, in which the state is held to be a protective power that guarantees the right of each and every person to be able to live from his labour.

---

66 GA I / 10: 272f.; AGN: 171.
67 GA I / 10: 198; AGN: 100.
68 GA I / 10: 203; AGN: 105.

In the Eighth Address, Fichte describes the state as also requiring 'merely restraint and training so that individuals may live peaceably side by side and the whole is turned into an efficient means for realising arbitrarily [willkührlich] posited ends that lie outside its proper sphere'.[69] This description again accords with Fichte's earlier view of one of the state's primary roles as being that of guaranteeing persons the possibility of exercising free choice in the sensible world, which demands only that they limit their natural freedom in relation to each other, irrespective of what actually motivates them to do so. Thus, if Fichte were to go no further than identifying the virtue of love of fatherland with the subordination of one's own immediate interests to the social whole to which one belongs, with the aim of preserving the state and making it perform the functions mentioned above more effectively, his position would be largely compatible with the one that I have suggested can be attributed to him in the writings from his Jena period, once his theory of right and his theory of ethical duties are read in the light of each other. However, since he claims that people and fatherland far exceed the state in the ordinary sense of the word, we must assume that the object of love of fatherland is not the state understood simply as the guarantor of a condition of right.

The first way in which Fichte thinks that love of fatherland ought to govern the state as a higher authority nevertheless gives the impression that his Jena theory of right, as long as it is viewed in the light of his theory of ethical duties from the same period, is compatible with his account of love of fatherland in the *Addresses to the German Nation*. For love of fatherland here serves to restrict the means that the state employs to achieve internal security, which could be most effectively achieved by limiting freedom as much as possible. Whereas it is only in a society in which freedom is given the widest possible scope that any 'higher culture' can develop, so that the tendency towards restricting freedom as much as possible is something that ought itself to be restricted, even though it may mean a lesser degree of peace and order within the state and may make the task of governing more difficult.[70]

In countering this tendency towards the suppression of freedom, love of fatherland can be thought to represent an example of the social or political form of virtue I identified in the previous chapter as a condition of the truly effective functioning and potential flourishing

69 GA I / 10: 204; AGN: 106.
70 GA I / 10: 203f.; AGN: 105f.

of the kind of state described in Fichte's theory of right, so that the exercise of such virtue turns out to be necessary if right is fully to meet its own intrinsic goals. In this particular case, love of fatherland could be seen as helping achieve the goal of guaranteeing persons a sphere of freedom in which they may exercise free choice, thereby providing them at the same time with the conditions in which they may develop as moral agents. For example, the state official who exhibits this virtue will be someone who seeks within the government itself to prevent any unnecessary restrictions being imposed on human freedom, despite the opposition he may experience from other members of the government. More generally, any person may be thought to demonstrate love of fatherland by attempting, in the face of the state's tendency to restrict freedom so as to make its task of ensuring internal security easier, to prevent the state and its officials from acting in ways that conflict with the end of guaranteeing persons a sphere of freedom. To this extent, Fichte's account of love of fatherland appears to correspond to what has been described as the 'patriotism of liberty', which is a form of patriotism based on classical republican models characterized by a civic virtue that manifests itself as a concern to protect the freedom of all the citizens of the republic as well as one's own.[71] Yet, in other respects, the position that Fichte develops in the *Addresses to the German Nation* concerning the virtue of love of fatherland goes far beyond this conception of virtue. This tendency is, in fact, already signalled by Fichte's claim that freedom 'is *only* for the higher ends that transcend the state'.[72]

Fichte claims in the Eighth Address that the state is only a means and condition of what love of the fatherland really requires, which is that 'the eternal and the divine may flourish in the world and never cease to become ever more pure, perfect and excellent'.[73] In the context of this particular address, the notion of the divine can be identified with the life of the nation as it develops according to the law that binds its members into a 'natural whole', a life whose development requires self-sacrifice on the part of its members, who may gain immortality, though only of an earthly kind, in sacrificing themselves for the nation.[74] Leaving aside the question as to how exactly we are to understand the

---

71 Cf. Viroli, *For Love of Country*. Viroli argues that this form of patriotism is essentially different from nationalism, of which he classes Fichte to be one of the main founders.
72 GA I / 10: 204; AGN: 106. My emphasis.
73 GA I / 10: 203; AGN: 105.
74 GA I / 10: 199ff.; AGN: 101ff.

process by means of which a nation develops, it should be noted that the reduction of the state to the status of a means to a higher end is equally a feature of Fichte's theory of the state and society from his Jena period, as is the idea of the sacrifice of individuality.

Another connection between the *Addresses to the German Nation* and the writings of Fichte's Jena period becomes apparent when we consider how the system of education that Fichte proposes aims at creating an ethical community whose intersubjective bonds are this time constituted by means of its members' common possession of an 'original' language and their shared experience of having undergone a German national education, which aims to instil in each and every pupil the idea of a common end and interest, and to produce in them the disposition to will this end and interest. The type of ethical community whose possibility Fichte seeks to explain in the *Addresses to the German Nation* can therefore be viewed as a possible candidate for a more concrete version of the kind of community based on relations of mutual recognition that has been discerned in his deduction of the concept of right in the *Foundations of Natural Right*, but which, it is claimed, Fichte fails to develop in the later parts of this work. Yet the way in which Fichte explains the generation of this ethical community and the end that its members are to pursue suggests that the idea of such a genuine ethical community is not necessarily something to be welcomed, so that in this respect the position that Fichte developed during his Jena period, which involved the separation of right from morality, might be preferred to his later attempt to moralize the idea of the state. This becomes evident, I believe, when we turn to Fichte's account in the Eighth Address of the second way in which love of fatherland must govern the state as a higher authority. This concerns putting before the state 'a higher purpose than the ordinary one of maintaining internal peace, property, personal freedom, life and the well-being of all'.[75]

Fichte immediately associates this higher end with the end that a state has in view when it assembles an armed force; and he goes on to claim that *only* when all the other ends of the state (that is, property, personal freedom, life and well-being) are put at stake, by which he presumably means in times of war, 'does a truly original and primal life take the helm of state'; whereas in 'maintaining the traditional constitution, laws and civic welfare, there is no truly authentic life at all

---

75 GA I / 10: 204; AGN: 106.

and no original decision'.[76] In this way, Fichte appears to glorify war, making it into the only means by which individuals are able to enter into a truly genuine relation with the life of the nation to which they belong. Fichte thus ignores the way in which he himself suggests only moments before that the virtue of love of fatherland might have a significant role to play in the life of a nation with respect to the very same ends of the state that are to be put at risk and sacrificed in times of war, such as that of guaranteeing personal freedom. Fichte's sudden denial of the significance and value of other, more peaceful expressions of the virtue of love of fatherland implies that for him the proper end of an individual's life is to sacrifice himself in war for the sake of the nation, and that there is simply no other way in which an individual can properly demonstrate his love of fatherland. This impression is strengthened by the following description of what love of fatherland consists in:

> Not the spirit of calm civic love for the constitution and laws [*der Geist der ruhigen bürgerlichen Liebe der Verfassung, und der Gesetze*], but the blazing flame of the higher love of fatherland that embraces the nation as the vesture of the eternal, for which the noble man joyfully sacrifices himself and the ignoble, who exists only for the sake of the former, should likewise sacrifice himself.[77]

Although such rhetoric can be attributed to the historical circumstances in which the *Addresses to the German Nation* were delivered, it provides a telling example of how the language of virtue, which has here assumed the particular form of the idea of love of fatherland, lends itself to being employed in the service of exaggerated, potentially fanatical claims, and that it consequently provides an example of the dangers inherent in the moralization of politics.

While Fichte's attempt to explain the possibility of a genuine ethical community already invites fears concerning the idea of such a community, in which the need for legal and political arrangements would, given the fully moral dispositions of its members, no longer exist to the same extent as it does in the case of his own earlier theory of right, I shall now indicate another problem that arises from Fichte's attempt in the *Addresses to the German Nation* to explain the possibility of a genuine ethical community. The problem in question relates to some claims that Fichte makes which suggest that the

76 GA I / 10: 204; AGN: 106.   77 GA I / 10: 205; AGN: 107.

German national education he has in mind aims to make moral action into something that occurs with necessity, rather than its being the result of genuine free choice, which always carries with it the possibility that an agent may not, in fact, choose to will that which morality commands. As we have seen, Fichte's theory of right and its relation to morality developed during his Jena period clearly allows for such a possibility. Indeed, it is largely based on the assumption that individuals may well fail to will that which morality demands. An example of the type of claim from the later *Addresses to the German Nation* that I have in mind can be found below:

> the new education would consist precisely in this, that, on the soil whose cultivation it takes over, it completely annihilates freedom of will, producing strict necessity in decisions and the impossibility of the opposite in the will, which can now be reckoned and relied on with confidence.[78]

This claim appears to be at odds with one of the basic intentions behind the theory of right that Fichte developed during his Jena period, namely, that of guaranteeing persons a sphere in which they may exercise free choice, thus providing them with a basic condition of moral agency. The key to explaining this claim nevertheless lies in the theory of moral judgement that Fichte sets out in the same period in *The System of Ethics* and, more especially, in the role that he assigns to conscience in this theory. One of the main aims of the German national education that Fichte proposes in the *Addresses to the German Nation* will be shown, in fact, to be that of eradicating the need for any genuine exercise of conscience in the case of many members of the German nation.

Conscience

The idea of conscience (*das Gewissen*) has an essential role to play in Fichte's theory of moral judgement in *The System of Ethics*. He introduces it in connection with the question raised by his claim that 'there must be an absolute criterion for the correctness of our conviction concerning duty'.[79] This is the question as to what is this absolute criterion for the correctness of our conviction concerning duty.

78 GA I / 10: 118; AGN: 23.
79 GA I / 5: 153; SE: 156.

Fichte's answer to his question starts with the claim that the moral law demands a determinate content which it then authorizes. The content of the moral law is not something that the moral law can itself provide, however, because it is a purely formal principle. This content must instead be found and determined by means of the reflective power of judgement, which belongs to theoretical rather than to practical reason.[80] We are therefore faced with the question as to how exactly the moral law can be applied to the content given to it by means of the reflective power of judgement. In order to answer this question, Fichte appeals to a feeling of truth and certainty. He argues that once the moral drive impels the reflective power of judgement to seek the content which the moral law cannot itself provide, but can only authorize or not authorize as the case may be, the free power of imagination wavers (*schwebt*) between different possible determinations. However, once the power of reflecting judgement discovers which of these possible determinations accords with the demands of the moral law, this wavering ceases, because the power of imagination is 'bound and compelled' and 'I cannot view this matter in any way other than in the way I do view it'.[81] This discovery of that which accords with the demands of the moral law is accompanied by a feeling of certainty. Fichte goes on to link this feeling of certainty with the voice of conscience, so that conscience turns out to be the absolute criterion for the correctness of our conviction concerning duty.

Fichte maintains, however, that although conscience 'never errs and cannot err',[82] the possibility exists that a person may allow his clear consciousness of duty to be obscured, because the clear consciousness of that which duty demands disappears if one ceases to reflect on the question of what one ought to do.[83] This leads Fichte to associate the notion of radical evil with inertia or laziness (*Trägheit*),[84] as opposed to any natural aversion to the good. Significantly, the system of education that Fichte proposes in the *Addresses to the German Nation* rests on the assumption that human beings are capable of becoming fully moral beings because 'there is at the root of man a pure pleasure in the good', and 'this pleasure can be developed to the extent that it becomes impossible for him to refrain from doing what he has recognised as

---

80 GA I / 5: 154f.; SE: 157.
81 GA I / 5: 156; SE: 159.
82 GA I / 5: 161; SE: 165.
83 GA I / 5: 177; SE: 182.
84 GA I / 5: 185; SE: 191.

good and instead do what he has recognised as bad'; while Fichte opposes this belief to the ideas that 'there inheres in man a natural aversion to God's commandments, and, secondly, it is simply impossible for him to obey them'.[85] These claims provide some indication that the theory of conscience which Fichte developed during his Jena period has an implicit, but highly significant, role to play in his later thoughts concerning how the German national education he proposes will produce truly virtuous citizens. Indeed, in the light of the emphasis that Fichte places on the significance of Protestantism in German history and in relation to the uniqueness of the German nation, we should not, perhaps, be surprised that it plays such a role.

The brief account of Fichte's theory of moral judgement that I have given above suggests, in fact, that this German national education will aim to produce moral subjects for whom a darkening of the consciousness of duty would not be possible, and who must therefore always judge correctly when it comes to determining what it is their duty to do in any particular case. For Fichte's belief in a human being's innate ability to recognize the good and the propensity to take pleasure in the latter implies that what a German national education needs to prevent above all else is the kind of darkening of the consciousness of duty which would corrupt this innate ability to recognize the good and pervert, if not altogether eradicate, the propensity to take pleasure in it.

Fichte goes beyond his earlier position, however, when he implies that the wavering between different possible ethical judgements, which he considers to be a normal part of the process of moral judgement in *The System of Ethics*, should not even be allowed to occur when it comes to a person with a truly ethical will. He does this in the Eighth Address, by stating that a German national education 'must bring forth this firm and no longer wavering will [*nicht weiter schwankenden Willen*] according to a sure rule that is valid without exception; it must itself produce with the same necessity the necessity that it intends'.[86] It is hard to see how Fichte here leaves any space for human freedom in the making of ethical judgements: for he appears not only to deny that it is possible for a truly moral person, who has undergone the German national education he proposes, ever to will anything other than that which morality demands, but also to turn the

85 GA I / 10: 139; AGN: 43f.
86 GA I / 10: 119; AGN: 24.

act of moral judgement itself into a quasi mechanical process. This problem can be highlighted with reference to Kant's account of the role of conscience in moral judgement given in the second part of his *The Metaphysics of Morals.*

For Kant, conscience is an 'unavoidable fact', which he describes as 'practical reason holding the human being's duty before him for his acquittal or condemnation in every case that comes under a law',[87] and as the consciousness of 'an *internal court* in man'.[88] This description shows that Kant associates conscience with the way in which each individual must decide for himself which of his maxims do or do not accord with the moral law. As with Fichte's theory of conscience in *The System of Ethics,* the general idea is that providing the moral law with a determinate content depends on individuals making the right moral judgement in particular circumstances. Each individual moral subject, however, can judge that he has done this only by listening to the voice of his own conscience, which for Kant expresses itself in the form of a sense of conviction, whereas for Fichte it consists in a feeling of certainty. Like Fichte, Kant also maintains that the idea of a conscience which errs is an absurdity, though this time on the following grounds:

> For while I can indeed be mistaken at times in my objective judgment as to whether something is a duty or not, I cannot be mistaken in my subjective judgment as to whether I have submitted it to my practical reason (here in its role as judge) for such a judgment; for if I could be mistaken in that, I would have made no practical judgment at all, and in that case there would be neither truth nor error.[89]

In this passage, Kant appears to be arguing that although I can be mistaken in judging a particular maxim to be a duty (the objective judgement), I cannot be mistaken in thinking that I have submitted the maxim in question to the judgement of my own practical reason, so as to determine whether or not it is a duty (the subjective judgement). For if I could be mistaken about this, I cannot be thought even to have made a judgement that can be right or wrong from an objective standpoint. In short, someone can be mistaken regarding the particular judgement that results from his attempt to determine whether or not a maxim accords with the moral law, which is of the

87 Kant, 'Die Metaphysik der Sitten', 400.
88 Kant, 'Die Metaphysik der Sitten', 438.
89 Kant, 'Die Metaphysik der Sitten', 401.

kind x is or is not a duty. Yet, having arrived at this judgement, it would make no sense for him to doubt that he has asked himself whether or not x is a duty and has judged it to be a duty or not to be a duty as the case may be. The person in question may, on reflection, begin to doubt that he has judged correctly; but this is not the same as doubting that he has judged at all. To this extent, all that can be reasonably asked of a person is that he earnestly seeks to arrive at the right moral judgement and that he is personally convinced it is the right one. To demand instead that a person's conscience should itself be subjected to some kind of test so as to determine whether or not it has judged correctly, would require the decision of another conscience, which passes judgement on the first conscience and would itself have to be judged, leading to an infinite regress. Conscience, in Kant's view, thus signifies a person's ultimate responsibility and independence when it comes to determining the morally right thing to do in any given situation. Moreover, given the impossibility of successfully applying any external objective criterion to the subjective judgement that a person makes without introducing another conscience, whose judgement would itself be subjective in the relevant sense, Kant thinks that this subjective judgement cannot itself be regarded as mistaken, as long as the person concerned is convinced that it is right.

Kant's account of conscience can be seen to stress two important aspects of human freedom. The first of these aspects concerns the fact that it must ultimately be the individual moral subject that decides whether something is or is not a duty, because otherwise human judgement would be made subject to an external authority, which would in turn rule out the possibility of morally autonomous actions. Secondly, in order to become better able to judge what is or is not a duty, a person will need to develop such qualities as independent judgement and a sense of responsibility for the decisions that he makes. Kant indicates what this might involve when he claims that I must not only be of the opinion that what I propose to do is right, I must also be certain of this. He then goes on to illustrate this point with the example of an inquisitor who appears to be firm in his belief that a supernatural will permits him to eradicate all supposed unbelief together with the unbelievers. Kant doubts, however, that the inquisitor could claim to be as strongly convinced of the rightness of what he proposes to do as would be required in the case of daring to destroy a human life. He therefore argues that the inquisitor would be acting unconscientiously if he were to risk doing something that would be wrong to the highest degree by acting on the belief in question.[90]

Although such a demand for absolute certainty arguably raises its own problems, such as indecision and a consequent inability to act in complex circumstances, Kant's example of the inquisitor nevertheless presents us with a heuristic device that serves to remind us of our fallibility when it comes to judging what we take to be the morally right thing to do. This may in turn lead us to think in a more independent, reflective and responsible manner when making such judgements and to avoid any sense of complacency in making them. Whereas part of the purpose of Fichte's German national education appears to be to remove altogether the need for moral judgement together with the possibility that it always contains of being in error in an objective sense, by producing individuals whose consciousness of duty is never darkened, so that they intuitively and infallibly know what is the right thing to do in the particular circumstances. This amounts to removing the need for independent thinking and a sense of genuine personal responsibility with regard to the moral judgements that one makes. Rather, the German national education that Fichte proposes appears to aim at ensuring that the verdicts of the consciences of each and every member of the nation inevitably agree with each other, because none of them suffers from the kind of darkening of the consciousness of duty and the inertia that might lead them to judge differently from how a person with a clear consciousness of duty would judge in the same circumstances.

This explains why Fichte feels himself entitled to suggest that the German nation as whole, and not just its individual members, may develop an unerring conscience, when he claims that once the Germans as a race have been formed by a German national education, they will be 'endowed with an understanding that is adequate for its standpoint and recognises the right unerringly on every occasion'.[91] Such a claim appears rather strange when it is viewed in the light of Fichte's claims that conscience never errs unless the clear consciousness of duty has been obscured through an individual's laziness and inertia, because conscience is here described in terms that imply it is something essentially personal in nature. Nevertheless, once the moment of wavering to which moral judgement is typically subject is

90 Kant, 'Die Religion innerhalb der Grenzen der bloßen Vernunft', in *Kant's gesammelte Schriften*, vol. VI, 186f. / *Religion within the Boundaries of Mere Reason and Other Writings*. The English translation contains the Akademie edition page numbers.
91 GA I / 10: 253; AGN: 154.

removed, as appears to be the aim of Fichte's German national education, and each person's knowledge of what duty requires is considered
to be infallible, we are confronted with the idea of an ethical community in which there can be no question of its individual members
failing to arrive at the right moral judgement. In this respect, we
might speak of a conscience of the nation. The quasi mechanical
nature of the process by means of which such an unerring, infallible
national conscience is produced and operates appears, however, to
leave little, if any, room for human freedom. Admittedly, making the
right moral judgement and acting in accordance with this judgement
are two different things. Yet the importance that Fichte attaches to the
process of shaping individuals by means of education in order that the
German nation might eventually regain its independence strongly
suggests that a German national education will aim at producing
people who not only always arrive at the right moral judgement but
also invariably act on the basis of their convictions concerning duty.

It looks, however, as if Fichte's German national education, insofar
as it seeks to produce individuals who are 'endowed with an understanding that is adequate for its standpoint and recognises the right
unerringly on every occasion', threatens to result in the kind of infinite
regress that leads Kant to stress the authority of conscience. This is
because certain fully virtuous individuals must be presumed already
to exist, individuals who, in the absence of any darkening of the consciousness of duty, are able unfailingly to recognize the good on every
occasion. For otherwise who would be in a position to judge whether or
not the pupils that undergo the German national education that Fichte
proposes have in fact developed an unerring conscience, and who
would know how this unerring conscience is itself to be produced?
Significantly, in the Tenth Address Fichte suggests that the pupil may
achieve an outward representation of his or her own good conscience in
the recognition accorded to his actions by the person among his or her
educators whom the pupil most respects and chooses to be his or her
confidant or 'keeper of his conscience' (*Gewissens-Rathe*), at the same
time as the pupil may receive counsel from this person when he or she
finds it difficult to do the right thing.[92] This implies that it is only by
means of the approval and guidance that the pupil receives from a
higher, external conscience that the rightness of the decisions of his or
her own conscience can be confirmed, or that his or her conscience can

92 GA I / 10: 232f.; AGN 133.

be directed in such a way as to lead him or her to do the right thing. Yet the idea of a higher, external conscience in turn raises the question as to how this conscience can itself be judged unfailingly to recognize the good on every occasion.[93] To stop this infinite regress, it seems that Fichte's only real option would be dogmatically to assert the existence of an empirical individual who instantiates the unerring conscience that is to be produced in every member of the German nation.

In the light of his views concerning the moral vocation of the scholar, which he attempts to fulfil in the *Addresses to the German Nation*, it is tempting to identify such an individual with the philosopher, and, more particularly, with Fichte himself. In the Eleventh Address, Fichte entrusts the task of executing his plans for a German national education to an impersonal entity, the state,[94] and, when

93 Fichte begins to develop the political implications of this problem in his 1812 *Rechtslehre*, when he rejects his earlier theory of the institution of the ephorate on the following three grounds. First of all, there is the problem that, in the absence of any constraints on its actions, the ephorate might begin a revolution even when the principles of right have not been violated. Secondly, the government can use the power entrusted to it to suppress the ephorate. Thirdly, the judgement of the people concerning the rival claims of the ephorate and the government may always be formally right, since there is no higher judge than the people, but this does not mean that it will be materially right, that is to say, with respect to its actual content. This last problem leads Fichte to claim that the judgements of a select group of the wisest are more to be trusted than those of any majority (GA II / 13: 283).

   Fichte thus appears to want to remove the only unambiguous expression of popular sovereignty found in his theory of right – the assembled people's right to decide between the claims of the ephorate and those of the government – and to replace it with a Platonic rule of the wisest and most virtuous. Yet he himself identifies various problems with such a solution to the problem of political authority, leading him to claim that 'the task of constructing right, which has now been led back to that of making the most just person of his age and nation into the ruler of the same, cannot be solved by means of human freedom. It is therefore a task for the divine governance of the world. Justice [*die Gerechtigkeit*] in the state depends, however, on the resolution of this task; this is therefore also a task for the divine governance of the world' (GA II / 13: 285). The matter is thus in the end to be decided by means of the historical process itself and the advance of culture that Fichte assumes it will bring.

94 This invites the question as to whether Fichte has in mind a German nation-state or the particular German states of his own time. In the Eleventh Address, he expresses the hope that rivalry between the separate German states will lead them to seek to outdo each other by introducing a German national education and making it work (GA I / 10: 247; AGN: 148f.). This does not mean, however, that for him the ultimate goal was not a German nation-state. It has been claimed, in fact, that evidence from other writings of the same period suggest that Fichte's recognition of separate German states in the *Addresses to the German Nation* is the result of consideration for the sensitivities of the particular existing powers and loyalties of the time, whereas his own hopes and

discussing the issue as to whether or not parents should be forced to enter their children into this system of education, he claims that the state as 'answerable only to God and its conscience, has the perfect right to compel them for their own good'.[95] Yet how can an impersonal entity such as the state have a conscience? It is evident from what he says shortly beforehand, however, that Fichte really has in mind not the state itself but its highest functionaries, leading him to express the following wish:

> May statesmen be found, and consulted on this matter, who have educated themselves [*sich selbst Erziehung gegeben haben*] by a deep and thorough study of philosophy and science in general, who take their business seriously, who possess a firm conception of man and his destiny [*Bestimmung*], who are able to understand the present and to comprehend what humanity urgently needs at this moment in time![96]

In addition to expressing the desire for the kind of statesman who has studied philosophy, this passage suggests the ultimate need for a philosopher who is answerable only to God and his conscience. For, as we have seen, a firm conception of man and his destiny, together with an understanding of the present and a comprehension of what humanity needs in the current epoch of human history, are all types of knowledge that Fichte thinks the scholar ought to possess, while the role that Fichte assumes for himself in the *Addresses to the German Nation* implies that he himself possesses such knowledge. The statesman whose existence Fichte so ardently wishes for consequently appears to be someone who has listened to and understood what the philosopher, in this case Fichte himself, has tried to teach his contemporaries.

Fichte manages in the *Addresses to the German Nation* to provide an explanation, though I here leave open the question as to its ultimate plausibility, of how a kingdom of ends might be created on earth, with each member of an ethical community coming to recognize and share the same moral ends as the other members, allowing Fichte to 'proclaim a transformation of the human race from earthly and sensuous creatures into pure and noble spirits'.[97] This does not mean that it would not be possible to develop an alternative theory of an ethical

---

wishes lay in the establishment of a German nation-state. Cf. Schottky, 'Fichtes Nationalstaatsgedanke auf der Grundlage unveröffentlicher Manuskripte von 1807'.

95 GA I / 10: 245f.; AGN: 147.
96 GA I / 10: 245; AGN: 146f.
97 GA I / 10: 264; AGN: 163.

community that was more compatible with the idea of human freedom, while overcoming the egoism that forms the basis of Fichte's theory of right. I would argue that Fichte's attempt to explain the possibility of a genuinely ethical community nevertheless shows that the notion of such a community, however attractive it may appear to be in principle, is not necessarily something that should be welcomed and allowed to supplant completely the legal and political relations that make up the sphere of right. In my view, the position that Fichte adopts during his Jena period must be considered to be preferable to the one he adopts in the *Addresses to the German Nation* because it not only acknowledges human fallibility, together with the reality of self-interest as a powerful source of motivation, but also understands the exercise of virtue to be a spontaneous kind of act. Fichte's separation of right from morality thus appears to be more compatible with the idea of human freedom than is the community of perfected moral beings which is to be created by means of a German national education.

This separation of right from morality also accords the sphere of right its own intrinsically valuable function, which is that of ensuring that individuals are able to enjoy an independent, meaningful existence, by being guaranteed the most basic means of acting effectively in the world so as to realize their capacities. This in turn provides them with the basis on which they can develop as moral beings, though in such a way that this process of moral development remains a genuine product of human freedom. I have suggested, moreover, that this moral aspect of human existence, in the shape of the social or political form of virtue that can be detected in Fichte's Jena theory of the state and society, will have an essential role to play if the sphere of right is to perform successfully the function that Fichte assigns to it. This social or political form of virtue is not the same as the kind of virtue that Fichte demands of the members of the German nation in the *Addresses to the German Nation,* in which sacrificing oneself for the sake of the nation is treated as an end in itself and as the ultimate expression of an individual's sense of moral duty.

Yet even here I would claim that what makes Fichte interesting as a political thinker is the way in which he tends to pursue fully the implications of certain ideas. As I believe I have shown, the continuity between some of the ideas that Fichte developed during his Jena period and some of those found in the *Addresses to the German Nation* demonstrates this tendency, making us into witnesses of the way in which a more radical standpoint may arise out of a persistent attempt to think through the implications of certain principles and concepts. In my view, Fichte's accounts of property and virtue provide the clearest examples of this tendency. This is turn presents the liberal interpreters of Fichte's theory of right and those who criticize Fichte for failing to develop his theory of recognition when he separates right from morality with a challenge, which is to show that he has not, in fact, consistently developed the implications of the parts of his social and political philosophy that they wish to keep, or that he has failed to consider equally justifiable alternatives. Otherwise, they will end up restricting themselves to a merely formalistic approach that fails to engage sufficiently with Fichte's own demand for concepts and principles to be 'applied', which is a task that philosophy must itself to some extent undertake.

In the case of Fichte's theory of property, I have argued that he consistently develops the implications of the concept of property which he introduces, a concept of property that is not the same as the modern liberal one. In the case of Fichte's attempt to explain the possibility of a genuine ethical community in the *Addresses to the German Nation*, the concept of recognition is made to rest on the more fundamental idea of a pre-existing unity based on the possession of a common 'original' language and on the cultural characteristics that result from it, at the same time as this unity must itself be created by means of a German national education. This creation of unity must be therefore taken to mean the process whereby the German people become conscious of a unity which already exists. This is why, in the First Address, Fichte speaks in terms that appear paradoxical insofar as he combines the ideas of a pre-existing unity and a unity that needs to be brought into being, when he claims that

> In the spirit whose emanation these addresses are, I behold the concrescent unity in which no member thinks the fate of another foreign to his own, a unity that shall and must arise if we are not to perish altogether – I behold this unity as already existing, perfected and present.[98]

This appeal both to a pre-existing unity based on language and culture and a unity that is to be created by means of a system of education, whose ultimate aim is to produce citizens who exhibit a form of virtue that appears to be of a quasi mechanical kind, can be said to involve a distorted form of recognition. Yet this simply invites the question as to how a more adequate form of recognition might be achieved in a given historically situated ethical and political community. In this respect, Fichte's own attempt to explain the possibility of a genuine ethical community, whose members recognize themselves in each other, if nothing else, presents us with a serious challenge, as does his theory of property insofar as it seeks to combine the right to exclude others from the use or benefit of something with the equal right of individuals to develop and realize their capacities, and, in so doing, raises the question as to how both of these rights can be properly guaranteed.

BIBLIOGRAPHY

Abizadeh, Arash, 'Was Fichte an Ethnic Nationalist? On Cultural Nationalism and its Double', *History of Political Thought* **26**(2) (2005), 334–59.

Batscha, Zwi, *Gesellschaft und Staat in der politischen Philosophie Fichtes* (Frankfurt: Europäische Verlagsanstalt, 1970).

Braun, Johann, *Freiheit, Gleichheit, Eigentum. Grundfragen des Rechts im Lichte der Philosophie J. G. Fichtes* (Tübingen: Mohr, 1991).

Breazeale, Daniel, 'Editor's Introduction: Fichte in Jena', in J. G. Fichte, *Fichte: Early Philosophical Writings*, ed. and trans. Daniel Breazeale (Ithaca: Cornell University Press, 1988).

Breazeale, Daniel and Rockmore, Tom (eds.), *Rights, Bodies and Recognition: New Essays on Fichte's Foundations of Natural Right* (Aldershot: Ashgate, 2006).

Buhr, Manfred, *Revolution und Philosophie. Die ursprüngliche Philosophie Johann Gottlieb Fichtes und die französische Revolution* (Berlin: VEB Deutscher Verlag der Wissenschaften, 1965).

Doyle, William, *The Oxford History of the French Revolution* (Oxford University Press, 1990).

Engelbrecht, H. C., *Johann Gottlieb Fichte: A Study of his Political Writings with Special Reference to his Nationalism* (New York: Columbia University Press, 1933).

Fleischacker, Samuel, *A Short History of Distributive Justice* (Cambridge, MA: Harvard University Press, 2004).

Frischmann, Bärbel, 'Die Herausbildung des Sozialstaatsdenkens im neuzeitlichen Kontraktualismus von Hobbes bis Fichte', *Zeitschrift für philosophische Forschung* **60**(4) (2006), 554–89.

Gans, Eduard, *Naturrecht und Universalrechtsgeschichte*, ed. Manfred Riedel (Stuttgart: Klett-Cotta, 1981).

Guéroult, Martial, 'Fichte et la Révolution française', in his *Études sur Fichte* (Paris: Aubier, 1974).

Hammacher, Kurt, 'Comment Fichte accède à l'histoire', *Archives de philosophie* **26** (1962), 388–440.

Hayek, F. A., *Law, Legislation and Liberty, vol. II: The Mirage of Social Justice* (London: Routledge & Kegan Paul, 1976).

Hegel, G. W. F., 'On the Scientific Ways of Treating Natural Law, on its Place in Practical Philosophy, and its Relation to the Positive Sciences of Right', in

Political Writings, ed. Laurence Dickey, trans. H. B. Nisbet (Cambridge University Press, 1999).

Foundations of the Philosophy of Right, ed. Allen W. Wood, trans. H. B. Nisbet (Cambridge University Press, 1991).

Philosophie des Rechts. Die Vorlesungen von 1819/20 in einer Nachschrift, ed. Dieter Henrich (Frankfurt: Suhrkamp, 1983).

The Difference between Fichte's and Schelling's Systems of Philosophy, trans. H. S. Harris and Walter Cerf (Albany, NY: State University of New York Press, 1977).

Vorlesungen über Rechtsphilosophie, vol. IV (transcription by K. G. von Griesheim of the 1824/25 lectures), ed. K. H. Ilting (Stuttgart and Bad Cannstatt: Frommann-Holzboog, 1974).

Werke, eds. Eva Moldenhauer and Karl Markus Michel (Frankfurt: Suhrkamp, 1969–71).

Higonnet, Patrice, *Goodness beyond Virtue: Jacobins during the French Revolution* (Cambridge, MA: Harvard University Press, 1998).

Hobbes, Thomas, *Leviathan*, ed. Richard Tuck (Cambridge University Press, 1996).

Höffe, Otfried, *Kant's Cosmopolitan Theory of Law and Peace*, trans. Alexander Newton (Cambridge University Press, 2006).

Kant, Immanuel, *Religion within the Boundaries of Mere Reason and Other Writings*, ed. and trans. Allen Wood and George di Giovanni (Cambridge University Press, 1998).

The Metaphysics of Morals, trans. Mary Gregor (Cambridge University Press, 1991).

Political Writings, ed. Hans Reiss, trans. H. B. Nisbet, 2nd edn (Cambridge University Press, 1991).

Kant's gesammelte Schriften, ed. Königliche preußische (later deutsche) Akademie der Wissenschaften (Berlin: Reimer/de Gruyter, 1900–).

Kersting, Wolfgang, 'Die Unabhängigkeit des Rechts von der Moral', in Jean-Christophe Merle (ed.), *Grundlage des Naturrechts* (Berlin: Akademie, 2001).

Kohn, Hans, 'The Paradox of Fichte's Nationalism', *Journal of the History of Ideas* **10**(3) (1949), 319–43.

Lampert, Jay, 'Locke, Fichte, and Hegel on the Right to Property', in Michael Baur and John Russon (eds.), *Hegel and the Tradition: Essays in Honour of H. S. Harris* (University of Toronto Press, 1997).

La Vopa, Anthony J., *Fichte: The Self and the Calling of Philosophy, 1762–1799* (Cambridge University Press, 2001).

Léon, Xavier, 'Le socialisme de Fichte d'après l'état commercial fermé', *Revue de metaphysique et de morale* **22** (1914), 27–71, 197–220.

Locke, John, *Two Treatises of Government*, ed. Peter Laslett (Cambridge University Press, 1988).

Macpherson, C. B., 'Liberal-Democracy and Property', in C. B. Macpherson (ed.), *Property: Mainstream and Critical Positions* (University of Toronto Press, 1978).

The Political Theory of Possessive Individualism: Hobbes to Locke (Oxford University Press, 1962).

Martyn, David, 'Borrowed Fatherland: Nationalism and Language Purism in Fichte's *Addresses to the German Nation*', *The Germanic Review* **72**(4) (1997), 303–15.

Marx, Karl, *Capital*, vol. I, trans. Ben Fowkes (Harmondsworth: Penguin, 1986).

Mouffe, Chantal, *On the Political* (London: Routledge, 2005).

Neuhouser, Frederick, 'Introduction', in J. G. Fichte, *Foundations of Natural Right*, ed. Frederick Neuhouser, trans. Michael Baur (Cambridge University Press, 2000).

'Fichte and the Relationship between Right and Morality', in Daniel Breazeale and Tom Rockmore (eds.), *Fichte: Historical Context/Contemporary Controversies* (Atlantic Highlands, NJ: Humanities Press, 1994).

Fichte's Theory of Subjectivity (Cambridge University Press, 1990).

Nietzsche, Friedrich, *Untimely Meditations*, ed. Daniel Breazeale, trans. R. J. Hollingdale (Cambridge University Press, 1997).

'Unzeitgemässe Betrachtungen', in *Nietzsche Werke Kritische Gesamtausgabe*, ed. Giorgio Colli and Mazzino Montinari (Berlin: Walter de Gruyter, 1967–), Abteilung III, Band 1.

Nomer, Nedim, 'Fichte and the Idea of Liberal Socialism', *The Journal of Political Philosophy* **13**(1) (2005), 53–73.

Pagden, Anthony, *Lords of all the World: Ideologies of Empire in Spain, Britain and France c. 1500–c. 1800* (New Haven: Yale University Press, 1995).

Renaut, Alain, 'Fichte: Le droit sans la morale?', *Archives de philosophie* **55** (1992), 221–42.

Le système du droit. Philosophie et droit dans la pensée de Fichte (Paris: Presses Universitaires de France, 1986).

Riedel, Manfred, *Between Tradition and Revolution: The Hegelian Transformation of Political Philosophy*, trans. Walter Wright (Cambridge University Press, 1984).

'Die Aporie von Herrschaft und Vereinbarung in Kants Idee des Sozialvertrags', in Gerold Prauss (ed.), *Kant. Zur Deutung seiner Theorie von Erkennen und Handeln* (Cologne: Kiepenhauer & Witsch, 1973).

Ritter, Joachim, *Hegel and the French Revolution: Essays on the Philosophy of Right*, trans. Richard Dien Winfield (Cambridge, MA: MIT Press, 1982).

Robespierre, Maximilien, *Œuvres de Maximilien Robespierre*, ed. M. Bouloiseau and A. Soboul (Paris: Presses Universitaires de France, 1958–67).

Rose, R. B., *Gracchus Babeuf: The First Revolutionary Communist* (London: Edward Arnold, 1978).

Rousseau, Jean-Jacques, The Social Contract *and Other Later Political Writings*, trans. Victor Gourevitch (Cambridge University Press, 1997).

Œuvres complètes, ed. Bernard Gagnebin and Marcel Raymond, 5 vols. (Paris: Gallimard, Bibliothèque de la Pléiade, 1959–95).

Schottky, Richard, 'Fichtes Nationalstaatsgedanke auf der Grundlage unveröffentlicher Manuskripte von 1807', *Fichte-Studien* **2** (1990), 111–37.

Siep, Ludwig, *Praktische Philosophie im Deutschen Idealismus* (Frankfurt: Suhrkamp, 1992).

Anerkennung als Prinzip der praktischen Philosophie (Freiburg: Karl Alber, 1979).

Simmons, A. John, *The Lockean Theory of Rights* (Princeton University Press, 1992).

Thomson, David, *The Babeuf Plot: The Making of a Republican Legend* (London: Kegan Paul, Trench, Trübner & Co., 1947).

Tully, James, *A Discourse on Property: John Locke and his Adversaries* (Cambridge University Press, 1980).

Verweyen, Hansjürgen, *Recht und Sittlichkeit in J. G. Fichtes Gesellschaftslehre* (Freiburg: Alber, 1975).

Verzar, Andreas, *Das autonome Subjekt und der Vernunftstaat. Eine systematisch-historische Untersuchung zu Fichtes 'Geschlossenem Handelstaat' von 1800* (Bonn: Bouvier, 1979).

Viroli, Maurizio, *For Love of Country: An Essay on Patriotism and Nationalism* (Oxford University Press, 1995).

Weber, Marianne, *Fichte's Sozialismus und sein Verhältnis zur Marx'schen Doktrin* (Tübingen: Mohr, 1900).

Williams, Robert R., 'The Displacement of Recognition by Coercion in Fichte's Grundlage des Naturrechts', in Daniel Breazeale and Tom Rockmore (eds.), *New Essays on Fichte's Later Wissenschaftslehre* (Evanston, IL: Northwestern University Press, 2002).

Recognition: Fichte and Hegel on the Other (Albany, NY: State University of New York Press, 1992).

Zöller, Günter, *Fichte's Transcendental Philosophy: The Original Duplicity of Intelligence and Will* (Cambridge University Press, 1998).

INDEX

INDEX 217

liberal political order
  defined 7–8
  Fichte's doubts about 8–9, 85–6
  positive and negative function 7
  property rights in 21–3, 37, 39, 67
  and value of individuality 6–8
liberal socialism 23
liberalism 6–8, 10–11, 43–5, 69–70,
    82, 85–6
  economic 43, 86
Locke, John
  compared with Fichte on property
    and freedom 21, 24, 44–55, 59
  *Essay Concerning Human
    Understanding* 45
  on legislation 31
  subject–centred approach 45,
    49–50
  The Second Treatise of Government 45,
    46–7
Louis XVI, execution 57
Luther, Martin 175, 180

Macpherson, C. B. 21–2
Marx, Karl 47, 49
mercantilism 100–1
merchants 77–8, 130
Minerva 56
Mirabeau, marquis de 94
money
  as absolute property 42, 43, 77, 80
  consent to the consequences of
    48–51
  as exchange 48–51
  and goods in circulation 79
moral agency
  freedom and 139, 193, 196
  right as a condition of 136–8
moral autonomy 131–2, 133–4, 200–2
  and right 113, 137–43, 155
moral development 189–205
moral judgement
  Fichte's theory of 196–207
  Kant on 199–202
moral law
  as a condition of self-consciousness
    113
  content of 197, 199
  and freedom 131–9, 200–2
  and nonmoral incentives 156–7
  and property rights 60

moral philosophy, Kant's 92–3
moral sense 83
morality 84
  absolute unconditional validity 121,
    127, 132
  concerns inner actions 117–18
  and duty 134
  and freedom 131–9
  political 146, 150
  'real' 132–3
  relation of right to 19–20, 112–61,
    132–3, 136–8, 155, 190
  separation from right 13–17, 18,
    59, 82, 85–6, 111, 113, 115,
    116–23, 132–3, 159, 194,
    205–6
  see also ethical duties theory (Fichte)
mutual dependence 123, 126,
    135, 138
mutual recognition 3–4, 17, 114,
    164, 194
  between states 96
  coercion by the state versus 13–18,
    74–6
  and the contract theory of state
    14–17, 30–44
  deduced as a condition of self-
    consciousness 12
  failure of 4, 6, 11–12, 28
  the possibility of 12–13, 15
  in property rights 28
  and the relation of right 46
  as a transcendental condition of
    right 13

Napoleon Bonaparte 162
nation
  conscience of a 202–3
  identification with state 163
  love of one's 191–5
  rights of a 87–8
nationalism, German 20, 162
natural law tradition 21, 31, 44–5,
    49, 103
natural right
  Fichte on 28–9, 35, 59–60
  Locke on 49–51
  theories of 5, 27
  to liberty, property, security
    and resistance to oppression
    67

For EU product safety concerns, contact us at Calle de José Abascal, 56–1°,
28003 Madrid, Spain or eugpsr@cambridge.org.

www.ingramcontent.com/pod-product-compliance
Ingram Content Group UK Ltd.
Pitfield, Milton Keynes, MK11 3LW, UK
UKHW020328140625
459647UK00018B/2072